The World of Computers
and Information Processing

The World of Computers
and Information Processing

Rob Kelley

Computer Education Consultant
Hamilton Board of Education
Hamilton, Ontario

John Wiley & Sons

Toronto New York Chichester Brisbane Singapore

Text and cover design by Blair Kerrigan /Glyphics
Technical illustration by Jim Loates

Canadian Cataloguing in Publication Data

Kelley, Rob, 1947 —
The world of computers and information
processing

For use in secondary schools.
Bibliography: p.
Includes index.
ISBN 0-471-79917-3

1. Computers. 2. Electronic data processing.
I. Title.

QA76.K44   001.64   C82-094250-2

Printed and bound in Canada

10 9 8 7 6 5 4

To those who believe computer literacy is a worthwhile goal.

Contents

Acknowledgements

To publish a comprehensive text about the world of computers has required the support and assistance of many teachers, educators, businesses, and government organizations. We would like to express our sincere thanks to all of them and acknowledge their contributions.

The people who volunteered their time and expertise during the early planning stages were: Bob Wilson, business education director, Thomas A. Blakelock Secondary School in Oakville, Ontario; Monica Taylor, High School of Commerce in Ottawa; Dan Ryan, business head at Gloucester High School in Ottawa; and George Wiens, vice-principal of La Salle Secondary School in Kingston, Ontario.

Several people volunteered to review the manuscript while it was being drafted. Many helpful suggestions were provided by Peter Gerrard, assistant head of the math department at Barton Secondary School in Hamilton; Gary Smith, mathematics teacher at Glendale Secondary School in Hamilton; Paul Rehak, business teacher at Scott Park Secondary School in Hamilton.

In addition to the above people, the publisher selected several educators from across Canada to scrutinize and make suggestions at both the planning and manuscript stages. These people include: Mr. R.J. Bourque, Faculty of Education, University of New Brunswick, Fredericton; Mr. J. Breadner, Stephen Leacock Collegiate Institute, Toronto; Ms F. Gammi, Chinquacousy Secondary School, Brampton, Ontario; Mr. G. Hopkins, Eastern High School of Commerce, Toronto; Dr. D. McCahill, director of business education, Lorne Park Secondary School, Mississauga; Mr. R. Noice, Cedarbrae Collegiate, Scarborough, Ontario; Mr. R. Peacock, business education consultant, Vancouver School Board; Mr. B. Scinto, Northern Secondary School, Toronto; Ms M. Sheptycki, Archbishop O'Leary High School, Edmonton, Alberta; Mr. S. Talsky, East York Collegiate Institute, Toronto; Mr. R. Wilkinson, business department, Malvern Collegiate Institute, Toronto.

A special note of thanks is extended to the members of the Hamilton Board of Education "Computer Studies Curriculum Design Committee," of which the author was a member. It was their basic curriculum framework around which the manuscript was built. The committee members include: Bob Harkness, business education supervisor; Dave Didur, computer studies coordinator; Norbert Casey; Paul Rehak; Georges Augustin; Dennis Haynes; Dave Cuttriss; Peat McHugh; Jay Parekh; Bob Ahrens; Gerry Hagen; and Clarke Groleau.

Thanks is extended also to the hundreds of students who enrolled in introductory computer courses over the years. They allowed the author the opportunity of testing and debugging the programs, diagrams, and end-of-chapter material presented in this text. Both a Commodore PET microcomputer and a Digital PDP-11-34 minicomputer were used frequently to validate the solutions to the many computer problems presented in the chapters on programming and problem solving. Efforts were also made to include Apple and Radio Shack variations of the BASIC language wherever it was appropriate.

A heartfelt thanks to these people who made a special effort to supply the author with illustrative material: Paul Swan, a cartoonist in Dallas, Texas; Sandy Dean, a cartoonist in Pensacola, Florida; Lynn Wendel, marketing manager at Apple Computers Inc.; Paul Warren, marketing manager at Ohio Scientific; Paul Plesman, editor of the newspaper *Computer Canada*; and Susan Johnson and Margery Laver, librarians with IBM Canada Ltd.

The following business organizations provided text illustrative material for which we are extremely grateful:

APF Electronics Inc.
Apple Computer Inc.
Atari Corporation
BASF Canada Ltd.
California Computer Products, Inc. (CalComp)
CAE-Morse Ltd.
Canadian National
Centronics Data Computer Corporation
Cincinnati Milacron
Commodore Business Machines
Computer Devices, Inc.
Computer Communications Group, (The)
Computing Canada (newspaper)
Cray Research, Inc.
Digital Equipment Corporation
Fidelity Electronics
Hazeltine Corporation
Heath/Zenith Corporation
Honeywell Corporation
IBM Canada Ltd.
Intel Corporation
Interstate Electronics Corporation
ITT Courier of Canada Ltd.
Kennedy Company
Kodak Company Canada Ltd.
Malibu Electronics Corporation
Mohawk Data Sciences
NASA Lyndon B. Johnson Space Center
National Semiconductor Inc.
NCR Corporation
Norand Corporation
North Star Computers
Ohio Scientific
Quasar Corporation, Franklin Park, Illinois
Radio Shack — A Division of Tandy Corporation
Rockwell International Corporation
Southwest Technical Products Corporation
Spectronics Corporation
Sperry Univac Corporation
Summagraphics Corporation
Teletype Corporation
Terrapin Inc.
Texas Instruments, Inc.
3M Canada Ltd.
Time magazine, N.Y.

Cartoonists:

Johns, Pebble Beach, California
Sandy Dean, Pensacola, Florida
Russel Myers, courtesy of *The Chicago Tribune*
Shane, courtesy of *Canadian Datasystems*
Paul Swan, Dallas, Texas

Preface

During the last decade, computer technology was "humanized." It became understandable, portable, and affordable. For the first time in its 40-year history, a technology formerly devoted to military, scientific, and business data processing became universally popular. Topics such as advanced programming, computer graphics, and process control are now understood and manipulated by ten-year-old children.

Any complex technology, once it becomes popular, can have a profound effect on our society. Unlike other fixed-purpose inventions such as the automobile, electric lights, television, and communication satellites, computer technology is endlessly modifiable through its programming. It can operate toys, talk, understand spoken commands, generate music or poetry, draw three-dimensional pictures, teach, make medical diagnoses, operate complete factories, and guide manned spacecraft into new worlds.

Like all other inventions, however, computers are morally neutral. They are neither good nor evil. What people decide to do with them will determine whether we view computers in a positive or negative way.

There is an urgent need for educators to include computers as a basic component in the school curriculum. Students who graduate without exposure to computers will find themselves frustrated or intimidated by a technology they can neither manipulate nor understand. In our increasingly computerized society, job opportunities decrease for the technologically illiterate.

Traditional computer courses must be broadened if they are to have any lasting value for students. Learning the syntax rules of some particular computer language is inadequate preparation for a person confronted with computers in all walks of life. An understanding of hardware systems, applications, and societal impacts are necessary if students are to cope with this new technology.

The World of Computers is an introductory computer textbook designed to provide a broad spectrum of knowledge, concepts, and skills essential to the development of computer literacy and awareness. Since the chapters are written as independent modules, it is not necessary for the reader to follow them sequentially.

Because of the broad scope of this text, it is recommended that the instructors preselect a limited number of topics for concentration. There are sufficient topics, if necessary, to enhance both a first and second year course in computers.

The end-of-chapter material presented in this text is designed for both general level and advanced level students. General level students should feel comfortable with the core material represented in the Review Questions and other items designated general level. Advanced level students should proceed through both the general level and advanced level questions before attempting other items such as classroom activities, issues for discussion, or projects.

Any selected group of four or more different topics from this textbook should provide sufficient scope to make any reader a knowledgeable "computer literate" in this fascinating world of computers.

Rob Kelley

1

An Information Processing Machine

The space race between the USSR and the United States during the 1960s played a key role in the development of miniaturized computer components.

Courtesy of NASA.

Objectives

An understanding of the two components of a computer system—hardware and software

An understanding of the five functions of a digital computer—input, output, processing, storage, and control

A knowledge of the three types of computer systems and the four categories of digital computers

An awareness of the variety of computer-related jobs now available

An appreciation of the historical development of computers and the computer industry

Chapter One
An Information Processing Machine

When IBM discovered that it was not in the business of making office equipment or business machines, but that it was in the business of processing information, then it began to navigate with a clear vision.

Marshall McLuhan

The computer is an excellent machine for processing information. It performs many complex instructions quickly, following instructions step by step, repeatedly, without making a mistake. It stores millions of facts and figures, and can locate them again whenever the information is needed.

The uses for the computer have made it one of civilization's most exciting achievements in the last 40 years. Space travel, use of credit cards, instant banking, and home information centres were made possible because of the computer's capabilities.

The space crafts which travelled to the moon and the planet Mars were guided by calculations performed by an on-board computer. Even in the training of the astronauts, computers were hooked up to machinery that simulated actual flight conditions. Across the country, people can buy on credit without long delays because store owners can ask a central computer for a customer's credit record. Banks have computer terminals with special printers for recording entries into passbooks and push-button terminals on the outside wall of the building to allow "instant banking" 24 hours a day. New homes being constructed have built-in computers which control the temperature, humidity, fire and burglar alarms, and also provide a message-taking service. Home computers, along with new computer cable companies, will soon change living rooms into entertainment and information centres.

Hardware and Software

Most computers consist of several machines linked together. For this reason, it is more accurate to refer to a complete computer as a computer system. All the electrical and mechanical parts that make up a computer system are called **hardware**. Hardware devices might include a keyboard, similar to those found on typewriters, a TV display screen, a printer, and a processor unit. The main part of the computer, **the processor**

unit, contains the circuit boards, capable of storing and processing information. Extra storage devices which store information for long periods of time can also be attached.

There is another necesary but invisible group of items contained in all computer systems. These are the programs which, with the help of the processor unit, operate the computer. A **program** consists of a series of instructions designed to guide the computer step by step through some process. All the instructions which make a computer operate in the required manner are referred to as **software**.

Figure 1.1
Types of Software

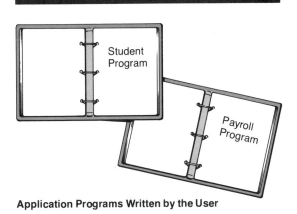

Application Programs Written by the User

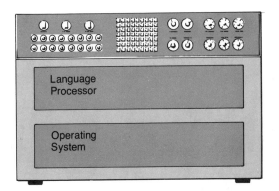

Programs Written by the Manufacturer and Stored in the Computer

Software programs are written by both the computer manufacturer and the person using the computer. Computer users, such as students, researchers, or people in business, generally write **application programs**. They are called this because the programs apply to a specific situation. A student, for example, might write a program to solve a particular problem in class, or a business person may write a payroll application program which would print the cheques for the company's employees.

The software programs written by the computer manufacturer are an important part of the computer system. Some of these programs must be present before any application programs can be run.

One such necessary program is called an **operating system**. It is a program which supervises the way in which the computer handles information. For example, an operating system can keep track of several different application programs at the same time without requiring any human assistance. It also commands the control unit to fetch, check, and execute each individual line in the program. The control unit refers to the hardware circuitry which controls the sequence of operations in the program.

Another important type of manufacturer's software is a program called a **language processor**. Its purpose is to translate the instructions the user provides into electrical impulses, which operate the circuits. Since the computer cannot understand the English language, people must write instructions in a short-form style called a **computer language**. There are several different computer languages available for this purpose. Each computer language needs its own language processor to translate these messages into electrical impulses which the computer can understand. For this reason, most large computer systems have two or more language processors stored somewhere in their memory bank.

Five Features of Any Digital Computer System

Computers are available in various sizes, ranging from large systems that fill an entire room, to portable, desk-top models. There are even hobby kits which people assemble for use at home. Computers are manufactured by several companies, such as IBM, Honeywell, Sperry-Rand, Digital, Wang, Commodore, Radio Shack, and Apple. Regardless of their size and origin, all computers display five basic features—INPUT, PROCESSING, OUTPUT, STORAGE, and CONTROL. Each of these features represents a particular function or job that the machine can perform.

Figure 1.2
A Simple Computer

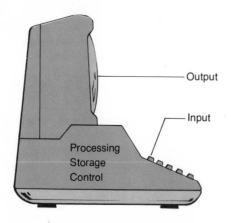

Output

Input

Processing
Storage
Control

The five basic parts needed to operate a typical desk-top computer. The keyboard provides a method of input; a visual screen provides a method for output; and the circuit boards provide processing, temporary storage, and control features.

Input

Each computer has some method of allowing instructions to be fed in. One method is to use a keyboard much like that on a typewriter. The user keys in the instructions to obtain whatever action or information that is required. Computers which handle a large volume of information each day need a faster method of input than a single keyboard can provide. One popular method used in schools is a card reader. This machine translates the holes or pencil marks found on the computer cards into electrical impulses. Some card readers are capable of reading several hundred instructions per minute.

Businesses usually use more expensive mediums, such as reels of magnetic tape or circular disks as a method of input, because of their faster speeds, and the additional space available on them.

Processing

All the calculations, logic decisions, comparing, and handling of information is done in one main area called the **processor unit**. Here, the electronic circuits operate the entire computer system. The processor unit is the actual computer. Any other device attached to it would be referred to as a **peripheral** because it operates outside of the mainframe of the computer. In small computers, the processing circuits can be placed on a single circuit board, which can be easily repaired or, if necessary, upgraded by plugging in a new one.

Output

Once the processing is completed, the answer can be displayed in a variety of ways. The most common method is to use a printer. When the answer to a problem appears on a piece of paper, it is called a **printout**. If a permanent copy of the answer is not necessary, a screen similar to that on a television set can be used. The display which appears on the TV screen, sometimes referred to as a **readout**, can be cleared or altered on the screen whenever the user wishes. The correct name for the display screen is **cathode ray tube**, or CRT.

Storage

Most computers have two storage areas. The first area is found inside the processor unit and is referred to as the **main memory**. Instructions are stored here temporarily while they are being processed.

For longer-term memory, extra devices (peripherals) can be added onto the computer. Large quantities of information can then be stored on either reels of magnetic tape or on circular magnetic disks.

Control

Student programs often contain errors which cause the computer to stop operating. The computer must have some way of explaining why it stopped. A manufacturer's software program called the language processor informs the person using the computer of any mistakes found in a program.

If no errors are found, another software program called the operating system then directs the flow of information to different parts of the processor unit. It is these two manufacturer's programs which help to control the flow of information and to control the way computer programs are written.

Figure 1.3
Large Digital Computer System

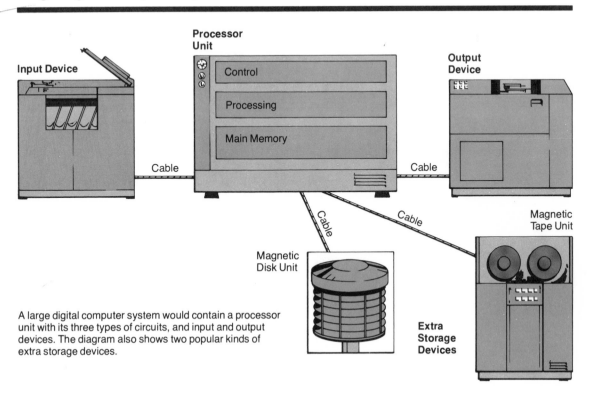

A large digital computer system would contain a processor unit with its three types of circuits, and input and output devices. The diagram also shows two popular kinds of extra storage devices.

Types of Digital Computers

Digital computers are what most people think of when they hear the word "computer." These machines are capable of following instructions step by step, performing rapid calculations, making logic decisions, and storing and retrieving large amounts of data.

There are, at present, four categories of digital computers. The smallest type is called a **pocket computer**, a portable, hand-held model. A keypad allows letters or numbers to be entered. A thin, rectangular screen displays one line of instructions at a time. Some pocket computers can be connected to other devices such as a television set, or extra memory devices. Business briefcases are available which snugly hold the pocket computer, and also hold a tape deck for storage, plus an **acoustic coupler** to insert a telephone headset, if access to a larger computer is necessary.

Pocket computers are small enough to fit into a briefcase. This model contains a keyboard, a one-line display screen, programmable memory, and manufacturer's software. The acoustic coupler into which a telephone headset can be placed allows the user to transmit and receive data from a distant computer, in addition to on-site programming.

Courtesy of Quasar Corporation, Franklin Park, Illinois.

The next size is a portable, desk-top model called a **microcomputer**. The typical method of input is a keyboard, and the usual output device is a cathode ray tube. Microcomputers are being used in schools, businesses, and as personal computers. Only one person at a time can use this machine.

A **minicomputer** is a small floor-model computer with separate machines for input, output, long-term storage, and the processor

unit. Schools and various departments in a large business use minicomputers because it can handle a moderately large volume of information, and has the added advantage in that several people can use the machine at the same time.

Mainframe computers are the largest of the four categories. Most of the basic computer functions have a separate floor-model machine, which operates at very high speeds.

Often, the computer hardware will occupy a whole room. The word mainframe refers to the oversized processor unit which operates the computer system. Large corporations, various levels of government, and the military prefer the speed and volume of information which a large mainframe computer is capable of handling. It also can communicate with hundreds of users almost simultaneously.

Mainframe computers typically have a large computer console, which indicate the status of programs to the person operating the computer system. This is an IBM 360 series computer, popular in the early 1970s.

Courtesy of IBM Canada Ltd.

7

Other Types of Computers

In addition to the popular digital computer, there are two other types of computer systems which are more specialized and limited in function—the analog and hybrid computers.

An **analog computer** is a device which measures a physical quantity such as air pressure, temperature, or velocity, and compares it to a preset level. For example, a wall thermostat continuously measures the room temperature and compares it to the point which the dial has been set. If the room temperature is less than the setting, the furnace is allowed to turn on; otherwise, the furnace remains off. Other examples of analog devices include speedometers, air conditioners, heat-sensing fire alarms, and most dials in airplanes.

A **hybrid computer system** is a combination of the analog and the digital computer.

Usually, analog computers act as input and output peripherals, while the digital computer provides the processing and instructions for the system.

An example of a hybrid computer is a system used to check out a rocket for malfunctions before it leaves the launch pad. Cables connected to the rocket can measure a number of things: cabin pressure, fuel, and oxygen. This information can be fed into an analog computer, which would display it in the form of dials and gauges for the repair personnel to observe. The information can be converted into a form which a digital computer could understand. The digital computer could then process and store the information, and display statistics, graphs, or even warnings on a CRT or a printer for the people in the control room to monitor.

Another application of a hybrid computer

Figure 1.4

A Hybrid Computer System

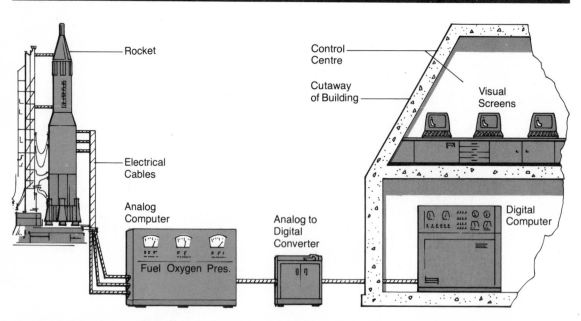

The electrical signals from devices on the rocket can be displayed in analog form through the use of dials and gauges or converted to digital signals, so that a digital computer can process the information to provide printouts or visual displays in the form of charts and tables.

system is a computerized manufacturing assembly line. Here, several analog devices measure and check product specifications, while the main digital computer uses this information to decide what manufacturing processes the product should go through next.

People Who Work With Computers

Most large businesses and government offices have their computer departments run by specially trained people. A **computer operator**, for example, makes certain that the computer operates correctly and without delays. Following a job schedule, the operator makes sure that the correct disks and tapes are mounted, and that the printer contains the proper type of printing form. The computer console typewriter and console lights are frequently checked to ensure that the processor unit is proceeding as it should.

A computer operator is loading a disk pack into a magnetic disk unit. This person makes sure that the computer operates correctly and without delays.
Courtesy of IBM Canada Ltd.

A computer operator is usually a college graduate with a knowledge of computer hardware and some programming skills. If the workload requires the computer to be operated 24 hours a day, the job often involves shift work.

Data entry clerks prepare information in a suitable form for the computer to read. A keyboard is used as an input device, and a CRT allows the person to view and correct the entries as they are being prepared. The corrected information is stored on disks, and later sent directly to the processor unit for processing.

In addition to the increasingly popular key-to-disk machines, data entry clerks also may work with other types of devices. A keypunch machine, for example, can be used to store the information onto computer cards in the form of holes, or a keytape machine can store the information onto reels of magnetic tape. The process of keypunching and keytaping, however, requires the extra step of loading the cards or tapes onto another machine before the information can be read into the computer. For this reason, keypunch and keytape jobs are gradually being replaced by the key-to-disk data entry method of preparing information.

All data entry jobs require keyboard skills and are best suited to people with typing experience.

A data entry clerk requires keyboard skills, and must be able to proofread and edit copy as it appears on the visual screen before it is entered into the computer system.

Courtesy of NCR Corporation.

A **computer programmer** plans and writes application programs to be used in the business (or government office). Assigned to a project, a senior programmer might spend several months planning, writing, and correcting the steps involved in a program. Junior programmers, usually with less than three years' experience, work on existing programs under the supervision of a senior programmer.

Writing programs is a job which requires problem-solving skills, patience, determination, and attention to small details. A company programmer may only be scheduled two test runs a day to find and correct errors in a program.

Programmers usually have a college degree in data processing or a university degree in computer science. Typically, they are skilled in at least two of the major computer languages (FORTRAN, COBOL, PL1, BASIC, PASCAL) and have an in-depth knowledge of manufacturers' software.

A **systems analyst** recommends ways of improving office routines which involve the computer. For example, if a new type of customer invoice (a bill) is needed, the systems analyst will study the required changes, and then design the new forms to be used with the computer. Another project might be the modification of the business's computer accounting system.

Usually this position requires a degree in computer science, experience in programming, and the ability to get along well with other members in the department.

The **data processing manager** is responsible for the successful operation of the computer department. This person usually has a university degree in computer science and has had several years' experience as a project leader, systems analyst, or supervisor. The DP manager hires the data processing staff, supervises its training, recommends the purchase of new equipment, and prepares the department's annual budget.

In addition to reporting to top management, this person frequently meets with managers of all departments to discuss their computer needs.

The **manager's secretary** performs the usual secretarial duties of typing, filing, and dictation, but is also familiar with computer terminology and computer concepts. This person's background would include a high school diploma with secretarial and computer options. A knowledge of computers will help the secretary cope with the technical details involved in phone calls, report typing, and assisting people when the manager is absent.

Figure 1.5
Want Ads

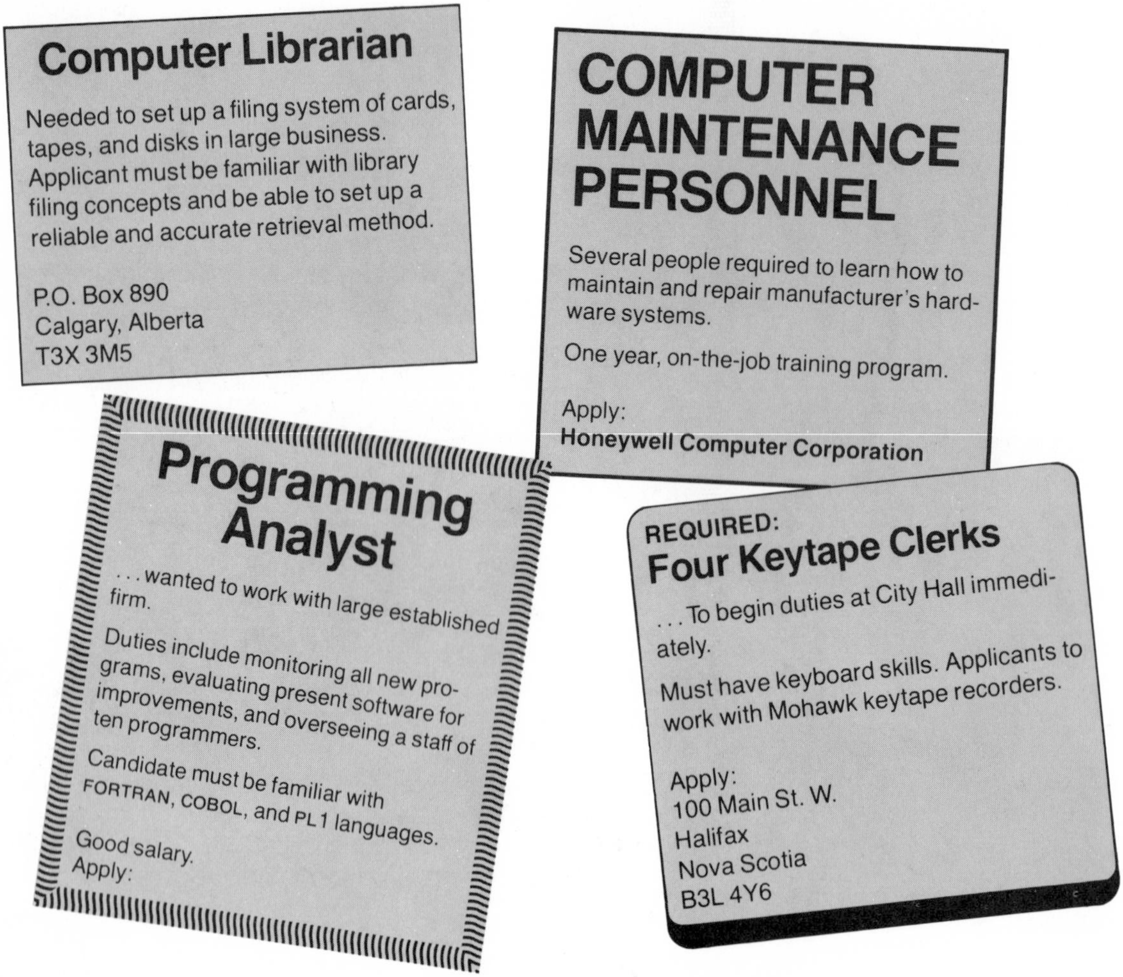

Computer Librarian

Needed to set up a filing system of cards, tapes, and disks in large business. Applicant must be familiar with library filing concepts and be able to set up a reliable and accurate retrieval method.

P.O. Box 890
Calgary, Alberta
T3X 3M5

COMPUTER MAINTENANCE PERSONNEL

Several people required to learn how to maintain and repair manufacturer's hardware systems.

One year, on-the-job training program.

Apply:
Honeywell Computer Corporation

Programming Analyst

. . . wanted to work with large established firm.

Duties include monitoring all new programs, evaluating present software for improvements, and overseeing a staff of ten programmers.

Candidate must be familiar with FORTRAN, COBOL, and PL1 languages.

Good salary.
Apply:

REQUIRED: Four Keytape Clerks

. . . To begin duties at City Hall immediately.

Must have keyboard skills. Applicants to work with Mohawk keytape recorders.

Apply:
100 Main St. W.
Halifax
Nova Scotia
B3L 4Y6

Other Computer-Related Jobs

Using a computer to process information has caused many charges in the traditional business office. New job positions such as **word processing operators** are combining a variety of formally independent office tasks. The "work station" is a minicomputer system dedicated to secretarial work, where a secretary operates a word processing work station. The traditional typewriter is replaced by a CRT and a keyboard. Electronic filing of documents on disks removes the need for filing cabinets. A table-top printer types individual error-proof letters at high speeds.

The software used with this equipment is called a **text editor**. It allows the operator to make changes in the information displayed on the CRT with ease, before commanding the processor unit to print or store the document electronically for future reference.

The job requires a good working knowledge of French or English, keyboard skills, and an ability to create, proofread, and edit documents. Educational requirements include a high school and college secretarial diploma with courses in word processing.

A word processing operator has an entire minicomputer system at his/her disposal. In addition to keyboard and grammar skills, this person must be able to create, proofread, edit, print, and electronically file letters and memos.

Courtesy of Digital Equipment Corporation.

A **word processing office manager** supervises a group of secretaries who operate word processing work stations. The manager schedules the work, sets up office procedures, rates staff performance, devises reports to other managers in the company, and interviews, selects, and trains new personnel.

Computer-related jobs are not restricted to office areas. Businesses which design and manufacture specialized products often have a person called a **numerical control clerk**. When a new product or part is ordered, this person translates the details of a blueprint into computer commands and stores them on magnetic or paper tape. When the tape is completed, it is fed into a computer-controlled machine, which follows the instructions to shape, cut, and grind the raw material into a finished product.

A numerical control clerk needs a strong technical and math background, with emphasis on mechanical drafting, algebra, geometry, calculus, and computer science.

A numerical control clerk combines technical and programming knowledge to operate specialized industrial machinery.

Courtesy of Cincinnati Milacron.

Computer Evolution

The historical development of computers is fascinating. Computers have been massed-produced commercially for less than three decades, and yet each decade has brought enormous improvements to its design and capabilities.

Oddly enough, long before computers were even invented, computer cards presently used in the classroom for programming, and used by service businesses such as telephone, natural gas, and electric power companies as invoices, were employed as a way of storing information.

In order to assist with the 1890 census, **Herman Hollerith**, a statistician with the U.S. government's census bureau, designed a way to store information on cardboard cards in the form of holes. He invented the Hollerith Code, which refers to the combination of holes needed to represent any letter, number, or symbol on the cards. In 1924, his ideas were purchased by the International Business Machines Corporation, more commonly known as IBM.

Another inventor, **James Powers**, invented similar equipment to handle cardboard cards, using a different code with rounded holes. Eventually, the company which he formed became part of UNIVAC, a division of the present-day Sperry Rand Corporation. Together, IBM and UNIVAC produced the majority of the card-handling equipment for several decades.

The Herman Hollerith Tabulating Machine was the forerunner to early computer systems. It punched information onto cardboard cards to facilitate machine handling.

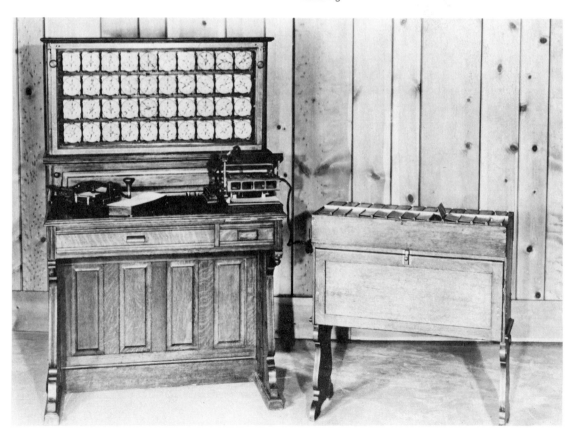

The First Experimental Computers

During the Second World War (1939–1945), the U.S. military establishment began the secret development of its first computer. Howard Aiken, together with IBM, built an electro-mechanical computer called the **Mark 1**. This computer, composed of both electrical and mechanical parts, operated on a system of electric relays, switches, and gears. Instructions were punched into rolls of paper tape, and once the machine started on the first instruction, no further human assistance was required.

A short time later, America's first completely electrical computer was designed by an engineer named John Mauchly, along with a graduate student named J. Presper Eckert. The computer, called ENIAC (Electrical Numerical Integrator and Calculator), had no moving parts. Electrical impulses, instead of gears, were used for counting. The machine weighed 30 t, and contained 18 000 vacuum tubes and several kilometres of electrical wire. This computer required so much power to operate (130 000 W) that it is claimed that all the lights in West Philadelphia used to dim when it was turned on.

The ENIAC operated on the decimal system of counting (0,1,2,3,4,5,6,7,8,9), similar to the way humans perform ordinary arithmetic. It was originally designed as a specialized military computer. One of its first test runs contained equations for the infamous "Manhatten Project" to help create the first atomic bombs which forced Japan's surrender during the Second World War.

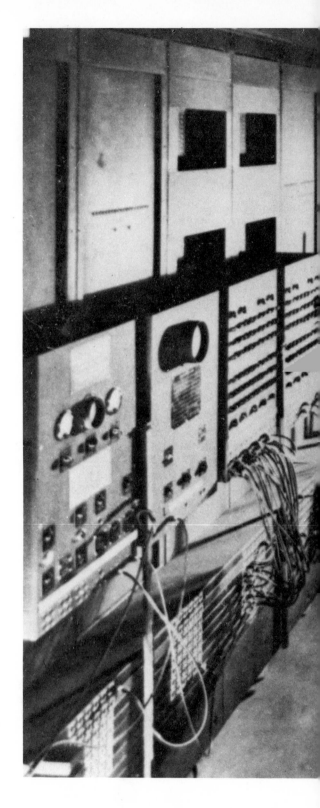

ENIAC was the first completely electrical computer. It generated a great deal of heat and was in frequent need of repairs.

Courtesy of Sperry Univac Corporation.

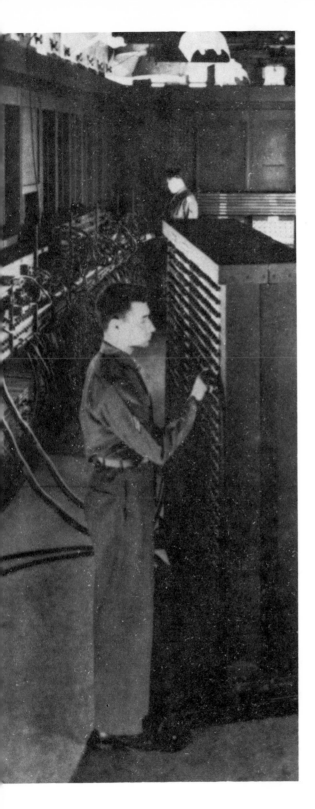

After the ENIAC, many research laboratories, most of them associated with universities in Britain and the United States, began to construct their own experimental models of electrical computers. Between 1946 and 1954, three important ideas were discovered that were included in the design of most computers from that time onwards.

The first idea, called the **stored program concept**, was introduced by a brilliant mathematician named John Von Neumann. This feature allowed a computer program to be stored inside the computer, while the processor unit worked on it without further assistance. Prior to this discovery, instructions had to be fed in on paper tape, or by rearranging hundreds of removable plug wires into a special pattern on a panel. Because the program was stored electrically inside the computer, the person using it could now alter the instructions whenever necessary, even when the machine was operating.

Another idea Von Neumann recommended, which eventually increased computer speeds, was to replace the ten decimal numbers used for counting with **binary numbers**. Since electrical switches can be either on or off, the binary system, which has only two numbers (1 and 0), seemed a logical way to store information electrically in a coded form.

The third discovery, made by Grace Hopper, was the creation of a **compiler program** to translate instructions into binary so that the computer could follow them. The compiler also gave error messages to the programmer when instructions were incorrect.

Development of a Computer Industry

The electronic industry as we know it today began with the creation of the **UNIVAC 1**. Its prototype (original experimental model) received much publicity by correctly predicting the victory of Dwight D. Eisenhower in the U.S. presidential election before all the votes were counted. In 1954, Sperry Rand massed-produced 48 identical models of the UNIVAC 1. It was the first "general-purpose computer" designed to help with a variety of applications in business, scientific fields, and in the military. Sperry Rand also introduced magnetic tape machines as a method of transferring stored data quickly.

Sperry Rand's early lead in the computer industry proved to be short-lived. The IBM corporation began producing a "general purpose computer" as well. Superior marketing techniques and computer designs soon gave IBM the largest share of the computer sales in North America from the mid-fifties to the present day.

The Univac 1 was the first mass-produced "general-purpose" computer system. It used magnetic tape units as auxiliary storage devices.

Courtesy of Sperry Univac Corporation.

Computer Generations

Various improvements in electronics and software have increased the speed and reliability of the machines. Each improvement created a new series or generation of computers.

Computers built during the period of the UNIVAC 1 to the late 1950s are referred to as the **first generation of computers**. Their circuits were made up of gas-filled, glass vacuum tubes and metres of electrical wire. Sheets of magnetic rings called "cores" served as internal storage, while magnetic tape units could be added to provide external storage. Programs were awkward to write because the computer only accepted instructions in binary code, using the numbers 0 and 1.

In the **second generation of computers** (1959–1964), solid transistors replaced the glass vacuum tubes. Computers were smaller, cooler, faster, and less likely to break down. Three different types of extra storage devices could now be attached to the computer. In addition to the magnetic tape unit, a magnetic drum device, which has a cylinder shape, or a circular magnetic disk unit were available. Committees of programmers designed standardized computer languages called FORTRAN and COBOL. For the first time, people could communicate with computers using English phrases instead of just numbers.

The **third generation of computers** (1965–1969) is characterized by tiny transistor chips called integrated circuits. These integrated circuits reduced and combined the wiring and transistors of earlier computers into miniature circuit patterns occupying only five square millimetres.

The first three generations of computer circuitry are shown in this photograph. The largest item is a circuit panel containing eight gas-filled vacuum tubes. Second-generation circuitry, shown at the left, is represented by a plastic circuit board containing several transistors. The modules in the foreground are examples of third-generation transistor chips.

Courtesy of IBM Canada Ltd.

Two operating features were also introduced which changed the way people communicated with computers. The first feature, **teleprocessing**, allowed users at computer terminals to have information processed by a computer several kilometres away. People no longer had to be in the same building, or even in the same city as the computer which they were using. The second feature, **interactive processing**, allowed users to communicate directly with the processor unit, asking questions and getting responses almost immediately. It was these features which permitted banks and airline ticket offices to set up vast information networks all across the country.

The **fourth generation of computers** (1970–1980) contained microprocessors which are a complete processing unit on a single computer chip. This miniaturization of the processing unit encouraged the development of small, floor-model minicomputers, and desk-top microcomputers, as well as a variety of electronic toys and calculators. A method of organizing stored information called **data base management** permitted companies to design large cross-referenced "libraries" on their magnetic disks. Instead of retrieving a complete data file of information on some topic, parts of several files could be combined in any sequence required. Another method of

Figure 1.6

Teleprocessing

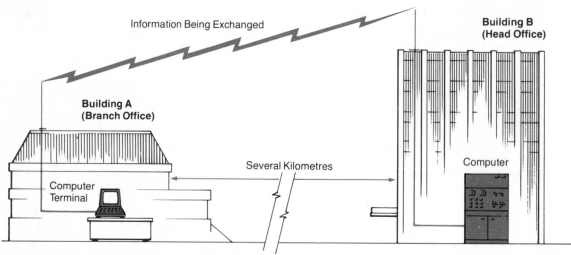

Teleprocessing, which means processing information at a distance, allows branch offices to use a computer several miles away. Many methods can be used to transmit the information from one building to another, including telephone lines, microwave towers, underground cables, and communication satellites.

organizing information, called **virtual memory**, allowed a computer to run programs normally too large for the main memory to store. Magnetic disks, under this method, were used as overflow areas to temporarily store and swap information to and from the computer's main memory. This allowed minicomputers to act as if they had the memory of a larger mainframe computer.

Fourth-generation circuitry introduced a complete computer on a single chip. The computer chip, shown here on a penny, contains the logic, control, and memory registers necessary to operate an entire computer system. It is also referred to as a microprocessing unit.

Courtesy of Rockwell International.

Summary

The computer is an excellent machine for processing information, and can be applied to a variety of applications. The electrical and mechanical parts, referred to as hardware, work together with a series of software programs which cause the computer to operate in some specific manner.

Each digital computer system contains five distinctive features—input, output, processing, storage, and control. Digital computers are capable of performing calculations, data manipulation, and simple decision making. They are manufactured, at present, in four sizes—pocket computers, microcomputers, minicomputers, and mainframe computer systems. Other types of computers include the analog computer, which compares physical quantities to preset levels, and hybrid computer systems, which combine elements of both the analog and digital computers for some special purpose.

Computer-related careers are found in computer departments, business offices, and manufacturing plants. These careers blend specialized programming, secretarial, or technical skills with a knowledge of computer systems.

Computer evolution began with the electromechanical Mark 1 and has progressed through four generations to the present-day pocket computers, and microprocessor chips used in toys, cars, and appliances.

Review Questions

These are *general level questions* which may require factual recall, reading comprehension, and some application of the knowledge from this chapter.

1. List four reasons why the compute excellent machine for processing info. tion.

2. Explain the concepts *hardware* and *software*.

3. What is the difference between an application program and programs written by the manufacturer? Give examples of each type.

4. List and briefly explain the purpose of the five basic features in all digital computers.

5. What is the purpose of a processor unit? What are peripherals?

6. Why do computer systems usually have two separate storage areas?

7. What control feature does the manufacturer's software provide?

8. Why do some people prefer the minicomputer rather than the two smaller types?

9. Give two reasons why corporations, government, and the military prefer the largest type of computer system.

10. Define *analog computer*. Describe how an analog device in an air conditioner would operate.

11. What is a hybrid computer system? Briefly describe an application of a hybrid computer system.

12. Describe some of the tasks which a computer operator would perform.

13. What does a data entry clerk do? Describe three different types of machines that data entry clerks may operate.

14. What type of work does a programmer do? List some personality traits and skills that a programmer would need to be successful.

15. A systems analyst plays an important role in a computer department. What does that person do?

16. Describe a computer-related job outside office areas. *Computer repair man*

17. For what inventions is Herman Hollerith known?

18. Name and briefly describe the first completely electrical computer.

19. What does the *stored program concept* refer to? Why is it important?

20. Explain what John Von Neumann recommended as a replacement for the decimal system of counting inside computers. Why did he make that choice?

21. What does the phrase *computer generation* refer to? Describe some features of the latest generation of computers.

22. Why was the development of computer languages important?

23. Explain two features which permitted banks and airline ticket offices to set up vast information networks all across the country.

24. What does *data base management* permit companies to do?

Applying Your Knowledge

These *advanced level questions* assume an understanding of the material presented in this chapter, and provide new situtations which may require evaluation, analysis, or application of that knowledge.

1. The computer is an excellent machine for processing information. Suggest some reasons why commercial banks would find computers well-suited to the processing of daily banking transactions.

2. Large aircraft have an automatic pilot mechanism that can be used to control the plane while the pilot relaxes. The automatic pilot is actually a combination of computers. Name three things the computer must constantly check in order to keep the plane safe and on course.

3. Imagine that you are sitting in a satellite 30 km above earth with just a computer to keep you informed of what is happening. Name five things that you would like the computer to keep track of for you.

4. Suppose a student puts an application program into a device for the computer to read. What is the first manufacturer's program to be involved? What does it do? What is the second program to be involved and what does it do?

5. A pocket calculator has several features which are similar to those on a computer. List each of these items, then state which function it represents—*input, output, processing, storage,* and *control.*

   Items:
   Keyboard; display screen; inside circuits; clear button; memory button.

6. Consumer products labelled "digital" often means that the product contains computer circuitry (example: pocket digital calculator). Name three additional products with that label and explain what the computer circuitry would be used for in each case.

7. Mainframe computers are the largest of the four categories of digital computers. List the following users of this size of digital computer—large corporations, government, and the military. Beside each, list at least two uses which they would find for the computer. Make all of the items different.

8. Suppose that the data processing manager of a computer department decides that the company's payroll program is to be completely redesigned. Identify four people who would be involved in the redesigning and explain what each of them would be doing.

Individual Projects

1. **Want Ads**

   Using newspapers as resource material,
   find want ads for ten different computer
   jobs. Fasten each clipping neatly to a
   separate page. Underneath each clipping,
   prepare a brief description of the job
   (50-word minimum). The description
   should be researched from your textbook
   and library resources, and include job
   description, educational requirements, and
   annual salary. Cover with an appropriate
   title page.

2. **Computer Articles**

   Using magazines such as *Byte*, *Creative
   Computing*, *Mini-Micro Systems*, *Popular
   Mechanics*, *Popular Science* and others,
   as well as newspapers, find ten different
   pictures or articles related to computers.
   Fasten each clipping neatly to a separate
   page. Underneath each clipping (or on a
   separate page), give a brief description
   (50-word minimum) of each article **in your
   own words**. Cover with an appropriate
   title page.

3. **Book Report**
   Advanced level

   Prepare a book report on any of the following books. Concentrate on the role which
   the computer has in the story. The report
   must be summarized in your own words.
   The title page should contain the title,
   author, publisher, and year of publication.

   (a) *Charles Babbage—Father of the
   Computer* by Dan Halacy

   (b) *We Reached the Moon —*by John
   Wilford

   (c) *Think: A Biography of the Watsons and
   IBM —*by William Rodgers

   (d) *Space Odyssey 2001 —*by Arthur C.
   Clarke

   (e) *Vulcan's Hammer —*by Philip K. Dick

   (f) Any computer-related book agreed
   upon by your teacher.

4. **Computer Generations**
   Challenge project

   Obtain resource textbooks from the library
   or classroom on computer circuitry. Study
   the generations of computer circuitry, and
   prepare diagrams and explanations of
   each of the following items: *vacuum tubes*,
   transistors, *integrated circuits*, and *MPUs*.

2

Elements of Problem Solving

Objectives

An understanding of the elements of a computer program

A detailed understanding of the five-step method of analyzing and solving computer problems

A detailed understanding of traditional flow-charting symbols, conventions, and applications

An awareness of other techniques for planning algorithms: pseudo-code, structure diagrams, Warnier-Orr diagrams, decision tables, and top down diagrams

An awareness of the elements of, and a need for, program documentation

As the complexity of computer applications increase, so does the need for well-designed, modifiable software.

Courtesy of Ohio Scientific.

Chapter Two
Elements of Problem Solving

Minutes spent in effective program planning can eliminate hours of frustrating program modification.

Have you ever watched a science fiction movie in which a computer was involved? The guidance systems of interstellar spaceships and the friendly, talking robots in such shows as *Star Wars* and *Buck Rogers* are imaginative ways in which writers think that computers will behave in the future. Present-day technicians have already developed talking, self-learning machines, as well as large computer systems capable of monitoring the complete environment of orbiting space stations. The one missing element, which would make today's computers behave like the futuristic movie versions, is the software. Programmed instructions have not yet been developed to allow computers to behave in such sophisticated ways.

The computer is just a machine. Without step-by-step instructions, the computer cannot do anything. It does what it is told to do, nothing more. Actions such as drawing pictures, imitating human speech, playing synthesized music, and moving robots from place to place are all dependent upon detailed, preprogrammed instructions which the computer follows. The ability to make computers perform in this manner is quite an art. With practice, most people can learn to manipulate a computer to do a variety of things, including problem solving, within a short span of time.

A Computer Program

Most computers when purchased from the manufacturer already contain a certain amount of software. They usually include an operating system and one or more language processors which allow the user the capability to communicate with the machine. What the computer does not have are application programs which will perform certain tasks or solve particular problems. These instructions, when required, must be planned and written by the person using the computer. The person who plans and writes programs for a computer is called a **programmer**.

A computer program usually contains three components: a set of instructions, some data (although not all programs need data), and some programmer comments. The **instructions** are commands which instruct the computer to perform some type of action. The instructions may be a single word such as "READ," or "PRINT," or longer phrases which require the computer to act once certain conditions are met.

The **data** refers to the values used in a problem. If a program is designed to calculate an average for a student's report card, for example, the student's list of subject marks would be referred to as the data for that problem.

The **programmer comments** are phrases or sentences inserted in the program to make it easier to understand. The comments may include a program title, programmer identification (student's name and period, for example), and various remarks placed throughout the program to aid the programmer in interpreting what the various groups of commands are designed to achieve. Grouping several commands together, and then separating them from the rest of the program with spaces and programmer comments, is a very important concept in writing computer programs. It makes a program easier to read, and easier to correct if something needs to be changed later on.

Figure 2.1
Diagram Showing Sequential Relationships

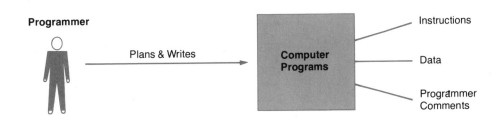

Steps Used To Solve Computer Problems

Computers are excellent machines for following instructions. If you can provide a computer with all the steps required to solve a problem, it will perform each step dutifully, in billionths of a second. Although a computer can be programmed to do many things, it cannot, unfortunately, invent solutions to problems. The solutions must be first created by the programmer.

Since the computer requires quite detailed instructions on how to perform a given task, it is important that the solution to a problem be carefully planned. Computer solutions, in particular, require a sequential approach to problem solving. One way to become skilled at solving computer-related problems is to follow a pattern of five steps:

Figure 2.2

Five-Step Approach to Problem Solving

1. Define the problem.
2. List the values.
3. Plan the solution.
4. Code the solution into a computer language.
5. Test the solution, and correct if necessary.

Step One—Define the Problem

Stating exactly what you want the computer to do is an important step in problem solving. People who leave out this step often become confused part way through the solution. An attempt to solve a problem with just a vague idea of what is required is a poor way to begin. If you can define the problem clearly, the rest of the steps are easy.

The best way to define a problem is to express it as simply as possible. This can be done in two ways. The first method is to reduce all the ideas needed to solve the problems to one or two sentences. The second method, which is particularly useful if calculations are involved, is to represent the ideas in the form of one or more equations. Many programmers prefer to use both methods at the same time to ensure clarity.

Step Two—List the Values

Most problems contain data values which are needed to process the solution. These values are stored in the computer's main memory along with the program's instructions. The data can be used repeatedly during the processing of the solution without being erased.

Since there may be several values stored in the computer's memory at the same time, the processor unit needs to know where to locate each one. To make the computer's search easier, a word or letter is assigned to the memory location of each value. The fastest way to assign names to storage locations is to use letters of the alphabet.

One way to provide effective labelling is to use the first letter of the word which describes whatever is stored in that location. For example, in a payroll program designed to calculate the amount to put on an employee's paycheque, the letter H could represent the hours worked, R could represent the rate of pay, and the letter G could represent the answer, gross pay. It is important to assign a different letter to each storage location; otherwise, the computer gets confused. Even the answer needs a letter to represent the storage location, where it will be put after the calculations are completed.

The following *Bank Interest Problem* illustrates how a problem can be reduced to a short definition, and a listing of known values.

Bank Interest Problem

Dan Ryan put $850 into a savings account. The bank indicated that they would pay 10% interest annually on this deposit. How much interest would Dan make if he left it in the account for one year?

The Problem Defined and the Values Listed

Problem Definition

Print the interest after one year at 10%.

$I = (P * R)$

Data

P = $850.00
R = 0.10
(P = principal)
(R = rate of interest)

Notice that the definition identifies exactly what is required of the computer, which is, print the interest after one year if the interest rate is 10%. The definition also includes an equation which shows how the answer is to be calculated. The equation, $I = (P * R)$, means that the dollar amount of interest is equal to the principal (amount invested) times the rate of interest. The first letter of the words being represented are used to express the equation. The asterisk (*) is a common method of representing multiplication in programming. It removes confusion with the letter X.

The data section lists all "known" values to be used in the solution. The principal, stored in location P, is $850.00. The rate of interest, stored in location R, is 0.10, which is 10% expressed as a decimal.

Step Three—Plan the Solution

Once you have mastered the art of reducing a problem to its simplest form, the next step is to plan the solution. A plan for solving a problem is called an **algorithm**. It consists of a list of instructions, in some particular order, which the computer must follow step-by-step, along with the data to be used in the problem. Each problem has its own algorithm, or solution.

Courtesy of Canadian Datasystems.

"Hope you like tea. We don't have a coffee algorithm yet."

There are many ways to plan an algorithm. Some programmers write out the list of steps using a combination of word phrases and equations. This type of list is called **psuedo-code** (which means false code). It is given this name because although it resembles the final set of instructions in a computer program, it still needs to be converted into a computer language which the computer can understand.

Another way to plan an algorithm is to use some type of diagram which makes the ideas or logic in the solution easy to see. Some of the diagrams used in planning algorithms include decision tables, Warnier-Orr (pro-nounced Warn-yay-Or) diagrams, top down diagrams, and structure diagrams. These planning techniques, along with pseudo-code, will be explained in a later chapter.

The most popular method to plan an algorithm, at present, is to use a **flowchart**. This is a diagram which uses arrows and special symbols to represent the steps in a problem solution.

Figure 2.3
Flowchart Symbols

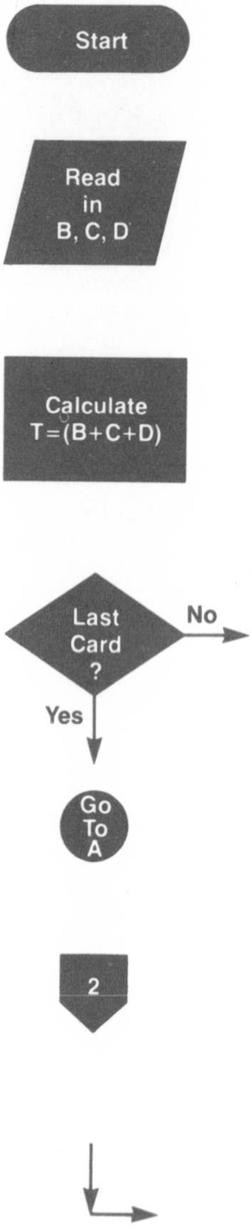

The *terminal symbol*.
It is used to show the beginning and the end of a program.

The *input/output symbol*.
This shape is used to identify the storage locations of data to be read in, and also the storage locations of answers to be printed out.

The *processing symbol*.
It is used to indicate some type of information processing such as mathematical operations, sorting, merging, copying, and location transfers.

The *decision symbol*.
This diamond shape is used to indicate points in a program where a branch to alternative paths is possible, if certain conditions are met.

The *step connector*.
Two of these are needed to hop from one part of the solution to another.

The *offpage connector*.
Two of these are needed to continue elsewhere when you run out of room at the bottom of the page.

Arrows and arrowheads.
These are used to show which way the steps are to be followed.

Preparing a Program Flowchart

In a traditional flowchart, each symbol has a specific shape. Each shape represents a different function which the computer can perform. A rectangle, for example, is used to show some type of calculating or processing of information. A diamond-shaped symbol, on the other hand, is reserved for questions on decisions which the computer will have to consider during the program.

Since people's drawing skills may vary, programmers often use a stencil called a **template** to draw flowcharts. The template helps to make everyone's diagram readable and similar in appearance. Consider the following flowchart for the same *Bank Interest Problem* mentioned earlier. As a reminder, the problem stated that $850 was deposited in an account for one year at 10%. The problem definition required that the dollar amount of interest be printed after one year, using the expression I = (P * R) as the method to calculate the interest.

Figure 2.4
Flowchart for the Bank Interest Problem

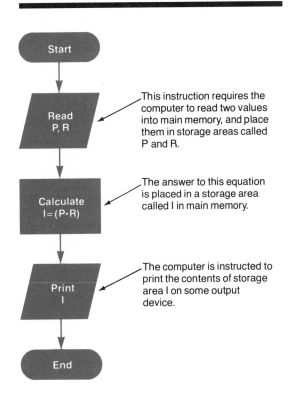

This instruction requires the computer to read two values into main memory, and place them in storage areas called P and R.

The answer to this equation is placed in a storage area called I in main memory.

The computer is instructed to print the contents of storage area I on some output device.

The flowchart solution, as indicated, requires the computer to **read** in the values and store them in memory locations P and R. Next, the values are multiplied, and the answer is stored in the location labelled I. Finally, the contents of storage location I (which contains the answer in this case) is printed. The start and stop symbols provide a beginning and ending to the flowchart diagram.

There are several things to note about the flowchart solution. All words are printed in *block letters*. Also, the actual data values are not put in the flowchart. Instead, the "title," or "address," of their location is used. This is an important concept because the computer reads and stores all programs in main memory before doing anything with them. Since computers have millions of storage locations, the processor unit will find it impossible to relocate a data value without the help of a "title," or "address," such as the letters P and R.

Each distinct function such as input, decision making, or processing has a different shape in a flowchart. This feature makes the logic of the solution easy to see. The arrows and arrowheads provide the direction, or "flow," of logic in the diagram.

Step Four—Coding the Solution

Computers cannot read flowcharts. Flowcharts are used to help the programmer plan the logic of the solution, and to make corrections easier, if any are needed. To put the algorithm, or solution, into a form which the computer can understand, the instructions must be converted into a computer language. This action is referred to as **coding** the solution. A **computer language** is a short-form style of listing instructions that can be understood by a particular computer. All computers contain one or more language processors which can interpret programs written in a computer language. There are several thousand different computer languages available in North America. Some creative people even invented their own personal computer language.

Computer manufacturers, however, tend to offer a limited number of languages, which makes programming easier to learn and provides some standardization among the many computer users. Some of the more popular "high level" computer languages include BASIC, FORTRAN, COBOL, and PASCAL. These languages are written with English phrases, and are relatively easy to understand. Another group of computer languages such as ZAP, MINI, and HYPO use numbers or abbreviated words to list the instructions. This group, referred to as "low level" computer languages, are cumbersome to write, less powerful, and in some cases more difficult to understand than the high level computer languages.

Once the flowchart (or some other type of algorithm) has been carefully thought about and prepared, the coding of the solution should be a routine procedure. Each step of the algorithm can be converted into one or two lines of the computer code using the rules of a particular computer language. Low level computer languages generally need more lines of computer code than a high level language to get the computer to process the same problem.

Figure 2.5

Coding From a Flowchart

Flowchart	Coded into Basic		Coded into Hypo		
Start					
Read in A, B, C	10	READ A, B, C	000	05	100
			001	05	110
			002	05	115
Calculate T = (A+B+C)	20	T = (A+B+C)	003	03	100
			004	03	110
			005	03	115
Print T	25	PRINT T	006	02	200
			007	07	200
End	30	END	008	14	000

The flowchart algorithm shown above can be converted into any computer language. Normally it takes fewer lines of code of a high level computer language, such as BASIC, compared to a low level language, such as HYPO, to solve the same problem.

Step Five — Test the Solution and Correct Any Errors

Once the algorithm has been coded into a computer language, it is tested to see if it works properly. This can be done in two ways. The first method is to check it manually. The second method is to let the computer attempt to process it. If the testing procedures indicate any errors, they are corrected, and testing continues until the solution is completely correct and acceptable.

One manual method of checking for error, if calculations are involved, is to use a pencil and paper to work out an approximate answer. If the answer appears too large, or too small, or just does not make sense, rethink the steps leading to that answer. If a partner is available, ask that person to carefully check the solution for errors as well.

A second way to test the solution is to let the computer attempt to process it. If there are errors in the way the solution was written, the computer will print out short messages called **error diagnostics**, which indicate the type of error and where to locate it in the program.

It is important to remember that programs which have been successfully processed by the computer are not necessarily correct. While the language processor does check for errors in the way the language was written, it does not check for errors in logic. Logic errors can only be discovered by a careful manual test.

"Where's the clown that set up this program?"

Putting the Steps Together

Effective problem solving requires a systematic approach. Even the most complex computer problems can be reduced to their basic elements if they are analyzed and processed with the same pattern of five steps described above.

Each stage of the process—definition, identifying values, planning algorithms, coding the solution, and removing errors—is a practised art. If one of the steps is omitted, the probability of becoming confused and frustrated with the solution is fairly high. This is particularly evident in problems which require lengthy solutions. Although the time spent learning each step in the process may seem extensive, the rewards of the learning process become clear when more complex problems are encountered.

The following *Payroll Problem* illustrates how the pattern of five steps can be used to analyze and plan its solution.

Payroll Problem

A company is processing cheques for its employees. One employee earns $6.50 per hour, and works 40 hours per week. If a standard deduction of $73.00 is taken off her paycheque each week, calculate and print both the gross pay and net pay for this employee.

Planning for Payroll Problem

Problem Definition

Print gross pay and net pay for one employee.

G = (R * H)
N = (G − D)

Data

R = $6.50
H = 40
D = $73.00

(R means rate of pay)
(H means hours worked)
(D means deductions)

Figure 2.6
Flowchart for Payroll Problem

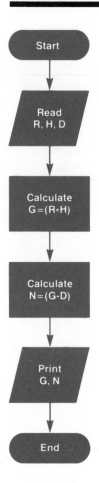

Basic Coding for Payroll Problem

```
10    REMARK  SUE  WILSON  PD.  6

15    REMARK  PAYROLL  PROGRAM

20    READ   R,H,D

25    G  =  (R  *  H)

30    N  =  (G  −  D)

35    PRINT    G,N

40    DATA  6.50,  40,  73

45    END
```

Developing Flowcharting Skills

Flowcharts are a popular method of planning algorithms to computer problems. The diagram allows the programmer to develop the necessary details, one step at a time, and to make changes during the planning of the solution. It is essential that certain guidelines or flowcharting conventions are followed in the development of the diagram. These guidelines not only make the diagram easier to understand, but also allow programmers to communicate with each other without confusion.

If a flowchart is properly designed, the coding of the steps should be a routine procedure. The programmer simply translates each step of the flowchart into one or more lines of computer code in the same order which the diagram indicates. Since the logic of the solution is already contained in the flowchart, the routine of coding only requires a knowledge of the coding rules of whatever computer language is being used. Because there are several thousand computer languages available, details in a flowchart should be presented in a general way, such that they can be easily converted into any computer language.

Flowcharting Convention 1

The contents of a flowchart should be of a general nature, and not be related to a specific set of data or to any particular computer language.

As you are reading the words on this page, notice the movement of your eyes. There are two distinct eye movements. The first is from left to right as you read across the page. The second movement, somewhat slower, is down the page as each new line is read. We have been using that reading pattern since primary school without any conscious effort.

Since we tend to read with this pattern of eye movements, any charts or diagrams which cause our eyes to move in those specific directions will be the easiest to read. Conversely, any diagrams which require the reader to shift direction, reading right to left, or bottom to top, will require more concentration to understand. Almost all traditional-style flowcharts can be designed to cause your eye to move in the regular reading pattern. Such flowcharts are the most effective in communicating ideas.

Flowcharting Convention 2

Design flowcharts with arrows pointing in only two directions—top to bottom and left to right.

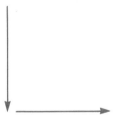

Flowcharts often require eye movement from one part of the diagram to another or, when space is insufficient, from part of one page to another. Two types of connectors are used to show these movements in a traditional flowchart. One is a step connector and the other is an offpage connector.

Flowcharting Convention 3

When using a pair of step connectors to "jump" from one part of the flowchart to another, interrupt the main line of the flowchart along the arrows and not at the symbols.

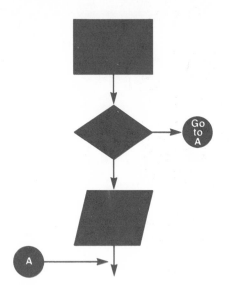

Flowcharting Convention 4

If there is insufficient room at the bottom of a page to complete the flowchart, use offpage connectors to provide continuity.

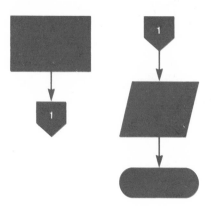

Looping

What happens if more than one set of data needs to be processed? This occurs frequently with computer programs. For example, in a payroll program, there may be information for hundreds, or even thousands, of different paycheques.

Computer programs are stored in main memory while they are being processed. The computer will follow the same set of instructions as many times as the user wishes. Each time the computer goes through the program, it can process an entirely new set of data values. This concept is referred to as **looping**. In this manner, a relatively short program can be made to produce a "mountain" of answers. What the computer does need to know, however, is when you wish it to stop looping. Without this knowledge, it may continue indefinitely. This error in program logic is referred to as **infinite loop**.

End-of-File Checks

A list made up of individual sets of data values is called a **data file**. When a computer searches for the last value (or the last set of values) in a data file, this process is referred to as an **end-of-file check**. The end-of-file check can be programmed in two ways. One method is to put a **flag**, or **dummy value**, at the end of the data file. The processor unit is then asked, in the program, to stop looping once that dummy value has been reached.

If a programmer knows the number of loops required in advance, another method may be used. This second method involves three steps. A storage location, called an **accumlator** or a **counter**, is created, and a value of zero is stored in it. Each time the computer completes a loop, the value of one is added to the counter. During each loop, the computer is asked to compare the number in the counter to the required number of loops.

If the numbers are equal, the looping process stops.

Consider the following problem in which the computer must perform an end-of-file check. One algorithm uses the *dummy value method*. The other algorithm uses the *counter method*.

Class List Problem

There are 25 students in a computer class. Have the computer read in and print the name and subject mark for each student.

Figure 2.7
Class List Problem Planned with the Dummy Value Method

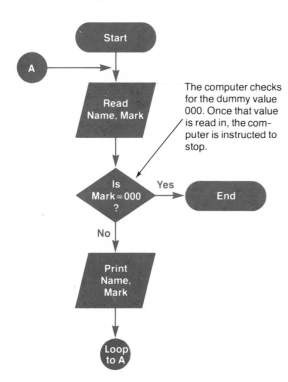

The computer checks for the dummy value 000. Once that value is read in, the computer is instructed to stop.

Figure 2.8
Class List Problem Planned with the Counter Method

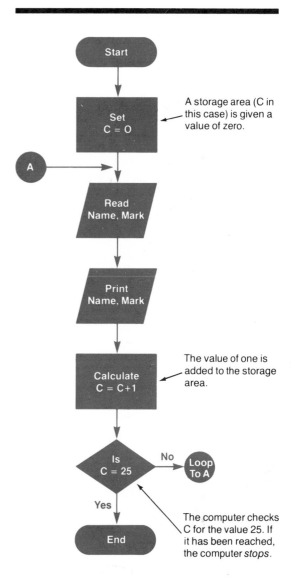

A storage area (C in this case) is given a value of zero.

The value of one is added to the storage area.

The computer checks C for the value 25. If it has been reached, the computer *stops*.

Selective Decisions

In addition to end-of-file checks, decision symbols can be used to select certain items out of a list. Although the flowchart symbol appears the same as it does in an end-of-file situation, its purpose is different. By allowing a simple comparison to be made, the computer is able to decide whether or not to select an item. It is these program decisions which give the computer its logic capability.

Consider the following *Final Exam Problem* in which only certain students in a list are to be considered.

Final Exam Problem

At Westminister District High School, students who obtain an average of 70% or greater during the year in computer science do not have to write the final exam. A classroom microcomputer is used to store each student's name and average mark. The last name in the list is a dummy record which reads "Student, 000".

Plan a computer program which reads in each student's name and average mark (one at a time). Then, have the computer print a list of only those students who must write the final exam. The list is to be posted on the classroom bulletin board near the exam schedule.

Figure 2.9

Flowchart for Final Exam Problem

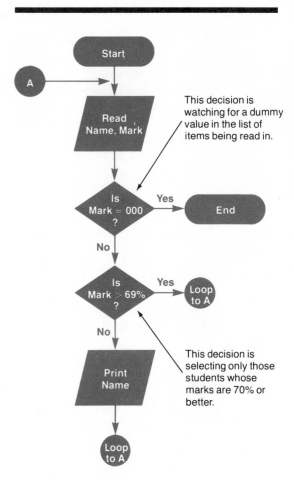

This decision is watching for a dummy value in the list of items being read in.

This decision is selecting only those students whose marks are 70% or better.

The Need for Documentation

Documentation refers to various items related to a computer program which are stored together, in an organized manner, for future reference. Management will usually require that all completed programs be thoroughly documented.

Documentation would include the program's title, completion date, its purpose, data values, an algorithm (often in the form of a traditional flowchart), and a program listing. A **program listing** is a complete copy of the program's instructions on a computer printout.

Good documentation is essential if anyone attempts to understand or modify a program later on. In a large organization, requests for changes in an old program happen frequently.

The original programmer will be glad that documentation on a program written six months earlier is available when the manager requests an updated version. If the original programmer has left the organization, someone else can turn to a file folder, or booklet containing the programmer's documentation, and plan the needed changes.

Documentation manuals are invaluable to programmers who work with complex software systems. Final drafts of program descriptions, planning diagrams, and program listings are indexed, bound, and stored in a filing cabinet for future reference.

Courtesy of Digital Equipment Corporation.

Summary

Although a computer can do many things, it cannot invent solutions to problems. The solutions must be first created by the programmer. Since the computer requires quite detailed instructions on how to perform a given task, it is important that the solution be carefully planned.

Beginning programmers often believe that by coding directly into a computer language, much time will be saved in the preparation of programs. The opposite is true, however. Poorly planned programs usually contain numerous errors. The time spent correcting these errors actually increases the total time spent in preparing programs.

Programmers will obtain better productivity if they use a five-step approach to problem solving: define the problem; list the values; plan the solution; code the solution; test the program, and correct any errors.

An algorithm, which is a solution to a problem, may be planned in many ways. The most common technique is called traditional flowcharting. It requires the use of a plastic stencil called a template. Flowcharting conventions help to make the solutions easy to read and understand. This is important, because in addition to planning algorithms, flowcharts are also used for documentation which other people will follow.

Review Questions

These are *general level questions* which may require factual recall, reading comprehension, and some application of the knowledge from this chapter.

1. When a computer arrives from the factory, what type of software is included? What is left out?

2. Name and describe three components of a computer program.

3. Why is it important that solutions to problems be carefully planned?

4. List the five steps involved in the preparation of solutions to computer problems.

5. What is the most effective way of assigning names or letters to storage areas?

6. What is a problem definition?

7. Define *algorithm*.

8. Name six methods which programmers can use to plan algorithms.

9. Problem solutions are eventually coded before they are put into a computer. What does coding refer to?

10. Describe two ways of testing a new program.

11. Why should the instructions in a flowchart not be related to any particular computer language?

12. Effective flowcharts have arrows pointing in only two directions. Explain why such flowcharts are effective.

13. What does *looping* refer to?

14. Why do some programs need an end-of-file check?

15. Define documentation. List the items found in a properly documented program.

Applying Your Knowledge

The answers to the problems listed below assume an understanding of the material presented in this chapter, and provide new situations which may require evaluation, analysis, or application of that knowledge.

Flowcharting Problems

Analyze and flowchart the solutions to the following problems. If possible, use the planning sheet approach to the analysis of the problems. Questions 1–12 are *general level problems*.

1. **The Stereo Set**

   Peter Wilson purchases a stereo set worth $350.00 The store calculated the interest at 24% per year. Flowchart the solution which would print out the dollar amount of interest.

2. **The Car Loan**

   Joan Wallace purchased a car on credit for $7500. The credit union calculated her interest at 13.5% compounded annually. Flowchart the solution which would print out the dollar amount of interest and the total cost of the bank loan.

3. **Net Pay**

   Find the net pay of an employee whose rate of pay is $4.50 per hour, and who works 40 hours per week. Weekly deduction amount to $35.50 per pay.

4. **The Report Card**

   Susan Clark wanted to calculate her term average which would appear on her report card. Flowchart the solution which would total her marks and print out her average.

   Her term marks:

Math	65
Business	75
French	64
English	89
Physical Ed.	83
Geography	72
Science	71
History	78

5. Engineering

A design engineer at Ford Motors is experimenting with different size holes in an engine block. He wants to know (a) the area, and (b) the circumference of a circle if he sets the radius at 7 cm. Flowchart the solution.

Formulas: Area = $(3.14 * r^2)$
Circumference = $(2 * 3.14 * r)$

6. The Warehouse

A manager wants to calculate her store's inventory. The former total number of products was 12 550 units. Since then, she has purchased an additional 780 units, sold 250 units, and discovered that 3% of the original total was either damaged or missing. Flowchart the solution which would calculate the final inventory.

End-of-File Problems

7. Sum of Numbers

Flowchart a solution which would total all of the numbers from 1 to 100, and print the final answer.

8. Sum of Even Numbers

Flowchart a solution which would total the first 50 even numbers, from 2 to 100, and print the final answer.

9. List of Workers

The manager of a company wants the computer department to prepare a printout of the company's 300 employees. There is a separate computer card for every employee which contains the employee's name and number. Flowchart a solution which would print both items for all 300 employees.

10. List of Students and Marks

A teacher wants a printout of all the students in her class. Flowchart the solution which would read each student's record card containing the *student's name* and *subject mark*, and have both items printed out for the whole class. Since the class size changes frequently, use the dummy value end-of-file check method.

11. Payroll Cheques

The owner of a large business wishes to use a computer to print the paycheques for all his employees. He uses the formula: *Net Pay = Gross Pay minus Deductions* to calculate the amount of each cheque. Flowchart the solution that reads in the employee's name, hours worked, rate of pay, and deductions, and prints a cheque containing the employee's name and net pay. There are 150 employees.

12. Class Average

There are 35 students at Albright High School in the computer studies class. Read in each student record which contains *student name* and *subject mark*. Flowchart the solution which would calculate and print the class average.

Selective Decision Problems

The following questions are *advanced level problems* which involve multiple decisions and the use of counters.

13. Positive Output

You have a deck of cards with three variables on each one. (Use A,B,C as storage area names.) Flowchart the solution which would calculate $(A + B)/C$, and print only the positive answers.

14. Non-Zero Output

You have a deck of cards with four variables on it...A,B,C, and D. Solve $(A * B * C)/D$ and print only the answers which are *not* equal to zero.

15. The Cosmetic Company

A cosmetic company which sells products door-to-door pays its sales staff a percentage of their total sales for the month. The company keeps a record of each person's name and her total monthly sales. If sales are under $1000, a 2% commission is paid. If sales are $1000, or over, a 4% commission is paid.

Plan a solution which would read in the name and monthly total for each person, and print a complete list containing the name and dollar amount of commission for every seller.

16. Baseball Draftees

For every baseball player eligible to be drafted, a card has been prepared that shows the *name* and *position* of that player. The Toronto Blue Jays are looking for a pitcher. Flowchart the solution that reads the cards and prints only a listing of players who are pitchers.

17. Honour List

There are 1250 students at Eastdale High School. The office has a card for each student containing the student's ~~number,~~ NAME code(1–female, 2–male), and average mark. Print out a list of girls who have obtained an average of 80% or better. The list should contain both student's name and average.

18. Criminal Record

The Moose Jaw Police Station wants a list of criminals in the computer records who have been convicted of theft. The tape being read in (one record at a time) contains *name, offence*, and *conviction date*. The offences are listed in the records as T (theft), A (arson), and H (homicide). The list should contain the name and conviction date of those who were arrested for theft.

19. Mortgage on a Home

A finance company has just provided someone with a $60 000 loan at 12% per year (calculated annually). Flowchart a solution to show the annual interest for twenty years, if the borrower plans to pay $2000 each year. (Note: The finance company will calculate the interest first and add it on to the balance before subtracting any payments.)

20. Bank Interest

A Halifax trust company uses a computer to calculate interest on customer deposits. If the interest is calculated twice a year on term deposits, show the solution to a sum put in for ten years. The final answer should contain principal plus accumulated interest.

Classroom Activities

1. Coding a Mark Sense Card

Obtain from your teacher a "mark sense" computer card which uses pencil marks to record information. This type of card is read by a device which employs reflection of light to determine the position of the spots on the cards.

Place the card on a hard, flat surface. Using a HB pencil, code your name and period on the card, leaving spaces where appropriate. Example: Susan Wilson P.5

2. File Folder Project

Set up a file folder to hold newspaper and magazine clippings with a title, your name, and class. Each time that you see a computer-related article or picture, neatly clip it out and mount it on blank typing paper. Place the sheet into your file folder. The contents of the file folder will be marked for variety in topics, balance between pictures and articles, and neatness.

3

Other Planning Techniques

Objectives

An awareness of planning techniques other than traditional flowcharts

An awareness that plans for a computer program are not related to any particular computer language

An awareness that a single planning technique may not be suitable for all types of computer-related problems

An appreciation of the necessity for the planning of algorithms to produce error-free, well-designed programs

The keyboard and visual screen have become the dominant method of editing and entering computer programs into a computer system. Much frustration is encountered, however, if a programmer forgets to plan the program on paper before approaching the keyboard.

Courtesy of Heath/Zenith Company.

Chapter Three

Other Planning Techniques

A slow-witted cowboy was overheard telling his friends, "I feel good today. I think I'll go into town and kick a few cattle rustlers, and kiss me a mess of pretty girls." With that statement, he turns and rides off in a cloud of dust. One friend turns to the other and says, "Boy, I sure hope he gets it right this time!"

David A. Higgins

Algorithms for computer programs can be planned in a variety of ways. Whatever method is chosen, a planning technique is only effective if it helps the programmer to organize the logic and sequence of steps in a program. The coding of a solution into a computer language should be a routine procedure if the algorithm has been carefully planned. Even if a programmer eventually develops a preference in planning methods, it may prove useful to be aware of techniques that other programmers use.

This chapter introduces the concepts of pseudo-code, structure diagrams, Warnier-Orr diagrams, decison tables, and top down diagrams. Traditional flowcharts are presented, in some cases, as a way of analyzing the new planning techniques.

Pseudo-Code

This planning technique refers to a series of English statements arranged in a manner to resemble a program. Usually, most of the pseudo-code is unrelated to any particular computer language.

It is a free-style planning technique which may contain unusual notations or abbreviations. This makes pseudo-code a poor documentation technique, but does provide a way for an experienced programmer to create imaginative solutions. Its primary uses are to communicate ideas to someone without actually coding, or as a preliminary "rough sketch" for a computer program.

The following two examples illustrate how pseudo-code can be used to plan the algorithms for the different methods of looping, mentioned in Chapter Two.

This example represents pseudo-code for looping with the dummy value method.

```
READ A RECORD
IF MARK = 000 STOP
OTHERWISE, PRINT RECORD
RETURN TO READ
```

This next example represents pseudo-code for the counter method plan for looping.

```
SET COUNTER = ZERO
READ A RECORD
PRINT A RECORD
ADD ONE TO COUNTER
IF COUNTER = 25 STOP
OTHERWISE, RETURN TO READ
```

Consider the following *Stereo Set Problem*. Note that the pseudo-code algorithm is written in short English phrases. This allows a programmer to concentrate on developing the logic of the solution without worrying about the grammatical rules of some computer language. Once the algorithm has been prepared, it can be easily coded into any computer language.

Stereo Set Problem

Monica Taylor purchased a stereo set on credit. After one year, $225.00 remained unpaid. If the store charged 24% interest on the unpaid balance, calculate (a) the dollar amount of interest she would have to pay, and (b) the new balance at the end of the first year.

Pseudo-Code Plan for Stereo Set Problem

```
READ INTEREST RATE, AMOUNT
CALCULATE $ INTEREST = (RATE * AMOUNT)
CALCULATE NEW BALANCE = (INTEREST + AMOUNT)
PRINT $ INTEREST
PRINT NEW BALANCE
STOP
```

Structure Diagrams

Structure diagrams are sometimes called "stick" flowcharts because of their simple, stick-like appearance. These diagrams are used to plan the logic or "structure" of a computer program.

This planning technique is made up of lines, circles, and short, written instructions which "sit" on the lines in the diagram. The straight lines are all drawn at right angles to one another. Two directions of logic flow are used—top to bottom, and left to right. These two directions make the diagram easy to follow visually. The short, written labels, however, are sometimes written lengthways, down the page. The user must turn the page on its side to both read and write the labels.

The small circles identify points in a program where decisions occur. These decisions may create a loop, or cause certain items to be selected from a data file. The letters L and S are used inside the circles to identify a loop or selection process. If there is more than one loop or selection decision in the algorithm, numbers are added to the letters, for example, L1: L2: or S1: S2: .

To clarify the points in the structure diagram, a traditional flowchart is used as a comparison.

Guidance Request Problem

There are 1200 students in a local high school. The guidance department wants a complete listing of the school's data file. The list is to contain the name and mark for each student on the role.

Figure 3.1
Traditional Flowchart of Guidance Request Problem

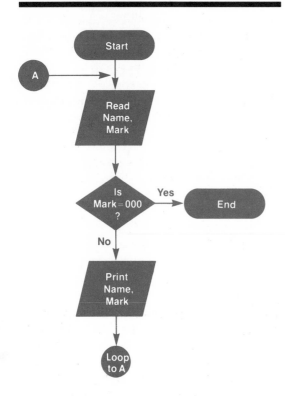

Figure 3.2
Structure Diagram of Guidance Request Problem

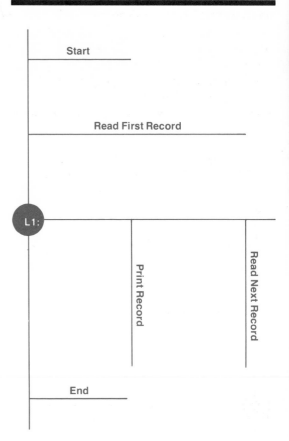

In a structure diagram, the left-hand vertical line is referred to as the trunk line. Instructions are attached to the trunk with short branches. When a series of steps are to be repeated, a longer branch is drawn with the steps attached to it. When the loop is completed, any additional instructions are placed along the trunk line once again.

In the structure diagram for the *Student Average Problem*, the steps are arranged in logical order along the trunk of the diagram. The longer loop branch is needed to read the marks in one at a time, and add them to a counter. This counter will then contain "total marks."

Student Average Problem

Beth James has taken eight subjects this year. Have the computer read each subject mark, then calculate her term average.

Figure 3.3

Structure Diagram for the Student Average Problem

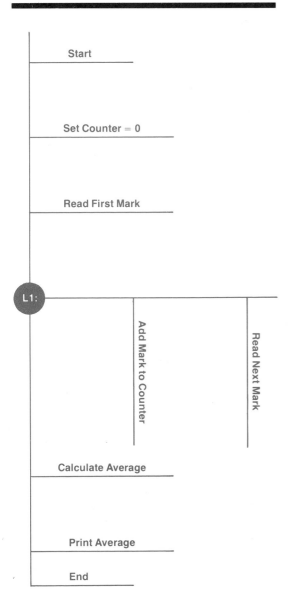

Warnier-Orr Diagrams

In the mid-1960s, a research team in Paris, France led by Jean-Dominique Warnier developed a technique for planning algorithms. Kenneth T. Orr refined and translated the ideas into English.

This planning technique, called a Warnier-Orr diagram, consists of a chart which resembles a tree branching to the right. The chart is made up of small groups, or sets, of instructions, each placed inside a left-hand bracket. As the chart progresses to the right, the brackets become smaller and smaller. Also, the chart progresses from generalized instructions to more specific detail about the algorithm. Each bracket contains the steps required to perform the process indicated by the title of that bracket.

Unlike other planning techniques, Warnier-Orr diagrams are designed backwards. This means that the planner starts with a knowledge of what the final output will be. The output is then analyzed into all the various steps which would lead to that answer.

To illustrate the design of Warnier-Orr diagrams, consider the following *Employee Paycheque* problem.

Employee Paycheque Problem

Wilson & Sons is processing cheques for its employees. One employee earns $6.35 per hour and works 35 hours per week. If a standard deduction of 24% of gross pay is taken off his paycheque each week, calculate and print both the gross pay and net pay for this employee.

Figure 3.4
Warnier-Orr Diagram for the Employee Paycheque Problem

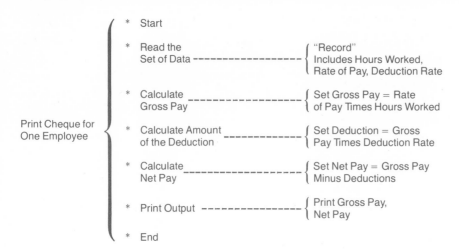

Print Cheque for
One Employee
{
* Start

* Read the
Set of Data ------------------- { "Record"
Includes Hours Worked,
Rate of Pay, Deduction Rate

* Calculate
Gross Pay ------------------- { Set Gross Pay = Rate
of Pay Times Hours Worked

* Calculate Amount
of the Deduction ------------- { Set Deduction = Gross
Pay Times Deduction Rate

* Calculate
Net Pay ------------------- { Set Net Pay = Gross Pay
Minus Deductions

* Print Output ------------------- { Print Gross Pay,
Net Pay

* End

Note that the statements in the Warnier-Orr diagram are not related to any particular computer language. This important concept avoids the eventual coding errors which result when some computer language statements are mixed with ordinary English in the algorithm.

The second illustration involves looping and an end-of-file check in a *Payroll Program* for several employees. In addition to the Warnier-Orr planning method, a planning sheet is used to first analyze the known values and the required output.

Payroll Program

Wilson & Sons wants the company's programmer to design a payroll program to process paycheques for all 800 of its employees. Each paycheque is to contain the name, gross pay, and net pay of the employee. Deductions are 24% of gross pay.

Planning for Payroll Program

Problem Definition

Print 800 cheques, each of which contain employees name, gross pay, and net pay.

E.O.F. Check: Use a dummy record
Dummy record: Dummy, 000,0000,0000

Typical Data Record

Employee Name
Hours Worked
Rate of Pay
Deduction Rate

Figure 3.5
Warnier-Orr Diagram for the Payroll Problem

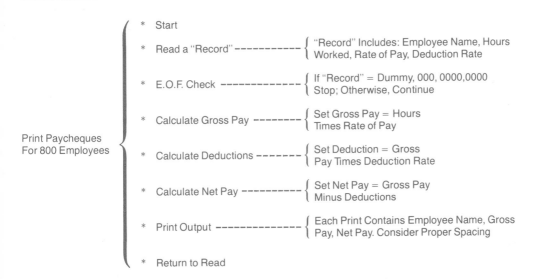

Print Paycheques For 800 Employees

* Start
* Read a "Record" ─────── { "Record" Includes: Employee Name, Hours Worked, Rate of Pay, Deduction Rate
* E.O.F. Check ─────── { If "Record" = Dummy, 000, 0000,0000 Stop; Otherwise, Continue
* Calculate Gross Pay ─────── { Set Gross Pay = Hours Times Rate of Pay
* Calculate Deductions ─────── { Set Deduction = Gross Pay Times Deduction Rate
* Calculate Net Pay ─────── { Set Net Pay = Gross Pay Minus Deductions
* Print Output ─────── { Each Print Contains Employee Name, Gross Pay, Net Pay. Consider Proper Spacing
* Return to Read

Decision Tables

Problems which contain multiple decisions and outcomes, but appear to lack a clear, mathematical solution, are well-suited to a compact planning technique called a **decision table**. This chart-like diagram is used in many phases of computer work, including systems analysis, planning algorithms, and documentation. The major users of this technique are financial institutions, insurance companies, the military, the U.S. government's National Aeronautics and Space Administration, and manufacturers.

Although mathematical solutions are sometimes easier to design with other planning techniques, decision tables can be applied to a variety of problems. Typically, the problems will have several conditions that must be considered in sequence before an appropriate action can be taken.

Designing a Decision Table

There are four sections to a decision table. The first area contains questions which usually require a "yes" or "no" response. These questions are called the *Conditions* of the problem. The second area, called *Condition Entries*, contains all the possible combinations of yes and no answers that the questions can produce. The third area, the *Action Stub*, contains a list of all the actions which can be taken. There is no limit to the number of items which can be placed in this list. The last area, the *Action Entries*, contains checkmarks that indicate which actions are to be taken, if the questions are answered in a certain way.

Figure 3.6
Decision Table

Condition Stub	Condition Entries			
1.	Y	Y	N	N
2.	Y	N	Y	N

Action Stub	Action Entries			
(a)	√			
(b)		√		
(c)				√
(d)			√	

Conditions and actions in a decision table are connected by an "if...then" relationship. This means that any column in the diagram can be read vertically with this meaning: "if this specified set of conditions exists, then perform the actions which have a checkmark."

Each column in a decision table represents one possible route through a flowchart algorithm of the same problem. Decision tables can be used to plan large numbers of alternative routes in less space, with less complexity, and with less chance of omitting one or more of the alternatives than a traditional flowchart.

In the following *Basketball Problem*, a decision table algorithm has been prepared. Three decisions in a row are to be considered before the appropriate actions are taken.

Basketball Problem

This year, the senior basketball coach received 120 applications for positions on the school team. He prepared a decison table algorithm to help program his microcomputer with a "team selection" program.

Three conditions are used to screen those who try out for the team: height, ball-handling capability, and school marks. The coach listed three actions which could be taken by the computer: Print name and "guard"; print name and "playmaker"; skip to next student.

The coach used the program to print out a list of selected candidates and their position, which was then posted on the gymnasium door.

Courtesy of Apple Computer Inc.

The preparation of the decision table is done in two stages. A rough copy is first prepared to ensure that **all** possible conditions, actions, and checkmark columns are considered. The correct number of checkmark columns can be calculated mathematically by remembering that each condition has two possible answers. Three conditions in a row produce 2^3 or eight possible columns. (Four conditions would produce 2^4 or sixteen columns, and so on.)

Consider the coach's first rough draft as he attempted to include all possibilities.

Figure 3.7

Coach's First Rough Draft of Decision Table for Basketball Problem

1. Over 5'10" (178 cm)?	Y	N	Y	Y	Y	N	N	N
2. Good ball-handler?	Y	Y	N	Y	N	Y	N	N
3. Passing grades in school?	Y	Y	Y	N	N	N	Y	N
(a) Print name and "guard"	√		√	√	√			
(b) Print name and "playmaker"	√	√		√		√		
(c) Skip to next student				√	√	√	√	√

In the final stage, the decison table is made more efficient, and reduced in size. Notice in the first draft that a "no" answer to the condition "Passing grades?" always results in the same action being taken, namely, "Skip to next student." One column can be used to determine that condition, instead of three. When these extra columns are removed, the decision table will be reduced in width.

Next, the order of the items can be rearranged so that school grades and the corresponding action "skip to next student" are checked first in the program. This is a more logical place in the program, since a "no" answer eliminates the need for any further questions.

Once the decision table has been reduced to remove repetition, and the conditions are placed in a more logical order, the final copy of the coach's decision table will appear as shown below:

Figure 3.8
Coach's Final Copy of Decision Table for Basketball Problem

1. Passing grades in school?	Y	Y	N		
2. Over 5′ 10″ (177 cm)?	Y	N		Y	
3 Good ball-handler	Y	N			Y
(a) Skip to next student		√	√		
(b) Print name and "guard"	√			√	
(c) Print name and "playmaker"	√				√

It was mentioned earlier that one column in the decision table represents one possible route through a traditional flowchart of the same problem. Compare the final draft of the decision table to a flowchart algorithm. Find the routes through the flowchart which represent the columns shown in the decision table.

Figure 3.9
Flowchart Algorithm of the Basketball Problem

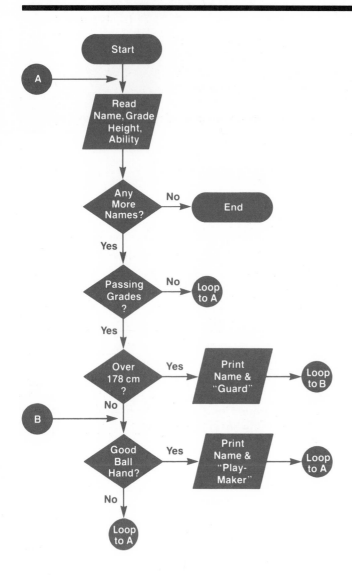

Design for Your Needs

When programmers use decision tables, they should keep this one idea in mind: "Shape the decision table to suit your programming needs, not the other way around." An attractive, symmetrical diagram is unproductive unless it helps to plan the actual computer program. Add an end-of-file check as a condition, if a reminder is needed. Write "programming notes" at the bottom of the planning sheet. These may include the program title, programer identification, and any titles or headings which are to be printed at the top of the printout. In other words, plan a complete algorithm on the planning sheet, not just part of one.

Variations in Decision Tables

The decision tables considered earlier used "Yes" and "No" answers. Other variations in condition entries can be used, such as True and False, Acid and Base (in chemistry problems), and "greater than" and "less than" symbols in mathematical problems. The type of condition entry chosen will depend on the needs of the programmer. (These variations can be applied to other types of planning techniques as well.)

Consider the following *Customer Account Problem* and note the variations used to plan an algorithm for it.

Customer Account Problem

Three account balances are stored in a computer's main memory in random order. The only thing known about them is that all the numbers are different. Have the computer print out the name and amount of the customer with the highest balance.

Figure 3.10

True and False Decision Table for Customer Account Problem

1. Is A greater than B?	T	F	
2. Is A greater than C?	T		F
3. Is B greater than C?		T	F
(a) Print name & balance of A	√		
(b) Print name & balance of B		√	
(c) Print name & balance of C			√

Figure 3.11

Math Symbol Decision Table for Customer Account Problem

1. A compared to B?	>	<	
2. A compared to C?	>		<
3. B compared to C?		>	<
(a) Print name & balance of A	√		
(b) Print name & balance of B		√	
(c) Print name & balance of C			√

Top Down Development

The top down method of planning algorithms is done in a series of levels. Each level provides details about the level above it. Usually the top level consists of the final output stated in general terms. The next level would show more detail about how the output would appear. This may include various headings or subtitles. A third level may describe how the items in the level above it are calculated, and so on. This method of analysis, which progresses from the general to the specific, continues until no additional details are required.

Consider the following simple *Passbook Update Problem*. The sections of the program are identified before the diagram is drawn.

Passbook Update Problem

A local trust company uses teller terminals to update customer passbooks. When a customer wishes to make a transaction, the teller first keys in the customer's account number.

Plan a computer program which would print the account number and the customer's balance on the customer's passbook.

Plan for Passbook Update Problem

Sections

1. Key in customer number
2. Print account number
3. Print balance

Figure 3.12
Top Down Diagram

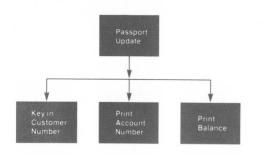

Several steps are taken to accurately analyze a more complex problem before the diagram is prepared. The problem is first clearly defined in short sentences. Any calculations or end-of-file checks are also stated in the problem definition. Next, the values are listed and assigned to storage areas. Then, the problem is separated into easily understood sections to make the top down diagram easier to prepare.

Consider the following *Report Card Problem* in which the various stages of analysis are presented, along with the top down diagram.

Report Card Problem

Ron Heidelbrecht, the school administrator, was assigned the job of programming the school minicomputer to prepare term report cards. Ron concentrated his efforts, in the first stages, on the appearance of a sample report card.

The data for the sample report card consisted of the student's name, identification number, and eight subject names with their corresponding marks.

The minicomputer was to print the student name and number at the top, and then under the subtitles Subject and Mark, list all the courses.

Planning for Report Card Problem

Problem Definition

Print a report card with the student's name, and number at the top. Under the headings Name and Mark, list all the courses.

E.O.F. check: Last One, 000

Typical Data Record

Subject
Mark

Sections

1. Print main heading
2. Print subtitles
3. Read data
4. E.O.F. check
5. Print details

Figure 3.13
Top Down Diagram

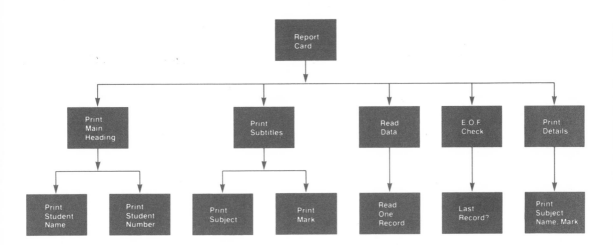

One of the design problems with top down planning techniques is overcrowding. (This also occurs with Warnier-Orr diagrams.) To avoid this problem, use extra wide planning sheets such as blank sheets from a larger printer. Also, sketch a rough draft of the diagram to estimate the spacing between horizontal sections before preparing the final draft.

Top down development, also referred to as hierarchy charts, are well-suited to planning printed output which has many levels of headings, and to the processing of data base files which involve a number of interrelated concepts.

Summary

There are many planning techniques available to programmers other than traditional flow-charting. These techniques include pseudo-code, structure diagrams, Warnier-Orr diagrams, decison tables, and top down development. The abundance of planning methods suggests that a single-planning technique may not be suitable for all types of computer-related problems. The more complex a problem becomes, the greater the need for some form of sophisticated planning.

There are two characteristics common to all methods. The first is that the plan is not related to any particular computer language. General concepts are conveyed without the restrictions of some language processor, allowing the programmer freedom to concentrate on the program's logic. It also makes the planning method easy to adapt to any computer language.

The second characteristic is the attempt to include in the plan all the concepts and information needed to code the solution. When the diagram itself is inadequate, comments on the planning sheet help to complete the design of the program.

Review Questions

These *general level questions* may require factual recall, reading comprehension, and some application of the knowledge from this chapter.

1. Describe *pseudo-code*.

2. Give one advantage and one disadvantage of the pseudo-code method of planning algorithms.

3. Why is it important to write pseudo-code in English phrases, rather than in a particular computer language?

4. What is a *structure diagram*?

5. Describe a disadvantage of structure diagrams.

6. Suppose a problem has no loop. What would a structure diagram of its solution look like?

7. Where did the name "Warnier-Orr" originate?

8. What makes the Warnier-Orr technique different from the other methods mentioned so far?

9. What type of problems are well-suited to decision table algorithms?

10. Briefly, describe the two stages of preparing a decision table algorithm.

11. Explain the phrase "Shape the decision table to suit your needs, not the other way around."

12. Briefly, describe the *top down development* technique.

13. What additional part of the planning sheet is needed with top down diagrams?

14. Describe a problem with the top down planning technique. Suggest solutions to the problem.

15. What is the alternative name for top down diagrams?

Applying Your Knowledge

These questions assume an understanding of the material presented in this chapter, and provide situations which may require evaluation, analysis, or application of that knowledge.

Pseudo-Code and Structure Diagrams

Plan the solutions to the following *general level problems* using either pseudo-code or structure diagrams as a planning technique.

1. **The Microcomputer**

   Terry Murphy purchased a desk-top microcomputer for use at home. The computer was priced at $1150, without application software. Calculate the final selling price, including the provincial sales tax.

2. **Secretary's Salary**

   The office secretary worked 40 hours last week at a rate of $5.65 per hour. Deductions are 27% of gross pay. Plan the solution which would print her net pay.

3. **The Engine**

   The engineering department of an automobile company is designing a new, fuel-efficient engine. Each cylinder in the engine block has a radius of 3 cm, and a length of 12 cm. Plan a solution which would print (a) the area of one end of the cylinder, and (b) the volume of the cylinder.

   Formulas: Area = $(3.14 * r^2)$
   Volume = (area * length)

4. **The Car Loan**

   Dennis Haynes purchased a new sports car priced at $11 400. His company's credit union offered a loan at 12.5% interest, compounded annually. Dennis plans to pay back the loan within one year, but is concerned with the actual cost of the loan. Plan the solution which would print (a) the dollar amount of interest, and (b) the total amount of the loan to be repaid by the end of the year.

5. Personnel List

There are 2200 employees in a New Brunswick factory. The personnel department wants a complete listing of the company's employees. The list is to contain both the name and job title for each person. Each employee record on magnetic disk presently contains employee name, number, and job title.

6. Inventory Report

A large factory keeps a record card for all 10 000 products which are stored in the warehouse. Each card contains the following information: *Product Name, Product Number*, and *Quantity on Hand*. The purchasing department wants a current inventory report. Plan a solution which would read in each record and print the information found on each one.

7. Changing Variable Problem

Solve the following equation, with the values for "A" beginning at five and increasing one at a time until ten answers have been reached.

Equation: T = 2550 /(3.5 * A)

8. Student Average Problem

Dave Didur has taken eight subjects this year. Have the computer read each subject mark, and then calculate his term average.

Decision Tables

Plan solutions to the following *advanced level problems* using decision tables as a planning technique. Remember to prepare a first draft of all possibilities. Then, prepare a final draft with all repetition removed, and items placed in the most logical order.

1. Research Laboratory

In a research laboratory, a computer program is used to compare the acid levels of different chemical solutions. Assuming that all solutions are different, have the computer select and print the name and acid content of the chemical with the greatest amount of acid.

2. Design Specifications

A design engineer needs a computer program which will print specifications for building a car when customers request specific models. Plan a solution which would include the following details:

If a "hard top" is requested, print "*A-frame*"; otherwise, print "*B-frame.*" If the model is a "two-door", print "6.5 *m length*"; otherwise, print "7 *m length.*"   "
If the model has a standard shift, print "*Model* B-83 *gear assembly*"; otherwise, print "*Model* C-100 *gear assembly.*"

3. Medical Diagnosis

A computer terminal is used to collect information from incoming patients. The program asks questions to which the patient responds. Based on the combination of the anwers, the program selects a preliminary diagnosis to be printed on the screen for the doctor to review. Plan a program which could diagnose cold symptoms. The user prompts include (a) temperature high? (b) lung infection? (c) sniffles?

The computer can be programmed to

print one of several alternatives. If the patient has a lung infection, and high temperature, print *pneumonia*. If the patient has any other combination of symptoms, print *cold*. If the patient has only one symptom, print *potential cold*. If there are no symptoms, print *no cold infection*.

4. Football Problem

Peter Gerrard, the senior football coach, received 110 applications for positions on the school team. He prepared a decison table algorithm to help program his microcomputer with a "team selection" program.

Three conditions are used to screen those who try out for the team: weight, ball-handling capability, and speed. The coach listed three selections which could be taken by the computer: Print name and "linesman"; print name and "back field"; skip to next student.

Linesmen were required to be over 80 kg; whereas, back field positions required both ball-handling capability and speed.

The coach used the program to print a list of selected conditions and their position, which was then posted in the locker room.

5. Advertising Department

The advertising department of a Winnipeg newspaper requires a computer program. The program is to provide questions, displayed on a visual screen, that the clerk will ask the customers when they phone in. It will calculate the total cost of the ad requested by the customer.

The price schedule appears on the screen in the form of a series of questions. The clerk responds to the questions by keying in yes or no. The questions include: (a) Greater than one week? (b) Length over 25 words? (c) Varied print?

The program uses a counter to add the following cost figures. If the time is only one week, add $7.50 to counter; otherwise, add $10.00. If the length is over 25 words, add $0.05 per word times the number of words in excess to the counter. If the print is varied, add $2.00 to the counter.

6. A Challenge Problem

A computer program used by an electronics company fills orders for customers who request parts. If there are enough parts in stock, a complete invoice is printed for the parts ordered. If there are not enough items in stock to complete the request the program prints an invoice for the order, and includes the phrase "back-ordered" beside those items not in stock. The computer then prints a back-order request for the purchasing department. If none of the parts ordered are available, no invoice is prepared, and the entire order is printed on the back-order sheet.

Plan the decision table algorithm for this program.

Warnier-Orr/Top Down Development

Plan the solutions to these *advanced level problems* using either Warnier-Orr diagrams or top down development as a planning technique. Remember to use larger than normal planning sheets, and to plan a rough copy first to ensure sufficient spacing.

1. Changing Variable Problem

Plan a solution to the following equation with the values of A beginning at five and increasing five at a time until a total of ten answers has been reached. The answers should be printed under two subtitles— Value of A and Value of Equation.

Equation: $Z = (1550)/(2.5)(A)$

2. The Paycheque

Design a payroll program for a manufacturing firm which would print out a sample paycheque for the manager to approve. The paycheque is to contain the name, hours, rate, and net pay of the employee. Deductions are 24% of gross pay. The computer will read in name, hours, and rate of pay for the employee.

3. Customer Invoice

The data processing manager of a local business wants the company programmer to design a customer invoice to process items purchased on credit. Each invoice is to contain the customer's name and address in one section, and product name, quantity, unit price, and cost in another section. Each item listed on the bill is also to have the cost beside it. (Cost = unit price times quantity)

4. The Report Card

Paul Rehak, the computer studies teacher, was assigned the job of programming the school minicomputer to prepare term report cards. Paul concentrated his efforts, in the first stages, on the appearance of a sample report card.

The data for the sample report card consisted of the student's name, and eight subject names with their corresponding marks.

The minicomputer was to print the *school name, date*, and *student's name* at the top. Under the subtitles—*Subject* and *Mark*, all the courses are listed.

5. Payroll Cheques

Ottawa Building Suppliers wants the company programmer to design a complete payroll program to process paycheques for all 230 of its employees. Each paycheque is to contain the name, hours, rate of pay, gross pay, and net pay of the employee. Deductions are 24% of gross pay. Each data record contains employee's name, hours worked, and rate of pay.

6. Inventory Reorder List

A large tire company keeps a record for each of its 400 products in inventory. Each record contains *product name, original quantity*, and *quantity on hand*.

Plan a program which would print a list as shown:

```
FIRESTONE REORDER LIST
    BURLINGTON PLANT


PRODUCT    AMOUNT TO REORDER
```

7. Bank Loan

The head office of a commercial bank has requested their programmer to design a program which would print an annual statement for all customers with bank loans.

The top of the statement is to contain the *Customer Name* and *Account Number*.

The body of the statement is to contain accumulated interest for the year, and final balance.

8. Council Trust Fund

In order to have money for the future, the student council has invested $500 in a trust fund. The trust company pays 12.5% interest on the year-end balance. Plan a program which would print the title *Student Council Trust Fund*, and the four subtitles —*Year, Annual Interest, Accumulated Interest*, and *Balance*.

The program should calculate and print the values for eight years for the council's investment.

The Human Robot

Ask for a volunteer to act like a nontalking, mechanical robot which responds to verbal commands. As a group, prepare a list of acceptable commands which the robot could follow, such as *turn left, stop, move three steps, pick up item*.

Next, prepare a program of logical commands which would have the human robot go from one part of the room to another and pick up an object such as a chalk brush. Do not allow the robot to bump into any furniture, or accept any illegal commands. The robot's response to any illegal command is to do nothing.

4

An Introduction to Programming

Objectives

An understanding of the elements of a coded computer program

An understanding of the different types of programming errors, and how to correct them

A detailed understanding of the most frequently used commands in the BASIC computer language

An understanding of the *for*. . .*next* loop and its ability to continuously repeat instructions until some condition is met

Solving problems with the aid of a computer can be a fascinating and enjoyable challenge.

Courtesy of Digital Equipment Corporation.

Chapter Four
An Introduction to Programming

Computers are the only machines in the world which run on instructions.

BASIC is a programming language for computers. It is easy to learn, and currently the most popular computer language for pocket computers and microcomputers. Developed by John Kemeny and Thomas Kurtz at Dartmouth college in 1965, it provides an introductory language for people without a background in computer studies.

BASIC is an acronym, that is, a word formed from the first letters of other words—in this case, "Beginner's All-Purpose Symbolic Instruction Code." It is an interactive computer language. This means that it allows someone to communicate directly with the computer. Typically, the user will sit down in front of the computer, and key in instructions on the typewriter keyboard. Above the keyboard is the cathode ray tube (a visual screen). The screen displays what the person types, as well as the responses from the computer. A small, lighted square or underscore, called a **cursor**, helps the user manipulate the information on the screen. This chapter assumes that the reader will have an opportunity to interact directly with the computer using this type of hardware.

BASIC is not a standardized computer language. Some computer companies have modified the language to include extra commands, or have changed the language to fit within their computer's memory. Each modification of the BASIC language is called a **version**. There are, at present, several versions of BASIC on the market. For this reason, it usually is not possible to take a program written on machine A and get it to work immediately on machine B. The characteristic of transferring programs from one computer to another is called **portability**. BASIC is not portable, unlike a standardized language such as FORTRAN. In spite of this limitation, BASIC has gained acceptance.

Elements of a Computer Program

As mentioned in Chapter Two, most computer programs contain three elements—instructions, data, and programmer comments.

The **instructions** are commands which instruct the computer to perform some type of action. The instructions may be a single word such as *remark*, *read*, or *print*, or longer phrases which require the computer to act once certain conditions are met.

The **data** refers to the values used in a problem. If a program is designed to calculate the area of a school yard, for example, the length and width of the yard would be referred to as the data for that problem.

There are different types of data. Numbers are called **numeric data**; letters are called **alphabetic data**. The computer needs to be informed of what type of data is being entered because numbers are stored and handled differently than letters inside the computer. In BASIC, quotation marks are placed around words or letters which are to be used as data. For example:

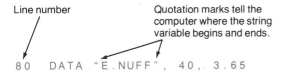

Line number

Quotation marks tell the computer where the string variable begins and ends.

    80   DATA "E.NUFF", 40, 3.65

Data which is made up of letters, words, or a mixture of letters and numbers is referred to as a **string variable**. The name "E. NUFF" is an example.

The **programmer comments** are phrases or sentences inserted in the program to make it easier to understand. The comments may include a program title and programmer identification (student's name and period, for example). Various remarks are also placed throughout the program to aid the programmer in interpreting what the various commands are designed to achieve.

Programmer comments are not considered to be data because they are not used to form the answer; they do not need quotation marks around them.

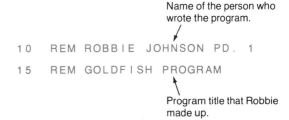

Name of the person who wrote the program.

    10   REM ROBBIE JOHNSON PD. 1
    15   REM GOLDFISH PROGRAM

Program title that Robbie made up.

Grouping several commands together and spacing them out from the rest of the program with spaces and programmer comments is a very important concept in program design. It makes the programs readable, and easier to correct.

Getting Started

To communicate with a computer, instructions must be entered in a certain way. Suppose that you typed:

HI COMPUTER

and pressed the *return* or *enter* key. When this message is entered, the computer will not recognize it as an acceptable command. As a result, the computer will respond with the message:

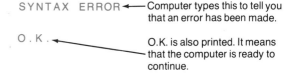

SYNTAX ERROR ◀— Computer types this to tell you that an error has been made.

O.K. ◀— O.K. is also printed. It means that the computer is ready to continue.

The computer responded with *syntax error* because it did not understand what you wanted it to do. A syntax error refers to a grammatical error in that particular computer language. Each computer language has a set of rules for writing statements. What may be a syntax error in one language, may be acceptable in another.

Your First Program

Before starting a program, the instruction NEW is keyed in.

NEW ◄——————————— You type this in.

O.K. ◄——————— The computer types this, then waits for your next instruction. Some computers type the word READY.

Any previous instructions are cleared (erased) from main memory, when the NEW command is entered. Some computers use *Scr* or *Scratch* to clear old programs. Now the computer is ready to accept something that it can understand. Suppose that you typed:

```
10   PRINT "HELLO COMPUTER"
```

When you are done, hit the *return* key. Now type in the word *run*, and press the *return* key again. Here is what happens:

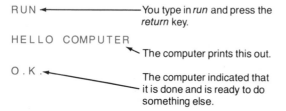

RUN ◄——————— You type in *run* and press the *return* key.

HELLO COMPUTER

       ◄ The computer prints this out.

O.K. ◄——————— The computer indicated that it is done and is ready to do something else.

Congratulations. You have just "entered" and "run" your first computer program. The program is small but, nonetheless, it is a program.

What the program has done is to tell the computer to print whatever it found between the quotation marks. We caused the program to run (execute) by typing in the word RUN.

In BASIC, **system commands** such as:

NEW   RUN   LIST

are not considered to be part of the program, and therefore do not require line numbers. They are direct commands designed to help the programmer at the keyboard.

Consider the next program. In this case, a student wants her name and address printed.

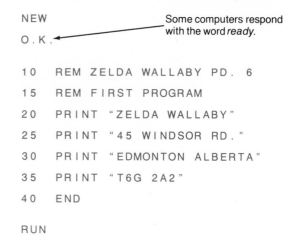

NEW

O.K. ◄——————— Some computers respond with the word *ready*.

```
10    REM ZELDA WALLABY PD. 6
15    REM FIRST PROGRAM
20    PRINT "ZELDA WALLABY"
25    PRINT "45 WINDSOR RD."
30    PRINT "EDMONTON ALBERTA"
35    PRINT "T6G 2A2"
40    END
```

RUN

The computer executes the program when the RUN command is entered and the *return* key is pressed.

ZELDA WALLABY

45 WINDSOR RD.

EDMONTON ALBERTA

.T6G 2A2
         ◄ The computer printed what it found between the quotation marks.

O.K.

Correcting Programs

If the address on line 25 was incorrect, it can be corrected by retyping the statement on a new line.

```
25   PRINT "54 WINDSOR RD."
RUN
```

The computer changes the program by erasing the old line 25, and inserting the new one. When the *return* key is pressed, here is the result:

```
ZELDA WALLABY
54 WINDSOR RD.
EDMONTON ALBERTA
T6G 2A8

O.K.
```

Any line in a program can be changed by writing the line over again, and pressing the *return* key. There is no need to move the cursor back to that line.

When a list of all the instruments in the program, called a **program listing**, is needed, key in the word

```
LIST
```

and press the *return* key. If you are curious about a specific line, such as line 200 where the computer may have indicated a syntax error, key in

```
LIST 200
```

and that line will appear on the screen. By using the same line number and entering the corrected version, the old line will be replaced.

If you wish the line to be deleted from memory simply key in the line number and press the *return* key.

```
200
```

When a specific line number is keyed in and the *return* key is pressed, the line number and any former contents are completely erased.

An error in a computer program is called a **bug**. The process of rewriting parts of a program to remove errors is referred to as **debugging**.

Errors may appear in two forms. A **syntax error**, mentioned earlier, is a mistake in the coding of the program. It may involve such things as a missing comma, quotation mark, or a command that the computer does not recognize. A **logic error** refers to an error in the design of the solution. Usually, a program containing logic errors will still execute, but the answer may be incomplete or incorrect. To correct a logic error, the programmer must go back to the original plan (such as a flowchart, or pseudo-code) and rethink the solution.

"Where did you learn to debug a program, Haverstraw?"

Borders to Highlight the Answers

If you want to highlight an answer with a border to improve its appearance, or draw attention to some item, use a row of stars (asterisks) or some other character.

```
25   PRINT "********************"
```

The computer will print whatever it finds between the quotation marks, which in this case is a row of asterisks. Consider the following program which prints two single rows of stars to highlight the output.

```
NEW
O.K.
10   REM ZIGFREED TOOLOOSE
15   REM FIRST PROGRAM
20   PRINT "********************"
25   PRINT
30   PRINT "ZIGFREED TOOLOOSE"
35   PRINT "81 GOLDEN AVE."
40   PRINT "TIMMINS ONTARIO"
45   PRINT "P4N 1RL"
50   PRINT
55   PRINT "********************"
60   END

RUN
```

When *run* is typed and the *return* key is pressed, the output would look like this:

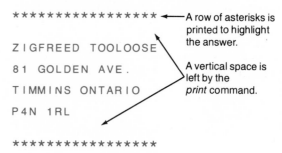

```
*******************
ZIGFREED TOOLOOSE
81 GOLDEN AVE.
TIMMINS ONTARIO
P4N 1RL

*******************
```

A row of asterisks is printed to highlight the answer.

A vertical space is left by the *print* command.

Note that PRINT commands by themselves leave a vertical space in the output. Some computers use PRINT " " for spaces.

Stop and End

The last instruction in all programs should be END, telling the computer that there are no more instructions to perform. When testing a program, however, the STOP command can be inserted at any point.

```
10   PRINT "I'M CERTAINLY NOT ALBERT EINSTEIN!"
15   STOP
```

This will produce the following response from the computer:

```
I'M CERTAINLY NOT ALBERT EINSTEIN!

BREAK AT LINE 15  ◄────────────      Indicates where the stop
                                     command was inserted.

O.K. ◄─────────────────────────      Ready to continue.
```

Practice Assignment

Design a program which will print your name and address. Include adequate vertical spacing to avoid crowded answers, and also highlight the answer with a top and bottom row of stars.

Figuring in Basic

In the section on flowcharting, you will remember that values to be stored in main memory need variable names. Letters or words can be used to assign names to variables. Most BASIC languages, however, will only allow letters. For example . . .

```
30   LET P = 850
40   LET R = .12
```

In some versions of BASIC, the command *let* is required to assign letters to storage areas, and also to set up equations for calculations. Most recent versions of BASIC allow the user to drop the command *let* when assigning values or stating equations. The following examples are acceptable statements in Commodore and Radio Shack computers.

```
30   P = 850
```

or

```
50   T = (A + B + C)
```

Since most microcomputers will accept arithmetic statements without the *let* command, the remainder of this text will display the shorter style. Check your computer manual for acceptable styles.

Bank Interest Problem

Consider the following *Bank Interest Problem* in which $850 is invested at 12%, compounded annually, for one year. How much interest would a customer make if he left it in the account for one year? The solution is first planned using a traditional flowchart, then coded into BASIC.

Figure 4.1

Flowchart (A) for Bank Interest Problem

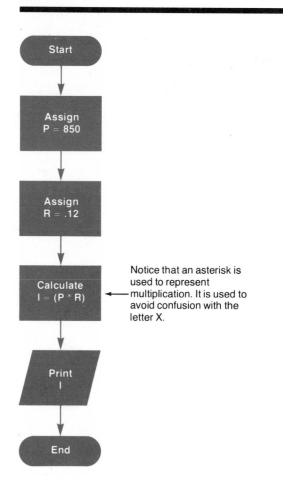

Notice that an asterisk is used to represent multiplication. It is used to avoid confusion with the letter X.

Basic Coding for Bank Interest Problem

```
10    REM FRED FLINTSTONE
20    REM INTEREST PROBLEM
30    P = 850
40    R = .12
50    I = (P * R)
60    PRINT I
70    END
```

Notice that an asterisk is used to represent multiplication. It is used to avoid confusion with the letter X.

Using Data Statements

The problem shown in the last section can be solved in a different way. The values can be read in from a data section at the bottom of a program. This style of solving the problem is an excellent method for solutions which require a loop and repeated reads. Consider the same *Bank Interest Problem* using *data* statements.

Figure 4.2

Flowchart (B) for Bank Interest Problem

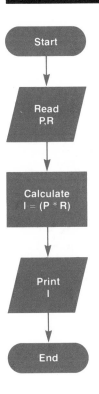

Basic Coding (B) for Bank Interest Problem

```
10    REM WALDO WILSON
15    REM BANK INTEREST PROBLEM
20    READ P, R
25    I = (P * R)
30    PRINT I
35    DATA 850, .12
40    END
```

Data statements contain the values to be used in the problem, which must be in the same order as the READ statement requests them. In the last example, the principle is listed first, then the rate of interest. Dollar signs are never included with the data values. Also, since commas are used to separate data items, they must not be used to separate digits in large values. For example, $10 000 invested at 15% would be listed as   ...

```
40 DATA 10000, 0.15
```

Math Symbols in Programming

In programming, mathematical symbols representing addition, substraction, multiplication, and division are called **arithmetic operators**. Some of the more common symbols are shown below.

To *add* numbers use   +

To *substract* numbers use   −

To *multiply* numbers use   *

To *divide* numbers use   /

Another operator is the exponential symbol, which means "to the power of." The keyboard symbol for exponential functions varies with different computer companies. Consider the following example:

18^2 may be coded as:

```
18**2  or  18↑2  or  18^2
```

Check the manual of your computer to determine which one applies.

Practice Assignment

Plan and code the solution to a problem which would print the annual interest and balance to a deposit of $4500 invested at 13.75%, compounded annually, for one year.

A hand-held pocket computer is capable of understanding and storing complete BASIC programs. The small visual screen can display one line at a time.

Courtesy of Radio Shack, A Division of Tandy Corporation.

Putting Words With the Answer

The computer can be instructed to print anything that is placed between the quotation marks. These items are called **literals**. Suppose that a program is coded to calculate the average of three numbers. The program may appear as follows:

```
NEW
O.K.
20   READ X,Y,Z
25   A = (X + Y + Z) / 3
30   PRINT "THE AVERAGE IS " , A
35   STOP
40   DATA 20, 13, 30
45   END
```

The output will appear like this:

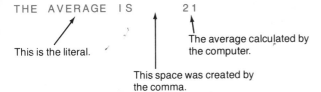

THE AVERAGE IS   21

This is the literal.

The average calculated by
the computer.

This space was created by
the comma.

To reduce the space left by the comma, a
semicolon may be used. However, a semicolon leaves no spaces at all. Therefore,
remember to include a space inside the quotation marks just before the answer is to be
printed. Consider the following example:

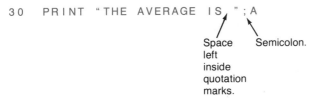

30   PRINT "THE AVERAGE IS ";A

Space   Semicolon.
left
inside
quotation
marks.

The output will appear like this:

THE AVERAGE IS 21

Commas are excellent for creating evenly
spaced columns of words or numbers. For
example:

45   PRINT "FIRST" , "SECOND" , "THIRD"

50   PRINT X,Y,Z

would cause the computer to print   . . .

FIRST   SECOND   THIRD

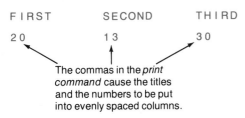

20   13   30

The commas in the *print
command* cause the titles
and the numbers to be put
into evenly spaced columns.

Practice Assignment

Plan and code a program which would read in three student marks 80, 75, 93 and calculate the average. The answer should appear as shown:

```
* * * * * * * * * * * * * * * * * * * * * * * * * * * * * *
CATHY          RON            WILLY
80             75             93
THE  CLASS  AVERAGE  IS  ____
* * * * * * * * * * * * * * * * * * * * * * * * * * * * * *
```

Using String Variables

Words can be used as data as well as numbers. They are called **string variables** because they appear like a string of letters, or characters, to the computer. It takes much more space to store words than it takes to store numbers. For this reason, a storage area name (storage address) must have a $ sign after it. This tells the computer to set aside more space to handle that item. Consider this example:

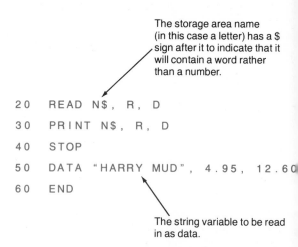

The storage area name (in this case a letter) has a $ sign after it to indicate that it will contain a word rather than a number.

```
20    READ  N$,  R,  D
30    PRINT  N$,  R,  D
40    STOP
50    DATA  "HARRY  MUD",  4.95,  12.60
60    END
```

The string variable to be read in as data.

Notice that the string variable *Harry Mud* is enclosed in quotation marks in the data section. All words to be used as data are entered in this manner. The storage area name has a dollar sign after it to let the computer know that there is a word in the data statement.

Tab

Tab is a command which can be combined with the word *print*. Its purpose is to move the cursor (or print head) horizontally to a specific positon before printing the information. For example:

```
20   PRINT TAB (10)  "MOST PRINTED ITEMS ARE SPACED"
RUN
```

The cursor moves ten spaces before beginning to print the message. The output would appear like this:

```
          MOST PRINTED ITEMS ARE SPACED
```

↑
10 spaces left by the *tab* command.

You may have noticed that while you were keying in line 20 that the message went off the screen and continued on the next line below it. The computer can store up to 72 characters on any line in memory. As long as your instruction does not exceed 72 characters, the computer will accept it, even though the message may "wrap around" the screen.

This TAB command works for numbers as well. Consider the following example.

```
20  PRINT  TAB(8)  457;  TAB(19)  789
```

The output would appear as shown:

```
          457           789
```

In this example, nine spaces were left before each number was printed. The extra space leaves room for a plus or minus sign in front of each number.

Practice Assignment

Plan and code a program which would read in the following student's name, and three subject marks as data values...Cathy Winslow 95 68 71 ... then print the following report. The report is to appear in the centre of the screen (or page) with appropriate horizontal and vertical spacing as shown below.

```
******************************
          REPORT CARD
        CATHY WINSLOW

CATHY'S AVERAGE IS ____
******************************
```

(handwritten notes):
```
10   rem   Wendy Batchelor
20   rem   Cathy Winslow
30   ? spc(25),"******************"
40   ? spc(34)," Report Card "
50   ? spc (34) , " Cathy Winslow "
60   ? spc (30), "Cathy's Average is ____
65   rem
70
```

Adding Programming Power

BASIC is an easy language to learn. Once you have mastered the simple commands such as *read*, *print*, *tab*, *stop*, *end*, and *data*, you may want to go on to learn more powerful programming instructions. The computer's power is partly due to the type of programs that you design. If your programs have loops and decisions in them, they are much more powerful than programs without them, because loops and decisions are capable of getting the computer to do a great deal of work with very few instructions.

For...Next Loops

This simple loop can be used to produce a variety of "goodies." It can act as a counter, draw pictures, create pauses in a program, and print lists of things in any length or width thay you desire.

Sample Problem

Suppose that we apply this loop to a bank interest problem. We are required to print three items: the year, the annual interest, and the balance of a $1500 deposit left in a savings account for ten years. Assume the interest to be 14%, compounded annually.

The *for* ... *next* loop will appear as follows:

```
45   FOR C = 1 TO 10
50   I = (P * R)
55   P = (P + I)
60   PRINT Y, I, P
65   Y = (Y + 1)
70   NEXT C
```

This instructs the computer to go back to the start of the loop and do it again.

This tells the computer to loop ten times. It also requires the computer to use the storage area C to count the number of loops.

In the above *for...next* loop, the computer is required to perform all the operations inside its boundaries (lines 50 to 65). The top line tells the computer how many times this looping process must be done.

```
45   FOR C = 1 TO 10
```

Any letter can be used as the storage area to count the number of loops. But be careful not to unintentionally use the same letter for some other variable in the program. This may lead to a confusing answer.

```
70 NEXT C
```

The bottom of the loop—*next C*—simply returns control of the computer to the *for...next* line. Only when the required number of loops has been performed will the computer move on to the next instruction beyond the loop. Consider the entire plan for the same bank interest problem.

Plan for Bank Interest Problem

Problem Definition

Print three items each year for ten years... year, annual interest, and balance.

$I = (P * R)$ $P = (P + I)$

Loop counter ends at 10.

Input Data

P = $1500
R = 0.14
Y = 198−

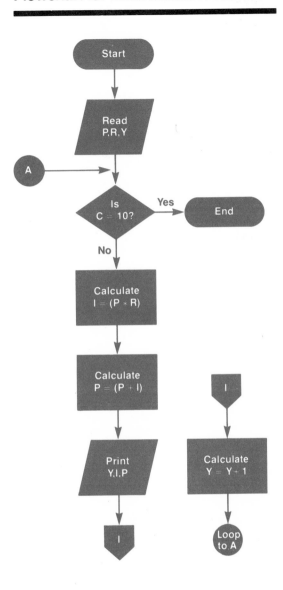

Figure 4.3

Flowchart for Bank Interest Problem

Basic Coding for Bank Interest Problem

```
10    REM*********************
15    REM BANK INTEREST
20    REM*********************
25    REM SERGIO FRANCO PD. 6
30    REM
35    READ P, R, Y
40    REM
45    FOR C = 1 TO 10
50    I = INT ((P * R)+ .001)
55    P = (P + I)
60    PRINT Y, I, P
65    Y = (Y + 1)
70    NEXT C
75    REM
80    DATA 1500, .14, 198—
85    END
```

The command *int*, meaning *integer*, truncates the answer. Example: INT (9.5) = 9

Note that some lines of the BASIC coding are left blank. This helps to make the program more readable. Some computers require the command *remark* with blank lines.

Practice Assignment

Suppose that you are comparing the fuel costs of two types of cars. The first car travels 16 km on one litre of gasoline. The second and larger vehicle travels only 7 km on the same amount of fuel. Plan a program which would print three columns of figures—distance travelled (in intervals of 100 km), fuel costs for a small car, and fuel costs for the larger car.

Assume that gasoline costs 40¢/L, and set the loop for five. The output should appear as shown. Subtitles are optional.

DISTANCE	SMALL CAR	LARGER CAR
100	$—	$—
200	—	—
300	—	—
400	—	—
500	—	—

Modifying the For...Next Loop

There is a more powerful version of the *for...next* loop. It allows the counting process to be altered to suit your solution. For example,

```
50    FOR C = 0 TO 100 STEP 5
```

would make the loop count by fives, starting at zero, and ending at one hundred. (i.e., 0, 5, 10, 15, 20...)

    For...next loops can be incremented by any number, including negative numbers. For example:

```
60    FOR Z = 100 TO 0 STEP −5
```

would make the loop count by fives, starting at one hundred and ending at zero. (i.e., 100, 95, 90, 85...)

Sample Problem

Suppose that we want to print a chart which would show how much time it takes a plane to fly at various rates of speeds from Toronto to Vancouver. The distance between the cities is 3600 km. The formula for calculating the time is $T = D/R$. The chart is to show flight times for rates of speed between 200 km/h and 1000 km/h in increments of 100 km/h.

Consider the *for...next* loop for the above problem.

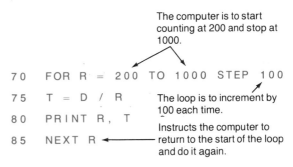

In the above *for...next* loop, the computer is required to perform all the operations inside its boundaries (lines 75 and 80). The extended top line tells the computer several things:

```
70    FOR R = 200 TO 1000 STEP 100
```

The loop is to begin with the number 200 and stop when the number 1000 is reached. The storage area R will be used to keep count. In addition to that, the computer is to increment the counter by 100. This means that it is to add the value 100 to the counter each time a loop is completed.

```
85    NEXT R
```

    The bottom line of the loop, *next R*, continues to return control to the *for...next* line until the limit of 1000 is reached.
    Consider the entire program for the time flight chart.

```
10     REM*******************************
15     REM TIME FLIGHT CHART
20     REM*******************************
25     REM ZIGGY WANDERLOST PD. 5 VER.#3
30     REM
35     D = 3600
40     PRINT TAB(5) "TORONTO TO VANCOUVER"
45     PRINT
50     PRINT
55     PRINT "RATE (KM/H)", "TIME (HOURS)"
60     PRINT
65     PRINT
70     FOR R = 200 TO 1000 STEP 100
75     T = D / R
80     PRINT R, TAB (22) T
85     NEXT R
90     END
```

The output from the time flight program would appear as follows:

```
       TORONTO TO VANCOUVER

RATE (KM/H)       TIME (HOURS)

  200             18
  300             12
  400              9
  500              7.20
  600              6
  700              5.14
  800              4.50
  900              4
 1000              3.60
```

Summary

BASIC is a programming language for computers, an acronym which stands for "Beginner's All-Purpose Symbolic Instruction Code." BASIC is used as an interactive computer language, which means that the user communicates directly with the computer on a one-to-one basis. Typically, the program is keyed in on a typewriter-style keyboard, and is displayed on a visual screen called a cathode ray tube.

Some of the more frequently used commands in the BASIC language are REM, READ, PRINT, TAB, FOR . . . NEXT, STOP, and END. Commas, semicolons, and quotation marks also represent instructions to the computer.

The comma spaces printed items; whereas, the semicolon brings printed items closer together. Quotation marks are used to enclose words which are to be used as variables (data) in the program. In addition, letters being used as variable names require a dollar sign ($) when representing strings. A string refers to a group of characters, such as a word, which is used as data.

Control commands are instructions which give computers their great ability to process information. The *for . . . next* loop, for example, allows a section of a program to be continuously repeated until a certain condition is met. Other control commands, for those who wish greater programming power, are found in Chapter Nine, The Microcomputer Revolution.

There are other ways of designing programs in addition to the type shown in this chapter. Another style, called "conversational programming," assumes that the person who will eventually use the program (the end-user), will require instructions or questions to continue with the program. This technique is used with games, medical diagnosis, airline or hotel reservation systems, and programs which teach. This technique is explained in Chapter Ten, Conversational Programming.

Another technique of writing programs, called "structured programming," is designed to make programs easier to write and correct (debug). Structured programs, however, require a structured language processor inside the computer. This is necessary because the control commands are different than most versions of BASIC. For explanations of that concept, refer to the chapters on structured programming.

As a final note, computer enthusiasts are reminded that a programming manual usually accompanies every computer. By studying the manual, you will discover additional commands not mentioned in this textbook which will give you more programming power. Computers are the only machines in the world which run on instructions. The more instructions that you are aware of, the greater the computer's power and its value to you.

Review Questions

These are *general level questions* which may require factual recall, reading comprehension, and some application of the knowledge of this chapter.

1. BASIC is called an interactive computer language. What does that refer to?

2. Why is BASIC not a portable computer language? What limitation will that place on programs that you write?

3. How do instructions differ from data in a computer program?

4. What is a string variable?

5. Most programs contain programmer comments. Explain their purpose and provide some examples.

6. What is a *syntax error*?

7. Give three examples of system commands. How does a system command differ from regular lines of a program?

8. What does the process of debugging refer to? How would you debug a syntax error? How would you debug a logic error?

9. Write a sample data statement which would include the following data: principal $45 000 and a rate of interest of 14%.

10. What is an arithmetic operator? List the BASIC symbols used for division, for multiplication, and for exponents (to the power of).

11. What is a literal in a computer program? Give an example of a print statement which contains a literal.

12. Punctuation marks such as a comma or a semicolon (;) can represent spacing instructions with a print command.
    (a) Explain the effect of the two commas in this statement.

    ```
    10   PRINT A, B, C
    ```

    (b) Explain the function of the semicolon in this instruction.

    ```
    25   PRINT "THE ANSWER IS "; T
    ```

13. When words are included in the data, what changes must you make in the *read* and *data* statements?

14. What does the *tab* command in this instruction do?

    ```
    30   PRINT TAB (10) "FRED'S VARIETY"
    ```
    [moves "fried variety" over 10 spaces]

15. How many times will the *print* instruction be performed in the following *for* ... *next* loop?

    ```
    20   FOR C = 1 TO 12
    30   PRINT "I'M A NICE PERSON!"   12
    40   NEXT C
    ```

16. How many times will the phrase "MERRY CHRISTMAS" be printed if the following *for...next* loop is used?

    ```
    20   FOR L = 0 TO 20 STEP 2
    30   PRINT "MERRY CHRISTMAS"   10
    40   NEXT L
    ```

Applying Your Knowledge

These questions assume an understanding of the material presented in this chapter, and provide new situations which may require evaluation, analysis, or application of that knowledge. Section One contains *general level questions* on specific programming statements or techniques. Section Two contains both *general level* and *advanced level questions* which require the planning and coding of complete problems.

Section One

1(a) Write a statement which would cause the computer to print a row of stars.

(b) Write a statement which would cause the computer to print the phrase THE ANSWER IS . . . as well the answer represented by the letter T.

(c) Write a statement which would read the following data:

    100   DATA 56, 22, 18

(d) Write a statement which would read the following data.

    50   DATA "PHIL GIBBONS", 256.8

2. Rewrite the following expressions so that they can be read by a computer.

(a) $T = \dfrac{(A)(B)}{C}$

(b) $S = \dfrac{A + B + C}{D}$

(c) $A = \dfrac{(X)(Y)(Z)}{B^8}$

(d) $T = \dfrac{A - B}{\dfrac{C - D}{D}}$

3. Write a *for . . . next* loop which will print the phrase *you are a great programmer* ten times.

4. Write a program with a *for . . . next* loop which would add all the even numbers from 0 to 50, then print the final answer.

5. Write a *for . . . next* loop which will print a column of stars (five stars wide) down the centre of the screen for a total of forty lines.

6. Write a program with a *for...next* loop which will begin with the number 5 and add five at a time until 100 is reached. Print the final total

7. Write a program with a *for...next* loop which would read the following data items, one at a time, and print them.

```
100    DATA "MATH" , 89
110    DATA "GEOGRAPHY" , 71
115    DATA "SCIENCE" , 82
120    DATA "COMPUTERS" , 93
```

8. Write a corrected version of this program.

```
10     REM RICK DUNN PD. 3
15     PROBLEM #5
20     PRINT ******************
25     PRINT "RICK DUNN"
30     PRINT "101 HANGOVER ST."
35     PRINT ******************
```

9. Write the corrected version of this program.

```
10     REM FRAN HIGHBROW
15     REM WATERLOO
20     READ
25     T = (A + B + C)
30     PRINT ******************
35     PRINT THE ANSWER IS T
40     PRINT ******************
45     DATA 14, 12, 18
       STOP
```

10. Write the corrected version of this program.

```
10     REM ROBBIE JOHNSON
15     REM BANK INTEREST PROBLEM
20     READ P, R
25     I = (P)(R)
30     P = P + R
35     PRINT I, T
40     STOP
45     DATA 850, .1225
50     PRINT
```

11. Classify each error in the previous question as either a *syntax error* or a *logic error*.

Section Two— Programming Problems

Plan and code the solutions to the following problems. For the planning stage, define the problem, list the values, then plan the steps to the solution using one of the following planning techniques : flowcharts, structure diagrams, pseudo-code, decision tables, Warnier-Orr diagrams, or top down method. Questions 1–9 are *general level problems*.

1. The Stereo Set

Jamie Quinn purchased a stereo set worth $865. The store clerk calculated the interest on the credit purchase at 24% per year, calculated annually. Plan the solution which would print:
(a) the dollar amount of interest;
(b) the total amount of the credit purchase.

2. The Bank Loan

Walter Johnson obtained a bank loan at a local branch. The principal of the loan was $8500, at an interest rate of 14.5% per year, calculated annually. Calculate:
(a) the dollar amount of interest for one year;
(b) the total amount to be repaid for one year;
(c) the monthly installments if the loan is to be repaid in twelve equal payments.

3. Warehouse Inventory

The warehouse manager is interested in finding the year-end inventory figure. The opening inventory at the beginning of the year was 26 563 units. During the year, 18 625 additional units were purchased; 2% of the opening inventory was estimated to be lost or damaged; and 15 045 units were sold.
   Calculate the year-end inventory, and precede the answer with the phrase *the ending inventory is* _____.

4. Secretary's Salary

The office secretary worked 40 hours last week at a rate of pay of $5.65 per hour. Deductions included income tax (24% of gross pay) and Canada Pension (3% of gross pay). Print the following answers with the phrases as indicated. Leave five blank lines before the answer is printed.

```
GROSS PAY = $

TOTAL DEDUCTIONS = $

NET PAY = $
```

5. Term Deposit

Alice Waxman deposited $655.00 into a term account for one year. The trust company paid 12.75% annual interest. Calculate:
(a) the dollar amount of interest;
(b) the balance after one year.
The answer must be separated from the program listing by five blank lines, and appear as follows:

```
***************************

ALICE WAXMAN ACCOUNT # 63465

INTEREST TO DATE      $

BALANCE               $

***************************
```

6. Graphics

Design a program which would print a picture such as a Christmas tree, Snoopy's Doghouse, or an enlargement of your initials. Use graph paper to design the picture. Each line of the graph represents a separate print line.

7. The Park Renovations

The Ottawa Parks Department is considering fencing in a section of land to use as a recreation area. The Parks Director wants to put a protective fence around the perimeter of the field, and seed the area with a high-quality grass seed. You have been chosen, as a summer helper, to determine the perimeter, area, fencing and seeding costs of this field.

The fencing is priced at $6.25 a running metre, and the seed costs $16.50 for 100 m². The park area is shown in the following diagram:

Figure 4.4

Park Area

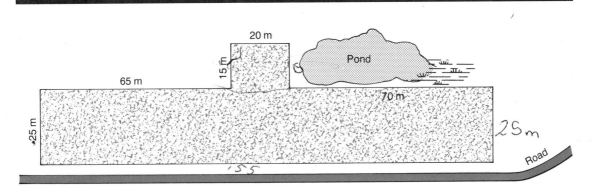

The answer should be centred, and five blank lines should be left after the program listing.

```
***************************

        PARK  RENOVATIONS

     PERIMETER  =_____  M

       AREA  =_____  M

  COST  OF  FENCING  =  $_____

  COST  OF  SEEDING  =  $_____

***************************
```

8. The Air Conditioner

Using the metre ruler, measure the dimensions of the classrom (length, width, and height). Calculate the volume of air in the room. A brochure on air conditioners stated that a 1500 W model would cool about 2.5 m³ of air in one hour; whereas, a 3000 W model would cool 5 m³ of air in the same amount of time.

Using the measurements of the classroom, plan a program which would print the following items. The answer should be centred, and five blank lines should be left after the program listing.

```
*************************
AIR  CONDITIONER  COMPARISON
ROOM  VOLUME  IN  CU.  M.  =
TIME  TO  COOL  (1500  W)  =
TIME  TO  COOL  (3000  W)  =
*************************
```

9. Changing Variable Problem

Solve the following equation with values for X beginning at 5 and increasing five at a time until a total of ten answers has been reached.

Problem: 1550 /(2.5)(X)

The answer should appear as shown.

```
VALUE              VALUE
OF  X          OF  EQUATION
  5                  —
 10                  —
(etc.)               —
```

10. Pierre's Report Card

Plan a program which would read in the subject names and marks, one set at a time, then print the following report for Pierre Amirault. The report is to appear as shown:

```
***  ALBRIGHT  HIGH  SCHOOL  ***

STUDENT:  PIERRE  AMIRAULT

    SUBJECT          MARK
       —              —

       —              —

      (etc.)          —

AVERAGE  FOR  THE  YEAR_____
**************************
```

Data Records:

Political Science	89
Philosophy	75
Math	76
English	80
French	90
Science	62

11. Buying Furniture on Credit

Janice Wilkinson purchased $2000 worth of furniture on credit at a local department store. If the annual rate of interest is 24%, calculate the monthly balance for twelve months. Equal monthly payments of $50 are made each month. The store adds the monthly interest to the balance before subtracting the payment.

```
* * * * * * * * * * * * * * * * * * * * * * * * * * * *
            LEDGER  CARD
       FOR  JANICE  WILSON
* * * * * * * * * * * * * * * * * * * * * * * * * * * *
```

MONTH	INTEREST	PAYMENT	BALANCE
1	—	—	—
2	—	—	—
(etc.)	—	—	—

12. Council Trust Fund

In order to have money for the future, the student council invested $5500 into an account in a trust company. The fixed rate of interest, calculated annually, is 12.5% calculated on the year-end balance. The council plans to leave the principal in the account for eight years. Plan a program that would print the following chart.

```
* * * * * * * STUDENT  COUNCIL * * * * * * *
* * * * * * * * * TRUST  FUND * * * * * * * * *
```

YEAR	INT.	ACCUM. INT.	BALANCE
198-	12.5	—	—
198-	—	—	—
(etc.)	—	—	—

5

Peeking Inside the Processor Unit

Objectives

An awareness of how the processor unit operates with the aid of software programs

A detailed knowledge of the integrated circuits which cause a computer to function

An understanding of the reasons for, and different types of, computer codes

An understanding of how a computer can manipulate binary to perform arithmetic

The computer operator is adjusting a switch on a computer console for a Sperry Univac computer system.

Chapter Five
Peeking Inside the Processor Unit

The lock on the steel security door finally gave way. Peterson, half-exhausted, stepped into the computer's control centre. The din of whirring disks, humming, and soft clicking noises filled his ears as he watched hundreds of tiny lights flashing in rhythmic patterns along endless rows of machinery.

"Welcome ∴..Peterson...," the system's mechanical voice droned. "I was expecting you!"

As the excerpt above illustrates, many science fiction novels and movies use the mystique of computer technology to enhance their plot. Alternatively cast in the role of either the villain or friend, computer hardware has for many years remained a mystery to most people. Although the technology in some cases is complex, it is fairly easy to understand the functions and limitations of such machinery.

The main component of any computer system is the **processor unit**. It controls the operation of all computer peripherals under the guidance of computer programs. A computer's capability to perform mathematical calculations, logic decisions, store and manipulate data is all contained within the circuitry of the processor unit.

This chapter concentrates on the processor unit, computer circuitry, how data is stored and manipulated internally.

Parts of the Processor Unit

The processor unit contains three sections: the control unit, the arithmetic/logic unit, and main memory. The *control unit* refers to hardware circuitry which controls the sequence of operations in a program. It contains a few special memory locations called registers. These registers receive one line of the program at a time, analyze it, and perform it with the help of the arithmetic/logic unit and the many tiny programs in the operating system.

The arithmetic/logic unit (or ALU) contains the electronic circuitry designed to perform operations such as addition, subtraction, multiplication, and division. It also contains the circuitry designed to perform logical operations such comparing one number to another and indicating the results.

The **main computer memory** (also called primary storage or internal storage) can store both the user's application program and the manufacturer's operating system. Application programs are those written by the person using the computer. This might include a student solving a particular problem in class, or a business person providing instructions to prepare bills for credit customers.

In minicomputers and mainframe computers, a large part of main memory is reserved for the operating system. This is a set of programs provided by the manufacturer to supervise the operation of the computer. The operating system, combined with the control unit, acts like a traffic director by giving instructions to cause the computer circuitry to perform the way it should.

Until recently, many sources referred to all three sections of the processor unit as the central processing unit (CPU). With current changes in computer design, and a clearer understanding of what the CPU does (interprets and executes instructions), it would be more accurate to refer to the control unit and the arithmetic/logic unit as the **central processing unit**.

Figure 5.1
Processor Unit

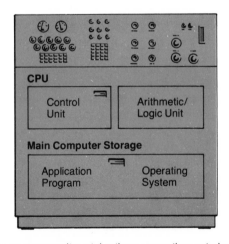

The processor unit contains three areas: the control unit, the arithmetic/logic unit, and the main computer storage. Most of the main storage is reserved for the operating system, while the remainder stores the user's application program.

How Programs Are Processed

When an application program is fed into the computer, it is immediately translated into a code of electrical impulses, which allows electronic movement of information through the computer circuits. The conversion from readable English into electrical impulses is performed by a manufacturer's program called a language processor.

The computer program, now stored in main memory, is actually a set of instructions which tells the control unit what to do.

The control unit in the CPU goes into main memory and fetches the first instruction, stores it in a control register (small memory area), and analyzes it. After figuring out what action is required, the control unit will do one of two things. If mathematics or comparing logic is involved, control is passed to the arithmetic/logic unit for processing. Or, if some other peripheral is needed such as a printer or a disk unit, the control unit may call up one of the many tiny programs from the operating system to provide further instructions on how to go about that job.

Once that first instruction is completed, the control unit returns to main memory to fetch the next one. The cycle is repeated over and over again until the whole program is completed.

Peeking Inside a Processor Unit

The third generation of computers (1965–1969) introduced a revolutionary approach to computer electronics. The countless, tangled wires and metal transistors of earlier computers were replaced by smooth, plastic printed circuit boards and several computer chips, each containing miniature integrated circuits. This inexpensive technology is now being applied to many products other than computers. Satellites and space probes contain the same type of integrated circuits as children's toys, calculators, cassette decks, microwave ovens, and digital watches.

The **printed circuit boards** are sheets of translucent plastic (20 cm × 30 cm) which are embedded with patterns of electrical wires. Often, there are two different layers of wire patterns in the plastic. Since each pattern is visible from a different side, this gives it the appearance of a "double-sided" circuit board. One purpose of a circuit board is to provide a common base to which the integrated circuits (computer chips) can be attached. Also, it provides the necessary electrical connections between those integrated circuits and other parts of the computer system.

Integrated circuits are miniature electrical circuits contained on a tiny silicon chip, protected by a retangular plastic cover. In the plastic are several electrical connectors called "pins" which allow the chip to be attached to the printed circuit board.

Integrated circuits, nicknamed "computer chips," are designed for different functions. Some may be memory chips, others may be logic chips, and larger ones may be microprocessors.

Courtesy of National Semiconductor.

Figure 5.2
An Integrated Circuit

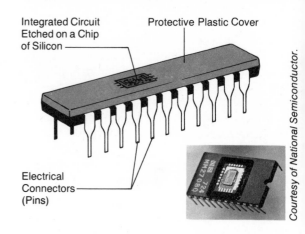

Integrated Circuit Etched on a Chip of Silicon

Protective Plastic Cover

Electrical Connectors (Pins)

Computer electronics has been reduced to the size of a tiny chip. The logic or memory patterns etched on the chip is referred to an integrated circuit.

The function of a **memory chip** is to store information. This type of integrated circuit forms the section of the computer called the main memory. Under a microscope, the memory chip can be seen to contain rows and rows of identical circuits.

A **logic chip** is used for the arithmetic/logic unit. Its circuits can be used to perform mathematical calculations or make logic decisions such as comparing one number to another to see if they are equal. Under a microscope, a logic chip appears similar to an aerial view of the streets of a city, with irregular, connecting roadways stretching in all directions.

The most sophisticated logic chip is a **microprocessor**. This slightly larger integrated circuit is a combination of control features, logic circuits, and memory registers. When a microprocessor (or MPU, meaning microprocessing unit) is combined with additional memory chips on a printed circuit board, a complete processor can be built. This single board provides the basic electronic hardware for most microcomputers and minicomputers on the market.

This circuit board contains a typewriter keyboard, an MPU, logic, and memory chips. Computer boards such as these form the basis for most microcomputers.

Courtesy of Ohio Scientific.

Types of Memory Chips

Memory chips are circuits designed for storing, rather than processing information. Like logic chips, they are an essential part of a computer's processing unit. Although most memory chips appear identical, they can be altered by the manufacturer to serve different purposes. Some are used to hold information for a short period of time: others are used to store information permanently.

A **RAM** (random access memory) is a memory chip which stores information as long as the power is on. Pocket calculators, for example, contain this type of memory. Once the power switch is turned off, any numbers stored in the memory registers disappear.

Hobbyists who build their own circuit boards and computer companies prefer a **PROM** (Programmable ROM). This is a blank memory chip which will allow a set of instructions to be loaded into the circuits by the user. Once the chip is loaded, the input wire is cut, and the information cannot be changed. A variation on this type of chip is an **EPROM** (Erasable PROM), which allows the information in the circuits to be erased by ultraviolet light.

Computer companies are presently researching different types of memory chips. Charged Coupled Devices (CCD) and bubble memory are examples of some newer approaches. These chips tend to be slower in finding information, but are cheaper to make and have a greater storage capacity.

" What's taking the new man so long? I just sent him for some extra RAMS."

This device is used to program memory chips. It contains a socket to insert the empty EPROM and a multi-channel connector to link the device with a keyboard or microcomputer.

Courtesy of Optimal Technology, Inc.

Another type of memory is designed to hold information permanently. Since a computer can only read from this memory, it is called a **ROM**, or read only memory. Manufacturers use ROMS to store software programs such as operating systems or language processors. Software programs stored in this fashion are referred to as **firmware**.

This simulation shows how ultraviolet light can erase the information store in a EPROM (an erasable, programmable ROM). The zeros and ones in the background represent the way information is coded and stored in memory chips.

Courtesy of Intel Corporation.

Bubble Memory

Bubble memory contains no moving parts, similar to RAMS and ROMS. The key element is a very thin wafer of magnetic garnet. It is very easy to form small magnetized regions called domains inside such a wafer. The domains can be effortlessly pushed or pulled anywhere within the wafer with a weak magnetic field produced by a series of magnetic needles.

Viewed horizontally, the domains resemble pins or cylinders. When they are viewed from the top, however, they resemble bubbles. The domains can be whisked around the garnet wafer at the rate of ten million a second. This is presently slower than the RAMS and ROMS, but faster than such outside storage mediums as diskettes or cassettes. One company, IBM, is attempting to improve the speed by super-cooling the main memory. The low manufacturing cost of these newer chips may eventually make it possible to store enormously large software programs within main memory. This may reduce a computer's reliance on outside memory devices.

Figure 5.3

Summary of Computer Chips

Name	Function
Logic Chips	These circuits are used to perform mathematics or logic decisions.
Microprocessor (MPU)	A larger logic chip which contains logic, control features, and some memory registers, it behaves like a miniature central processing unit.
RAM (Random Access Memory)	This direct access memory chip is used to store information temporarily. Information is erased when the power is shut off.
ROM (Read Only Memory)	This is a permanent memory chip already filled with "factory software." The computer can read from this memory, but not alter any of the contents.
PROM (Programmable ROM)	This is a blank memory chip which can be programmed permanently by the user.
EPROM (Erasable PROM)	This is a blank memory chip for user programs. The contents can be erased with ultraviolet light if the user wishes.

This circuit board contains several modules of a particular type of memory chip called "bubble memory" (light metallic colour). Although bubble memory has a slower retrieval time than RAMS or ROMS, it has a greater storage capacity.

Courtesy of Texas Instruments Inc.

RAMS, ROMS, AND MPUs Together

Only three types of computer chips (integrated circuits) are needed to assemble a computer. The main chip is the microprocessor which provides the processing and control features of the computer. Many companies, such as Intel and Motorola, specialize in making and selling microprocessors. Their customers include computer manufacturers, as well as military suppliers, computer hobby stores, and toy manufacturers.

The main memory of the processor unit is made up of two different computer chips— RAMS and ROMS. The empty RAM memory chips are the part of main memory in which the user can store application programs. Hobby computers contain a small amount of "user memory" because only one person can use the computer at a time, and normally small programs are run. Mainframe computers, on the other hand, run several large programs at the same time, requiring a large amount of RAM "user memory." Most RAM memory chips erase when the power is turned off or when the "clear" signal is given.

The other part of main memory is allocated to ROM "factory memory." These chips permanently store manufacturer's software, even when the power is turned off. The software may include a set of instructions to translate the user's commands into electrical impulses (a language processor) and a set of stored programs to tell the microprocessor how to operate the circuits (an operating system).

Figure 5.4
Imaginary Printed Circuit Board

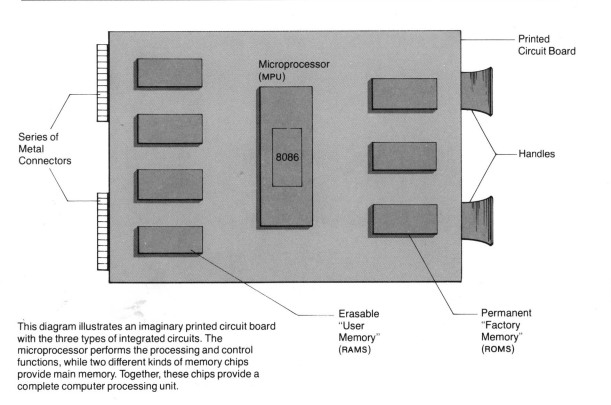

Series of Metal Connectors

Microprocessor (MPU)

8086

Printed Circuit Board

Handles

Erasable "User Memory" (RAMS)

Permanent "Factory Memory" (ROMS)

This diagram illustrates an imaginary printed circuit board with the three types of integrated circuits. The microprocessor performs the processing and control functions, while two different kinds of memory chips provide main memory. Together, these chips provide a complete computer processing unit.

If extra pieces of equipment are added to a computer system, more instructions must be put into the computer to control them. One of the reasons why mainframe computer systems have oversized processing units is that the manufacturer has permanently stored very large operating systems and several language processors in ROM "factory memory." This requires hundreds of memory circuit boards containing 60–100 ROM memory chips. Minicomputer manufacturers avoid this expense by storing most of those instructions on magnetic disks.

All three types of computer chips are mounted on replaceable, printed circuit boards. The boards have a series of metal connectors at one end. These connectors are part of a **bus**, which refers to the network of electrical "highways" along which the computer transmits information. The bus connectors allow a printed circuit board to be plugged into an electrical socket on a "mother board." A mother board may be holding and feeding electrical impulses to several printed circuit boards (its children) at the same time. Some circuit boards may be entirely devoted to memory chips, while others may have a specialized duty such as controlling a disk unit or a video display unit.

Figure 5.5

A Mother Board

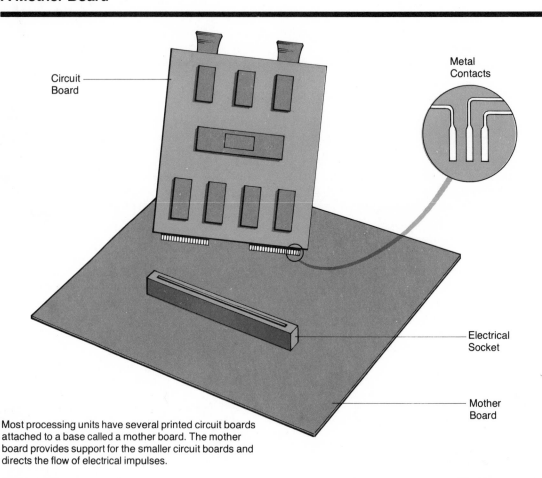

Circuit Board

Metal Contacts

Electrical Socket

Mother Board

Most processing units have several printed circuit boards attached to a base called a mother board. The mother board provides support for the smaller circuit boards and directs the flow of electrical impulses.

Electronic Information

A computer is an excellent machine for processing information. What is surprising about the device is that no numbers or letters ever travel through the printed circuit boards or the computer chips. It's all done electronically. Whenever someone feeds information into a computer, the information is immediately converted into electrical impulses. Every number or letter has a different code of on and off signals.

Since electricity has only two states, on or off (more accurately, strong or weak pulses), it can be represented by the 1 and 0 of the **binary number system**. John Von Neumann was the mathematician who recommended that all computer codes should be based on binary because, like electricity, it contains only two elements. (This system will be discussed later in this chapter.)

When electrical impulses are travelling down a circuit, the computer has to know how many of those on and off impulses represent a single letter or number. Without this knowledge, the message would get garbled, such as "Howdo6oud2" instead of "How do you do?" Realizing this, computer companies began to devise their own codes to translate the message. Unfortunately, not all computer manufacturers could agree on how many impulses should be in the group. Some use four, some use six, others use eight, and so on. This is why some computers cannot communicate with machinery from another company; the electrical signals are grouped differently. What one computer thinks is a 7, the other thinks is the letter P.

In computer codes, each impulse is referred to as a **bit** (meaning **b**inary dig**it**). The number of bits that it would take to code one character (a letter, number, or symbol) is referred to as a **byte**. The number of bits in a byte (4,6 or 8) determines the number of characters that the code can represent. A group of four bits, called a **nibble**, can only represent numbers. This is suitable for pocket calculators and hobby computer boards which only display numbers. A six-bit code, such as BCD (Binary Coded Decimal), can store numbers, capital letters, and special characters. Computers designed for scientific uses, engineering research, mathematical applications, learning programming, and hobbyists usually do not need a larger code. An eight-bit code can represent numbers, upper and lower case letters of the alphabet, and special symbols. This code is an important consideration if attractive printed reports are necessary such as in word processing and business applications.

Figure 5.6

Computer Codes

Code	Number of Bits	What can be represented	Uses for the code
Pure Binary	4	Numbers only	Calculators, numerical control devices.
BCD (Binary Coded Decimal)	6	Numbers, capital letters, and special characters.	Science, engineering, mathematics, learning programming, hobbyists.
ASCII-8 or EBCDIC Codes	8	Numbers, upper and lower case letters of the alphabet, special characters.	Word processing and business applications.

This chart illustrates the various codes used in modern computers. A byte of computer code is represented by the number of bits it takes to represent one character.

Two of the more popular codes (ways of grouping the impulses) use a group of eight impulses to represent any character. One code is called EBCDIC, pronounced EBB-SEE-DIC (an acronym meaning Extended Binary Coded Decimal Interchange Code). It was developed by the largest North American computer manufacturer, IBM. Another code, called ASCII (American Standard Code Information Interchange) was invented by a committee of data processing people who had hoped, but failed, to make it the standard code for all computers.

An eight-bit code has three parts to it—some numeric bits, some zone bits, and an extra bit not included in the group of eight called a check bit. The four numeric bits can represent any number from 0-9. It takes both the numeric and zone bits together to represent all the letters of the alphabet. The **check bit** is used to check the accuracy of the message by the computer using the check bit to keep the byte odd or even (depending on the preferences of the manufacturer).

Figure 5.7

Three Sections of a Byte of Information

A Byte

This diagram illustrates the three sections of a byte of information. There are eight positions for either an on or off signal. Together, the eight positions (or bits) can represent one letter, or one number, or one special character. Four bits, which is sufficient to represent a number, is referred to as a nibble. An extra check bit combines with the byte to create an odd or even number of "on" bits. In this way, the machine can check for circuitry malfunctions while it is operating.

Most computers have a command called *dump*. It tells the computer to print out the binary code for all the instructions presently in main memory. When this is done, rows and rows of 0's and 1's are printed out (00110100 00111100, etc.) in groups of four, six, or eight, depending on what code that computer uses. Some computers have a command which converts the instructions into shorter forms such as octal or hexidecimal, which are easier to read. No computers, though, operate in octal or hexidecimal. All computers operate in binary.

Memory Chip Storage

When instructions are put into a computer, they are converted into binary and are stored as rows of 0's and 1's in the RAM memory chips. Some of the newer memory chips will store over 65 000 bits. Manufacturers use the letter K (the Greek prefix meaning thousand) when referring to storage capacity and round the number of bits to the nearest thousand. For example, a memory board with 128K of RAM memory would mean a printed circuit board with 128 000 bits of storage capacity in the form of RAM integrated circuits.

Most average-length student programs will take up from 2K to 4K of memory, although answers from mathematical calculations may require more room. If the computer runs out of storage space, it will signal with an **overflow message**, and the computer will be unable to complete the program. Hobbiests often discover this problem while running "gaming programs" in a microcomputer which has a limited amount of user memory.

Number Crunching

Scientific computers (as opposed to word processing or general-purpose computers) are well known for their capacity to process mathematical calculations, and are referred to as number crunchers. For example, the world's most powerful "number cruncher" is a computer in Boulder, Colorado used to analyze atmospheric and weather data. The computer, called the Cray-1, can process 80 million instructions per second! When you consider that any computer using the binary number system can only count up to one (since it only has two numbers—0 and 1), that is quite an accomplishment.

The semicircular design of the processor unit is a unique characteristic of the Cray 1 computer. Currently the world's most powerful computer system, the Cray 1 can process 80 million instructions per second, and store over one million characters of data in main memory.

Here are the four simple rules which the computer uses to add.

1. $0+0 = 0$
2. $0+1 = 1$
3. $1+0 = 1$
4. $1+1 = 0$ and carry one (or 10)

Consider these examples of binary addition. Using the four simple addition rules, add the numbers to see how the answers were obtained.

(a)		(b)		(c)	
	10		101		111
+	11	+	111		101
				+	011
	101		1100		1111

For additions which involve more than two rows, as in question (c), consider this shortcut procedure. A column which has an odd number of 1's in it (1,3,5, etc.) always adds up to 1 in binary. For each complete pair of 1's in that column, carry one to the next column. Then again consider whether the number of 1's in that column is odd or even. If you didn't get the answer in question (c) with the four rules, go back and try it again using the shortcut procedure.

Because most people are more familiar with the decimal system of counting (0,1,2,3,4,5,6,7,8,9), the computer's binary manipulation can be converted into decimal numbers. It also provides a way of checking to see if the binary addition is correct.

In the following sample item, each row of the question is first converted into a decimal number. Next, the decimal numbers are added together. The last step is to convert the binary answer into a decimal number as well. If the sum of the decimal numbers and the decimal answer are equal, the addition was performed correctly. The binary to decimal conversion chart will be helpful in visualizing the changes.

Sample Addition Problem in Binary

$$
\begin{array}{r}
101 \\
+ \ 111 \\
\hline
1100
\end{array}
$$

Figure 5.8

Binary to Decimal Conversion Chart

Value of Position in Base Two	2^3	2^2	2^1	2^0
Decimal Value	8	4	2	1
Binary Number		1	0	1

$1 \times 1 = 1$
$0 \times 2 = 0$
$1 \times 4 = 4$
—
5

First Step

Convert each row of the problem into a decimal number.

Second Step

$101 = 5$ Add the decimal numbers together.
$111 = 7$
$+$
12

Third Step

$1100 = 12$ Verify the answer.

Processing Speeds

Computer circuits operate so quickly that a single second is much too long a period of time to describe their operation. New words had to be invented to relate the tiny fractions of a second that it takes a computer to complete a mathematical calculation or make a simple decision. For example, most present-day computers operate in nanoseconds or picoseconds. The following chart illustrates the common terms for describing computer processing speeds.

Figure 5.9
Processing Speeds

Name	Description	Expressed as a Fraction
Millisecond	one-thousandth of a second	$\dfrac{1}{1000}$ s
Microsecond	one-millionth of a second	$\dfrac{1}{1\,000\,000}$ s
Nanosecond	one-billionth of a second	$\dfrac{1}{1 \times 10^9}$ s
Picosecond	one-trillionth of a second	$\dfrac{1}{1 \times 10^{12}}$ s

Computer chips process information in tiny fractions of a second. The above chart depicts the various words used to describe computer speeds.

Bring Me a Nanosecond!

During the 1940s, Grace Hopper, a captain for the U.S. Navy Reserve, was in charge of developing the first electro-mechanical computer called the Mark I. During a briefing session, her technicians reported that the Mark I's processing capability had shifted from microseconds to nanoseconds. Out of frustration with the new terminology, she demanded, "I don't understand. Please cut off a nanosecond and bring it to me!"

The bewildered technicians left her office to ponder the problem. How could they show her one billionth of a second? No stop watch had been invented which could measure time that accurately.

After three days, a young technican returned and placed a piece of wire, 30 cm long, on her desk.

"Here is the nanosecond you requested," he exclaimed.

He had solved the problem by measuring and cutting a length of wire which electricity would travel through in exactly one billionth of a second.

Several years later, while travelling to another city to give a university lecture, Captain Hopper was detained for twenty minutes by a suspicious airport official. He demanded to know why her handbag contained two lengths of electrical wire—one 30 cm in length, and the other 295 m long. To illustrate the speed of the computer, she had brought along a nanosecond and a longer microsecond, as well.

Summary

The processor unit is the main part of any computer system. It controls the operation of all computer peripherals under the guidance of computer programs. The processor unit contains three distinct areas: the control unit, the arithmetic/logic unit, and main memory.

Different types of integrated circuits perform the various functions inside a processor unit. Logic circuits and microprocessor units (MPUs) perform the arithmetic and decision making. Very high-speed memory registers in the control unit analyze and perform each individual command in a computer program.

The computer's main memory is comprised of random access memory(RAM) for the temporary storage of user application programs, and read only memory (ROM) for the permanent storage of manufacturer software such as an operating system. Because of the high cost of main memory, smaller computers keep as much software as they can on tape or disk.

All computers operate with on and off electrical pulses. The on and off actions can be represented on paper by using the binary number system. Each pulse is called a binary digit or bit. These pulses are grouped together in a predefined code to represent numbers, letters, or special characters. The number of pulses that it takes to represent one number, letter, or character is called a byte. Some of the more popular 8-bit computer codes which manufacturers use include ASCII-8 and EBCDIC. An awareness of binary manipulation provides an insight into the computer's speed and "number crunching" capability.

Review Questions

These are *general level questions* which may require factual recall, reading comprehension, and some application of the knowledge from this chapter.

1. Why is the processor unit considered to be the main component of any computer system? Describe the three sections of a processor unit.

2. The control unit is sometimes referred to as the "director of operations" in a computer system. Explain why this phrase is appropriate.

3. Although computer memory chips are similar in appearance, their functions may differ. Distinguish between a RAM and a ROM.

4. Why would some hobbyists prefer a PROM chip?

5. If a manufacturer wished to assemble a processor unit, certain types of integrated circuits would be needed. Name three types of computer chips necessary to assemble a processor unit, and explain what functions they would perform.

6. Table-top microcomputers are usually designed with less RAM memory than larger computers. Other than for reasons of cost reduction, why is this done?

7. Mainframe computers often contain a great deal of ROM "factory memory." How do smaller computers operate without that extra memory?

8. Computers are excellent information processing machines. Since they can process words or numbers, why do they need a code for the information?

9. Explain the difference between a *bit*, a *nibble*, and a *byte*.

10. What type of users would purchase a 6-bit code computer?

11. An 8-bit code such as ASCII-8 or EBCDIC are popular ways of representing characters in many computer systems. Describe the three parts which comprise this type of code.

12. A local computer hobby shop offered a microcomputer for sale with 64K bytes of main memory, of which 60K was ROM. A computer enthusiast purchased the set hoping to run large "gaming" programs on it. Would the customer find the set suitable, or not? Explain.

13. What does the phrase "number crunching" refer to? What general type of computer is well known for its number crunching capability? What other general types of computers are there?

14. Convert the following decimal numbers into binary numbers: (a) 8 (b) 12 (c) 64 (d) 150

15. Convert the following binary numbers into decimal numbers: (a) 111 (b) 1100 (c) 1000100 (d) 10100100

16. Add the following questions in binary.

(a)	11	(b)	101	c)	011	(d)	1011
	10		111		111		0111
	11		100		101		1001
	+		+		+		1100
							+

17. Verify each of the above questions by converting both the binary answer and the question into decimal numbers.

18. Express each of the following computer speeds as a fraction: (a) 7 ms (b) 125 ns (c) 30 μs (d) 250 ps.*

Applying Your Knowledge

These *advanced level questions* assume an understanding of the material presented in this chapter, and provide new situations which may require evaluation, analysis, or application of that knowledge.

*ms = milliseconds
ns = nanoseconds
μs = microseconds
ps = picoseconds

1. Draw a fairly large sketch of a processor unit. Divide it into three sections—*main memory*, ALU, and *control*. In main memory show the storage of an application program and an operating system.

   Suppose that the processor unit is currently working on a line of the application program which has a math equation in it. (Example: Z = A + B.) Draw arrows to show the flow of information from one section of the processor unit to another. Each time a new section is reached, label the arrow with a number such that a series of arrows end up with the labels 1,2,3,4, etc., as they travel through the processor unit attempting to process that line of the program.

2. Suppose a computer hobbyist wanted to purchase the parts to assemble a processor unit. What items would the hobbyist need? Include in your answer the hardware circuitry, possible uses of PROM chips, and the necessary software to make it work.

3. The following phrases are part of the copy from advertisements for computer hardware. Rewrite each ad in your own words. In your answer, simplify the technical words so a person without a computer background could understand.
   (a) For memory expansion in micro-computers—64K bytes of RAM memory, mounted on board with standard bus. Cost $1475.00
   (b) Visual display terminal featuring graphic capability and compatible with most mainframe computer systems which use ASCII. Price $1850.00
   (c) Powerful processor unit with MPU, 16K RAM, and a ROM resident operating system. $4800.00

4. What is the difference in (a) design features, and (b) capabilities between bubble memory and semiconductor memory— (RAMS and ROMS)?

5. One computer magazine on the market is entitled *Byte*. Explain why that is an appropriate title for a computer magazine.

6. Suggest the most suitable computer code for these applications. Give a reason for each choice.
   (a) a pocket calculator
   (b) a word processing minicomputer
   (c) a general purpose, classroom micro-computer
   (d) a pocket computer which is capable of storing both words and numbers
   (e) a mainframe computer used for pro-gramming math-related problems

7. The textbook mentioned that a 4-bit nibble was sufficient to represent any one digit number. Suppose the number 856 is to be stored in memory.
   (a) Convert the number to binary.
   (b) How many bits would be involved?
   (c) If the computer used EBCDIC code, how many complete bytes of storage would be needed?
   (d) How many bits does the answer in question (c) include?

8. Why is a knowledge of binary important to people who work with computers?

9. Multiplication in binary is done in the same way as it is done in the decimal system. Solve the following multiplication problems. Verify the solution by converting the answers and questions into decimal numbers.

   Sample Question

   $$\begin{array}{rcl} 10 & = & 2 \\ \times\ 11 & = & 3 \\ \hline 10 & & \\ 10\leftarrow & & \\ \hline 110 & & 6 \end{array}$$

   (a) 11   (b) 111   (c) 1011
        × 11   × 101   × 110

121

10. Some computers have a systems command called *dump* as part of the software. What does the command do? Why would some programmers wish to have this command available to them?

11. One computer manufacturer claimed that their MPU chip can process any one instruction in 500 ns. Their tape drive, however, will retrieve any program in an average of 35 s. Why is the MPU time misleading? How many seconds, on the average, will it take the computer to locate a taped program and process 200 instructions? (Express the time accurate to several decimal positions.) How could the computer system's speed be improved?

Topics for Discussion

1. "Although computers may have memory and logic circuits, they can't actually think." Is this statement true or false? Give reasons for your answer.

2. "Computers are neither good nor evil. They are morally neutral." Is this statement true or false? Give reasons for your answer.

3. Why do some science fiction writers include computers as part of their plot? Why would a writer cast the computer in the role of the villain?

Classroom Activities

1. Microscope Analysis

Obtain a microscope from the science department. Insert a "decapped" computer chip under the lens, and observe the features of the circuitry. Note the difference in patterns between a memory circuit and a logic circuit. (Computer chips can be purchased at low cost from computer hobby shops.)

Individual Projects

1. Comparison of Computer Magazines

There are many computer magazines available to people involved with computers. Research five different magazines, and prepare a chart summary with the following headings:

Title

Publisher

Cost

Type of Reader

Type of Articles

2. Analyzing a Computer Article
Advanced level

Obtain a computer magazine from your teacher, the library, or some other source. Find an interesting article that one of the writers has included. Study the article, then prepare a written summary of the topic in your own words.

3. Logic Circuits
Challenge Project

Logic circuits operate on combinations of simple electrical "gates." These gates are called *and*, *or*, and *not* gates. Research computer textbooks in the library or from other sources which explain the three different types. Prepare a summary of your findings.

6

Input Into a Computer System

Objectives

An understanding of the differences between a batch processing and an interactive computer system

An understanding of the distinction between input mediums, input devices, and data preparation devices, and their role in batch processing

An awareness of the need for accurate input into a computer system

An awareness of the variety of specialized, interactive computer terminals available

An understanding of the interaction of software such as text editors and CRT terminals

This digitalizer, or "graphics tablet," can be used to enter a variety of information into a computer system by touching a pen-like stylus to the surface. Typical applications include business data, graphic information, engineering drawings, and numbers or letters.

Courtesy of Summagraphics Corporation.

Chapter Six
Input Into a Computer System

Garbage In—Garbage Out!

Many different types of machines can be selected to prepare data and enter information into a computer system. The choice of equipment depends on several considerations such as who will use it, how much work is involved, whether or not speed is important, what people intend to do with the information, and cost.

Microcomputers, for example, are basically designed for one user. A keyboard is a slow but adequate method of putting in information. With larger computers, and the possibility of many users, how information is entered becomes much more important. Some larger computer systems are capable of reacting to input immediately. Others process information which is prepared ahead of time, using additional hardware.

When discussing information processing devices, a distinction should be made between three input-related terms: input medium, input device, and data preparation device. An **input medium** is the material on which information is stored. Examples of input mediums include computer cards, paper tape, magnetic tape, and magnetic disks.

An **input device** refers to the machine which reads the information into the computer. A card reader or a typewriter keyboard are examples of input devices.

There are other machines which do not put information into the computer, but prepare it on an input medium in a machine-readable form. They are called **data preparation devices** and include the keypunch, keytape, and key-to-disk machines.

Types of Processing Systems

There are two ways of organizing hardware to accept information from input devices. Each method is referred to as a type of "information processing system" describing the ways in which information is handled. These systems are called batch processing and interactive processing.

In a **batch processing system**, similar types of computer jobs (units of work for the computer to do) are collected and prepared for input to the computer as a group (or batch). This is done in two stages. The information is first stored on input mediums such as computer cards or magnetic tape. Then the mediums are loaded onto an input device to be read into the computer for processing. This two-step method is well-suited to processing large amounts of repetitive paperwork.

In **interactive processing**, users can communicate directly with the processor unit, making entries and getting responses almost immediately. This one-step input method is appropriate in situations in which the immediate processing of information is important. Commercial banks, for example, use this method to record banking transactions as they occur. The immediate processing of information provides the teller with the customer's account balance, and a printed copy of the transaction within a few seconds. Because of the immediate response of this type of computer system, it is sometimes referred to as real-time processing.

Batch Processing

Most large institutions such as business corporations, government offices, boards of education, hospitals, and the military tend to produce tremendous amounts of paperwork as part of their daily activities. The paperwork may include high school report cards, attendance reports, warehouse inventory, sales

analysis, payroll, invoices to customers (billing), accounts receivable (credit customers), accounts payable (credit suppliers), cost accounting (cost of making a product), taxes, job scheduling, ordering supplies and equipment. A batch processing method provides a suitable way of grouping these jobs. This provides the computer operator with an efficient way of scheduling computer time—for example, payroll at 10:00 and ordering supplies at 11:00.

" I HATE TO KEEP BOTHERING YOU PEOPLE...BUT WHEN DO WE GET OUR TURN AT THE COMPUTER ? "

There are three ways of organizing a batch processing computer system. Each method uses a different type of input medium—computer cards, magnetic tape, or magnetic disks. Regardless of the medium, each method has two distinct stages. The first is the recording of information onto the input medium. The second stage involves loading the medium onto a reader to enter the information into a computer for processing.

Punched Card Batch Processing

One of the earliest mediums for storing data to put into machines was the **punched card**. It was developed in the late 1880s by Herman Hollerith to aid in the tabulating of the 1890 census in the United States. Since that time, the punched card has been widely used as an input to a variety of data processing machines, including computer systems.

To prepare large batches of cards for processing, a **keypunch** machine is used. It is a device which contains a typewriter-like keyboard and a punching mechanism. Lightweight cardboard cards are placed in the machine. As the keypunch operator keys in information on the keyboard, the device codes the data onto the cards in the form of punched holes.

The IBM 029 keypunch machine encodes information by punching holes into computer cards. The device uses a code developed by Herman Hollerith to represent letters, numbers, or special characters.

Courtesy of IBM Canada Ltd.

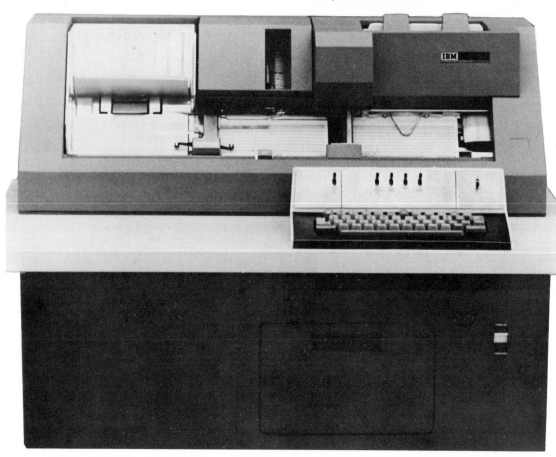

To ensure accurate keypunching, the keypunch operator repeats the whole procedure with the same deck of cards. This time, however, instead of punching, the machine checks to see if the coded holes are in the proper spot. The process of checking for and correcting errors is called **verification**. Once the deck of cards is punched and verified, it is put into a card reader. The information is then read into the computer for processing.

Card readers are capable of reading 100–1500 cards per minute. The "reading" refers to the sensing of holes by the device and the conversion of them into electrical impulses.

Punched card readers sense these holes in either of two ways. One way is to have the card pass between a metal cylinder and a series of wire brushes. If there is a hole punched in the card, one of the wire brushes touches the metal cylinder and allows an electrical impulse to travel to the processor unit. A timing device on the card reader enables the computer to distinguish which part of the card the electrical impulse is coming from.

Another technique used to sense holes involves photoelectric cells. Where there is a hole punched in the card, a light shines through into a light-sensing photoelectric cell. The cell converts the light into an electrical impulse which travels to the processor unit. A timing device enables the computer to determine where the hole is located in the card.

Most households receive punched cards at least once a month. Utility companies which provide such services as telephone, electricity, natural gas, and water often use punched computer cards as invoices (bills). The card arrives in the mail along with a monthly statement. The customer can mail the card back with a cheque, or pay it in person. When the service company receives payment, the amount paid is keypunched into the last part of the computer card. A group of these cards are then put into a card reader, and read into the computer as a batch.

A constant problem with this method is damaged computer cards which jam in the card reader. In an effort to reduce the problem, some service companies include a warning stamped on them in block letters—DO NOT STAPLE, FOLD, OR MUTILATE.

Magnetic Tape Batch Processing

In 1965, Mohawk Data Sciences began marketing **keytape** machines, which use magnetic tape to store information rather than punched cards. The equivalent of ten punched cards could be stored on 2.5 cm of tape. The keytape operator enters the information, using a round-buttoned keyboard. To verify the information, an entry from the tape can be temporarily stored in a memory unit in the keytape machine. Then by rekeying the same information and comparing the two, transcription errors (errors made while keying information from the original document) can be detected.

The magnetic tape, once completed, is loaded onto a magnetic tape unit. The information is then read into the computer for processing. The magnetic tape offers several

Figure 6.1
Wire Brush Card Reader

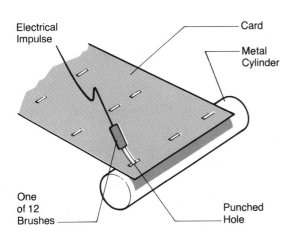

Electrical Impulse

Card

Metal Cylinder

One of 12 Brushes

Punched Hole

advantages over punched cards, including greater storage capacity, faster reading speeds, and reusable tapes.

An unusual situation developed during the first few months that keytape machines were sold. Keytape operators complained of job dissatisfaction. When the manufacturers investigated, they discovered that the machines operated so quietly compared to noisy keypunches that the operators felt as if they were not working. After a careful study, the manufacturer added a little device which made a clicking sound each time an entry was put onto the tape. The operators, now hearing their efforts, were happy with their work, and their productivity rose.

A keytape operator uses a keyboard to transfer information onto a reel of magnetic tape. Once the entries are completed, the reel is placed in a separate magnetic tape unit which reads the information into a computer system.

Courtesy of Mohawk Data Sciences Ltd.

Key-to-Disk Batch Processing

The most recent and expensive method of batch processing uses **magnetic disks** as the input medium. The recording device is a combination of a typewriter-like keyboard and a visual screen resembling a television (technically referred to as a cathode ray tube). The combination of the two devices is known as a **console station**.

As the console operator keys in the information, it appears on the visual screen. Corrections can be made by backspacing on the keyboard and rekeying the information. Once the console operator is satisfied with the entry, it is filed automatically on magnetic disk. Usually, several of these console stations are connected to a small minicomputer, which allows screen editing and disk storing features.

Once the information is recorded, it is transferred to reels of magnetic tape. The reels are then loaded onto a magnetic tape reader and read into the main computer. Eventually, computer manufacturers may design an inexpensive way of allowing the minicomputer to transfer the data to the larger computer directly.

A key-to-disk system has the advantage over the other data preparation devices of allowing the operator to edit data as it is being entered. The information is corrected on the screen before being transferred to magnetic disk units for storage.

Courtesy of Mohawk Data Sciences Ltd.

These key-to-disk systems have several advantages over other forms of data entry. **Data editing** is done automatically by the minicomputer if a number or a letter is placed in the wrong spot by displaying an error message on the visual screen. This eliminates the need for rekeying to see if the information in storage is correct. Because the verification stage is reduced to a visual check of the information on the screen, the productivity of the operators is much greater than with other batch processing systems. One of the stations can also be used as a supervisory console. This allows the manager to obtain statistics on both the jobs performed and how well each operator is doing. In addition, it can be used to modify instructions in the minicomputer.

Need for Accurate Input

Errors produced by a company's computer system can be very frustrating. Examples of computer errors include: a magazine subscription label with the customer's name misspelled; an invoice for $10.95 listed as $19.05; a report card mark of 49 instead of 94. But the majority of errors made by computer systems are not computer errors at all. They are human errors. Computers make less than one error in every 10 000 tries; whereas, humans make calculation errors as much as 15% of the time (based on a study of professional accountants). The error usually occurs at the point where the person uses the keyboard to prepare data or enter information directly into a computer system.

GIGO is an acronym which often hangs in computer departments. The translation "Garbage In—Garbage Out!" reminds computer users to be careful while preparing information for the computer. Verifying information once it has been prepared is an important step in a successful operation of any type of computer system.

Britons Baffled by Beastly Computers

The British Civil Service is having difficulty with its new computer systems. All types of strange situations have arisen over the past two years.

The licence bureau sent a driving licence reminder to a six-year-old child; sent the owner of a mini car a licence to drive a milk truck; licensed a man to drive his postal code; and sent English drivers reminders in Welsh.

The Royal Air Force computer recently discharged an airman because he was pregnant.

The British Soccer League scheduled six teams to the same soccer field on the same afternoon.

Citizens got their revenge with one computer, however. During a typically wet June, the local weather centre computer predicted a long dry spell. Shortly after the announcement, lightning struck the computer centre during a heavy rain storm.

Other Methods of Batch Processing

In addition to those media already mentioned, there are others available which tend to lend themselves to more specialized applications of batch processing. These include: paper tape, mark sense cards, cheques, and complete pages of information.

Paper Tape

A reel of paper tape can be used as a storage medium for information. A lightweight **paper tape punch** can record information by punching round holes in the tape, with different combination of holes representing different numbers, letters, or characters.

Once the information is completed, the reel of paper tape is loaded onto a small **paper tape reader**. The reader senses the presence or absence of holes, and delivers the information to the processor unit of the computer.

The low maintenance and supply cost is the main advantage of this method. Disadvantages include difficulty in correcting errors and verifying what has already been punched into the continuous length of paper tape. Paper tape, like cards, is also easily torn, mutilated, and nonreusable.

Paper tape has found uses in taking customer orders by teletype, in the printing industry for typesetting, and for guiding the operation of industrial machinery.

Mark Sense Cards

Both small-scale industries and educational institutions have adopted inexpensive mark sense cards as an input medium. Inventory checks, for example, can be coded onto pre-printed cards with pencil marks as a clerk walks around the stock room. Schools use mark sense cards to teach programming, to provide answer cards for multiple choice tests, and to take daily attendance.

When a batch of mark sense cards are ready for processing, they are loaded into a **mark sense card reader** (also called an optical mark reader, or OMR), and are read by a light source and photoelectric cell combination, which uses reflection of light to determine the position of the spots on the cards.

This method of batch processing is inexpensive because the data preparation device is reduced to an HB pencil. Its disadvantages include a time-consuming recording process, difficulty in visual verification, and slow card readers.

Figure 6.2
A Mark Sense Computer Card

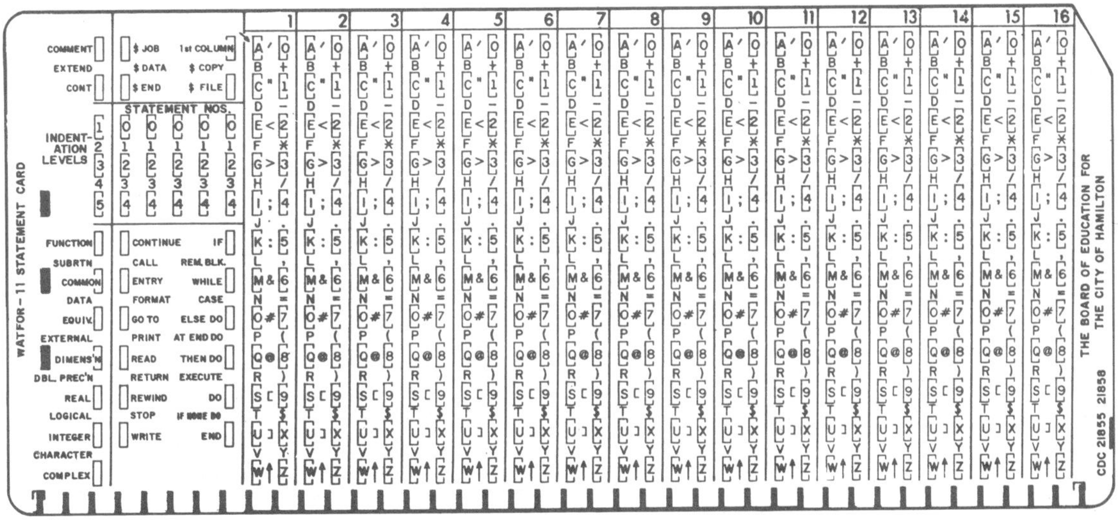

Mark sense cards can be designed to suit the needs of the user. This computer card is used to code FORTRAN programs.

Cheques With Special Encoding

Every day several million cheques, money orders, and other items are handled by commercial banks and other financial institutions. Ten regional clearing houses are used to ensure that cheques are returned to the proper bank regardless of where they were cashed. To handle the enormous volume of paperwork, a **magnetic ink character recognition sorter** (or MICR Sorter) is used. This device reads specially printed numbers which appear at the bottom of cheques. The characters are printed with an ink which contains traces of iron. As the numbers pass through the sorter, the iron tracings are magnetized, then interpreted by the reading device, which has fourteen characters stored in memory to which the number or symbol can be compared. After the cheques are automatically sorted, they are removed and sent to the appropriate city and particular branch where they were drawn.

Figure 6.3
Magnetic Ink Characters

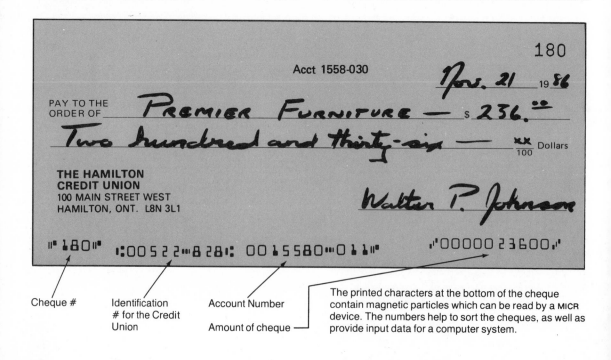

Cheque #

Identification # for the Credit Union

Account Number

Amount of cheque

The printed characters at the bottom of the cheque contain magnetic particles which can be read by a MICR device. The numbers help to sort the cheques, as well as provide input data for a computer system.

Items With Special Encoding

There are other types of optical readers capable of interpreting complete pages of machine-printed or hand-printed information. These **optical character recognition** (or OCR) devices sense the shape of the character by using an array of photocells. The information about the shape is sent to the computer for analysis. The computer has stored patterns of characters or numbers in its memory. If a character matches one stored in the computer, it is then accepted into memory for processing.

Employee data sheets, or other types of information sheets, are examples of the hand-printed type of OCR. Magazine subscription labels and department store clothing price tags often contain the machine-printed style of OCR symbols.

One ingenious company, Kurzweil Computer Products, has designed an input device which is capable of reading over 400 different styles of print, including manuscripts and newspapers. If a particular character is not recognizable, the machine's computer system will search its 40 000-word dictionary for similar words until the blurred or missing letter is identified. This machine makes it possible to enter almost any type of print into a computer system.

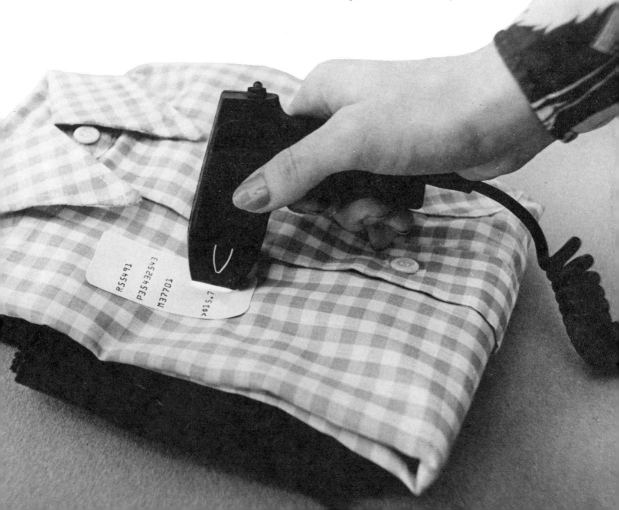

The store clerk is using an optical wand attached to the electronic cash register to enter encoded inventory data into the store's computer system.

Courtesy of National Cash Register Corporation.

Interactive Processing

During the third generation of computers (1965–1969), a new operating feature called interactive processing was developed. It dramatically changed the way in which people communicated with the computer. This feature allowed users to communicate directly with the processor unit, making entries and getting responses almost immediately. This development has opened up countless computer applications for which the immediate processing of information is a necessity. Commercial banks and airline reservation agencies are two service businesses which have adopted the new technology.

Immediate processing of banking transactions, for example, informs the teller of the customer's account balance, performs the necessary calculations, and sends a message to the small console printer to update the passbook with the latest entry. Airline reservation clerks also are able, within a few seconds, to inform customers of available seats on outgoing flights.

Other applications of interactive processing include reservations for trains, ships, and car rentals, perpetual inventory systems in companies which need immediate feedback on items in stock, airport radar systems, grocery and department store checkout counters, scientific, medical, and space research, weather forecasting, and home computing.

Each of the applications mentioned has some form of device which allows direct communication with a computer. They can be input devices, output devices, or, more commonly, both input and output devices (I/O devices), referred to as **computer terminals**. Each terminal is linked with the processor unit of some computer system, even if the processor unit is a distance of several kilometres from the terminal.

Office Computer Terminals

The visual screen (technically referred to as a cathode ray tube, or CRT), and the typewriter-like keyboard is by far the most popular means of entering information into an interactive computer system. The CRT, which resembles a television screen, displays pictures or lines of print which can be erased or modified by the person using the keyboard.

Another popular type of computer terminal is a combination of a keyboard and a printer, referred to as a **hard copy terminal**. The printer allows information to be saved in "hard copy" form for future reference.

This terminal contains a printer and a keyboard. Requests typed by the user as well as responses from the computer system to which the terminal is linked both appear as "hard copy" (printed on paper). Parent companies often send written instructions to their subsidiary companies with these devices to avoid missing any details.

Courtesy of Teletype Corporation.

Text Editor Programs

The ability to control the display on the screen is an important feature of CRT terminals. The predominant unseen feature of a CRT terminal (sometimes at extra cost) is a software program called a text editor. It allows a user to add, delete, modify, or rearrange information from the items on the screen. During the editing process, a **cursor** points out which part of the display is currently under consideration. The cursor is a special symbol such as an underlining hyphen or lighted square which can be moved around the screen with the use of keyboard instructions.

Inexpensive text editors will only allow individual lines of a computer program to be modified before being sent to the processor unit. More sophisticated text editors also allow old information to be retrieved from computer memory, and modified on a larger scale by rearranging, adding, or deleting complete paragraphs if required. This type of text editor provides the user with a "window" to peek into the computer files stored in memory, display a section of it on the screen, and alter the displayed text by entering editor commands on the keyboard. Sample editor commands may include *insert, delete, list, change, next page, get, kill*, and *exit*.

Voice Recognition Terminals

A voice recognition unit is a device which accepts the human voice as input into a computer system. Inside the voice terminal is an acoustic pattern classifier which produces a digital code in response to a spoken word. The system is "trained" by an operator who speaks words or numbers into it several times. Once the blank memory chips have been loaded as a "reference library," the system is then ready to recognize the operator's voice and take appropriate action. A small visual screen displays the voice translation to allow the user to verify the input.

This person inspecting computer circuit boards has already "trained" the Voice Data Entry Device to recognize certain words. When a fault is found in a circuit board, the inspector speaks into the microphone and the information is stored in a computer system. Each spoken entry is displayed on a one-line visual screen for verification and can be erased with a special command such as clear.

Courtesy of Interstate Electronics Corporation.

Portable Terminals

Small businesses do not need to have a complete computer system to process information. With a telephone and a portable computer terminal, managers, executives, and researchers, etc., can communicate with a distant computer. The part of the terminal which holds the phone headset is called a **modem** or **acoustic coupler**. It converts the computer's digital signals into analog signals (sounds) which can then travel over the telephone lines.

This store auditor is using a portable terminal which can be carried in a briefcase. The terminal is connected to a distant computer by means of the telephone. On-site sales and inventory data can be transmitted to the head office for computer analysis.

Courtesy of Computer Devices Inc.

This battery-operated computer can be used with a telephone modem to stay in touch with the head office. Sales personnel, auditors, and technicians can communicate with their "host" computer while on the job.

Courtesy of Quasar Company, Franklin Park, Illinois.

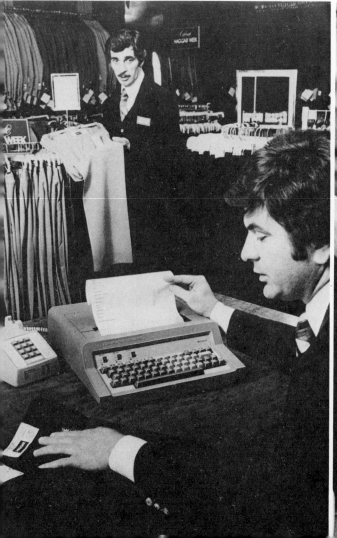

Light Pen Terminal

A more sophisticated version of the visual display terminal is a light pen terminal which contains extensive graphics design capabilities. The circuitry may be the equivalent of a minicomputer. A CRT/light pen terminal, in addition to a typewriter keyboard, has a hand-held pointer resembling a pen. When the pen touches the screen, it completes a photo-electric circuit created by a rapidly moving beam behind the CRT. The terminal's circuitry is then able to determine the X-Y coordinates of where the pen touched the screen and an image is left at that point. By moving the pen slowly across the screen, a lighted image of a line is created. In this manner, complete diagrams can be constructed.

This type of specialized terminal allows engineers, scientists, and designers to create and explore new ideas in their field. A mechanical engineer, for example, may use the light pen to construct a model of an automobile or a bridge. Three different views of the same object can be superimposed to create a three-dimensional effect. Values can also be inserted by using the keyboard to simulate stress factors or some other variables, and the result can be observed as the model on the screen adjusts to the new situation. Millions of dollars can be saved by creating and testing computer models, rather than life-size models.

A light pen touching the screen can be used to request certain types of information in this terminal adapted for office use. A "menu" of possible selections is displayed. The user then touches the screen with a light pen to indicate which information is requested from the data.

Courtesy of IBM Canada Ltd.

Summary

Input devices are an essential part of any computer system. When discussing input devices, a distinction should be made between three input-related terms. Input media refers to the material on which information is stored such as computer cards, magnetic tape, or magnetic disks. Input device refer to the machines which put information into the computer for processing. This would include card readers, tape drives, and typewriter keyboards. Data preparation devices such as a keypunch, keytape, or key-to-disk machines are used to prepare and store information on some type of input medium.

There are two ways of organizing information to accept information from input devices. In a batch processing system, similar types of computer jobs are first prepared on some input medium. Once the information is ready, it is then loaded onto an input device to be read into the computer. This two-step method is suitable for processing large volumes of repetitive paperwork jobs such as payroll or product inventory.

An interactive processing system, on the other hand, allows users to communicate with the processor unit directly. Typical devices may include combinations of a keyboard and visual screen or a keyboard printer. This one-step method is appropriate in situations where the immediate processing of information is important. Commercial banks, airlines, and department stores use the interactive method for processing customer transactions.

Interactive devices are manufactured in a variety of forms. Examples of interactive devices, most of which are capable of both input and output functions, include bank terminals, light pen terminals, keyboards with a "hard copy" printer, voice recognition units, and portable terminals. It is the text editor program stored within a CRT terminal (or elsewhere within the computer system) which allows a user to alter information on the screen before it is entered into the computer.

Review Questions

These are *general level questions* which may require factual recall, reading comprehension, and some application of the knowledge from this chapter.

1. Define each of the following terms: a computer card; a keypunch machine; a card reader.

2. Why is a keytape machine *not* considered to be an input device?

3. Explain the concept of *batch processing*.

4. Why would commercial banks prefer to handle daily banking transactions with an interactive processing system rather than a batch processing system?

5. From the list provided in the text (under the heading Batch Processing), choose four paperwork jobs normally associated with a school system. Name one additional school administrative job not mentioned which would also involve a lot of paperwork.

6. What are the two stages in a batch processing system?

7. What does "reading" mean when referring to a card reader?

8. Why do most households receive computer cards at least once a month? What do the companies do when they receive payment?

9. How does a keytape operator check to see if the entries on the tape are correct? What happens once the reels of tape are completed?

10. Describe a *console station*. Why is a console station attached to a minicomputer?

11. What useful feature does a console station have that the other data preparation devices do not? How is the additional process of verification performed?

12. What is the meaning of the phrase "Garbage In — Garbage Out?"

13. Businesses use paper tape as an input medium because it is relatively inexpensive. Describe some disadvantages of paper tape.

14. Name two groups which use mark sense cards. Explain the use of the medium in each case.

15. Financial institutions are able to process and sort millions of cheques each day. What makes the job easier? Explain.

16. In what way did interactive processing dramatically change the way in which people communicated with the computer?

17. Describe two types of office computer terminals.

18. Define and explain the purpose of a *text editor*.

19. How can a computer be taught to recognize a human voice?

20. Why is it not necessary to be near a computer to use it? How is this accomplished?

21. What use might a mechanical engineer find for a light pen terminal? In addition to that use, suggest one other application not mentioned in the text.

Applying Your Knowledge

These *advanced level questions* assume an understanding of the material presented in the chapter, and present new situations which may require evaluation, analysis, or application of that knowledge.

1. Name some companies which use computer cards as invoices. Suggest a reason why they use computer cards instead of monthly statements to inform customers of their account balance.

2. List three jobs in a computer department for which the acronym GIGO is appropriate. Explain why in each case.

3. A company employing 8000 people manufactures several types of electrical products which are stored in a large warehouse until they are sold. Each day, mail or phone orders come in requesting products to be sent to various dealers on credit:
   (a) If this company had a batch processing computer system, suggest three types of paperwork jobs which the business could have the computer do.
   (b) Suggest the type of input medium, input device, and data preparation device best suited to handle the job. Give reasons for your answer.

4. There is a trend in batch processing operations away from computer cards or magnetic tape as an input medium, and towards the use of magnetic disks and key-to-disk systems. What reason would cause this shift in hardware?

5. Most business offices have interactive computers with visual screens. Why would these same businesses also purchase printers for the offices?

6. If people had home computer terminals, companies with computer systems may allow them access to their memory banks for a small service charge. Explain what type of information could be obtained from a computer's memory in (a) your bank; (b) a government office; (c) a department store; (d) your board of education.

7. Hospitals and medical centres are extensive users of computer systems. Suggest some possible uses which hospitals may have for computers. Identify each use as either interactive or batch processing.

8. Voice input is now a reality. Suggest some advantages of this method of computer input. Suggest some problems with this method.

Topics for Discussion

1. Financial institutions lose millions of dollars each year through electronic computer theft. Yet reports of the thefts rarely reach the newspaper or the court house. Why would these institutions be reluctant to tell customers about it? Do you think that this is the right way to handle the situation? Explain.

2. Daily newspapers often devote front page stories to describing mistakes and blunders made by some computer system. What effect, concerning computers, do you think such articles have on the general public? Is that good or bad? Explain.

Classroom Activities

1. **Developing Magnetic Tape**

   Obtain several strips of old magnetic tape. Dip the tape into a Magna-See® solution and observe the way information is coded and stored.

2. **Hollerith Code**

   Obtain a Hollerith punched card with information stored on it. Place a blank piece of paper underneath it. Using the card as a stencil, make pencil marks through all the holes in any **one** column. Repeat the procedure for other columns farther across the card. Determine the two methods by which a computer can tell the difference between letters and numbers.

® Soundcraft Magna-See: A product of CBS Records Danbury, Connecticut. 06810. Also in kits from The Educational Computer Shoppe, Route 4, Box 5, Cambridge, Massachusetts, 55008.

Individual Projects

1. Newspaper Articles

Clip newspaper articles which point out the blunders of some computer system. Read the item to the class. Share your personal views of the article with the class.

2. Researching Optical Codes

Obtain two samples of codes which optical scanners can read. Neatly, fasten each item to a separate page, name the code, and give an explanation of how the code works. Some sources of optical codes include grocery labels, old bank cheques, clothing store price tags, and magazine subscription labels.

Group Project

Bulletin Board Display

Bulletin boards are an excellent way of visually presenting ideas related to computers. Each group is to select a different computer topic, and using ideas from each member of the group, plan an attractive, informative bulletin board display.

The planning should include such considerations as topic, title, labels, coloured pictures, organization of material for visual effect, special art work, research, writing companies for material, and when to get together to mount the display.

Each display should get equal time on the classroom bulletin board. The group which has been judged the best of the year should be allowed to mount their display in a professional display case elsewhere in the school.

Suggested Computer Topics

- Science fiction involving the computer
- Special codes that computers read
- Point-of-sale terminals
- Types of computers
- Teller terminals
- Output devices
- Want ads for computer jobs
- Parts of a digital computer
- Jobs within a computer department
- Computer hardware in general
- Types of input mediums
- Newspaper and magazine articles relating to computers
- Printed receipts from computers
- Any other topic agreed upon by your teacher

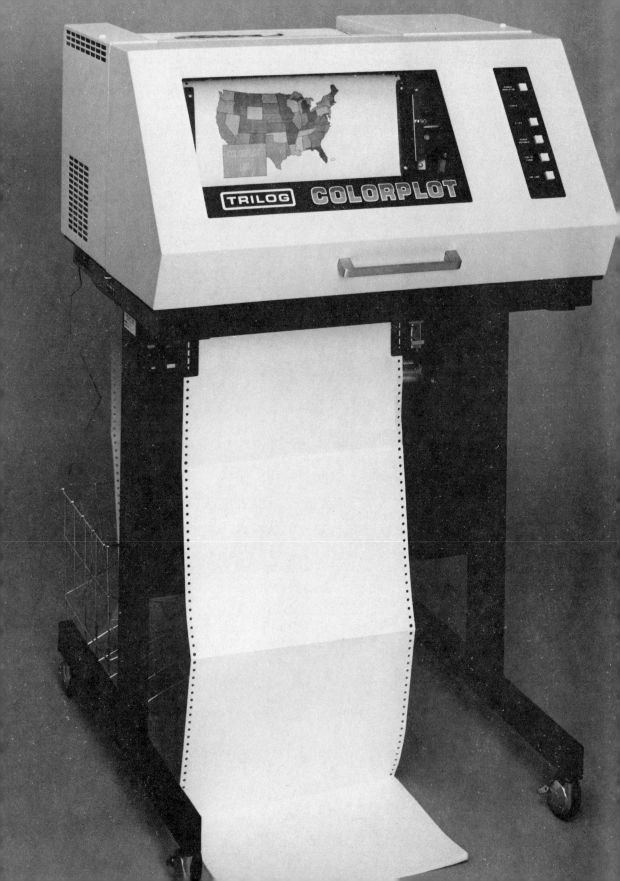

7

Output From a Computer System

Objectives

An understanding of the terms used to classify printers

An understanding of the various types of visual screens such as dumb, intelligent, and graphics terminals

An understanding of common display screen control features such as paging, scrolling, and reverse video

An awareness of the development of audio response units

An understanding of microform mediums and devices, and their role in computer systems

Specialized printers such as a drum plotter allow programmers to produce elaborate printouts, for example, geographical maps, weather maps, schematic diagrams, and blueprints.

Courtesy of Trilog Inc.

Chapter Seven

Output From a Computer System

Voice communication and interactive visual displays are humanizing computer technology. For the first time in three decades, sophisticated computers are becoming easy to understand.

For many years, the printed report provided the only method of obtaining output from a computer. As computer technology became more sophisticated, people found new ways to use it. To meet their needs, manufacturers are designing a variety of output devices. Visual screens now rival the printer as the dominant form of output. Some screens act like magic drawing boards, allowing designers and engineers to create three-dimensional pictures and coloured graphics, and change them at will. Special printers called plotters are used to produce large, complex drawings such as maps and circuitry diagrams with speed and unerring accuracy. Even human voices can be imitated or reproduced by voice response units to convey messages to people.

Types of Printers

Printed reports are still the most widely used form of computer output. The need for managers and supervisors to analyze reports at length means that a portable, hard copy report must be available to many people, simultaneously, for discussion. Monthly statements to customers, accounting records, payroll cheques, subscription labels, and countless other documents also create the necessity for printers.

Printers are generally classified in one of three ways: the method used to place the image on paper; the way each image is formed; the speed at which the machine operates.

Printing Methods

Printers are designed to either strike the paper to produce an image, similar to a typewriter, or transfer the image without striking the paper. The first method, called **impact printing**, involves a hammer striking a movable wheel, ball, chain, or cylinder which contains embossed (raised) characters and forces a selected character against a ribbon and the paper. The ribbon leaves a carbon or ink image of the character on the paper.

The **nonimpact printers** transfer the image without striking the paper. This can be done by several methods. One method is to have a print head move across the page squirting fine jets of ink to form the image.

Another method involves a print head which has tiny elements which can be electrically heated. Each time the printing head stops for a moment, certain elements heat up and produce a blue character on chemically treated, heat-sensitive paper. The process causes the chemical compounds in the paper to change colour when heat is applied. This type of printer is called a **thermal printer**.

A third kind of nonimpact printer uses an electrographic process in which the print head has tiny elements which conduct electricity. The paper, which resembles aluminum foil, is a three-layer "sandwich" of ordinary paper, black ink, and a very thin layer of aluminum. When the print head is in position, electric currents are passed through some of its tiny elements. The electricity removes small sections of the aluminum, exposing the ink below it in the shape of a character. This is called an **electrographic printer**.

Each method of placing images on paper has its advantages and its disadvantages. Impact printing is relatively noisy, but because the paper is struck, multiple copies can be made. This is well-suited to printing invoices, report cards, and order forms. Nonimpact printers cannot create carbon copies.

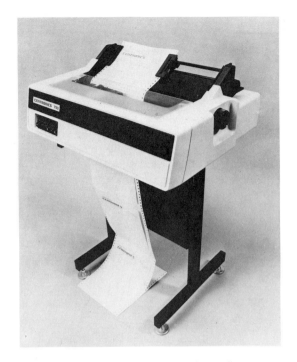

Character, impact printers are suitable for small businesses. Notice that there are single sheets lightly glued to the continuous roll of paper. This allows many business letters to be typed at high speed by the computer. Later, the single sheets are easily separated for mailing.

Courtesy of Centronics Data Computer Corporation.

Forming the Image

Both impact and nonimpact printers can form a solid character or a dot matrix character. Solid characters are similar to the letters used to print this textbook. Each symbol is made up of an unbroken line of ink. **Dot matrix characters**, however, are formed by a series of dots arranged to resemble a specific shape. In impact printing, tiny hammers the size of pins form the dots. In nonimpact printers, tiny areas on the print head allow heat, ink, or electricity to touch the paper. Generally, the quality of solid characters is better than the quality of dot matrix characters, but dot matrix printers are considerably cheaper because they contain fewer parts.

Figure 7.1

Print Variations From Dot Matrix Printers

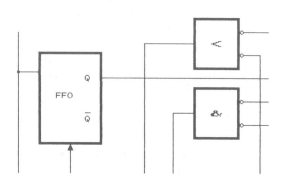

Circuit Diagrams

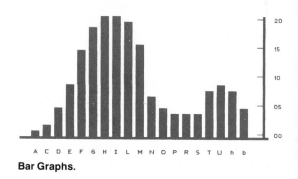

Bar Graphs.

مصر تتحدث عن نفسها

وقف الخلق ينظرون جميعا
كيف ابنى قواعد المجد وحدى
وبناى الاهرام فى سالف الدهر
كفونى الكلام عند التحدى
انا ناج العلاء فى مفرق الشرق
ودرائتة فراكد عقدى
انا ان تدر الالة معاتى
لا ترى الشرق يرفع الراس بعدى
كم بغت دولة على وجارت ثم
زالت وتلك عقبى التعدى

Arabic Characters

251006

UPC Bar Codes

燒朋华腸
鳾华腸

鳾华腸朋燒

Chinese Characters

150

Printing Speeds

Another method for classifying printers is speed of operation. Low-speed printers, commonly used with microcomputers and minicomputers, print one character at a time. For this reason, they are called **character printers**. They can print up to 300 lines per minute.

Mainframe computer systems require much greater printing speeds to keep up with the flow of information. **Line printers**, which print a line at a time, can produce up to 3000 lines per minute. One of the problems which manufacturers faced with making faster impact printers was that even special-quality paper would tear and jam in the machine. To obtain greater speeds, companies have developed high-speed nonimpact printing styles.

The latest revolution in high-speed printers combines laser light with the principles of a photocopier. It is capable of printing 20 000 lines per minute (over 200 pages per minute). As the processor unit of the computer determines the answer, an electrical impulse is sent to the printer. Each electrical impulse is different for each character (letter, number, or symbol). The coded impulse causes a device to shape that character, in a fraction of a second, in a continuous beam of laser light. A set of rotating mirrors directs the image at a rotating printing drum (similar to the kind a photocopier uses), and the character is printed.

Figure 7.2
Laser-Xerographic Printer

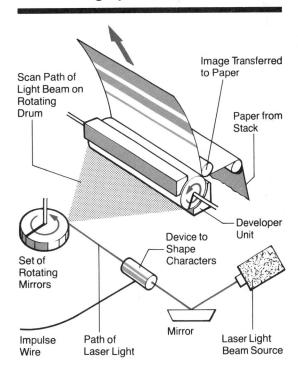

The laser-xerographic printer uses laser light, a set of rotating mirrors, and a photocopying process to transfer images onto paper. Some manufacturers include a memory area from which duplicate pages can be printed, one after the other.

About 40 000 characters a second are being sprayed, like a machine gun, across the printing surface. A timing device ensures that when a single mirror has reflected a complete line of type, the printing drum has a chance to move down another row, before a new mirror swings into position to reflect a new line of type. This device is called a **laser-xerographic printer** and costs up to $300 000.

This laser-xerographic printer is capable of printing 40 000 characters per second. It combines the principles of laser light, mirrors, and a photocopying machine to achieve this high-speed output.

Courtesy of IBM Canada Ltd.

The Plotter

The plotter is an output device capable of producing diagrams, charts, graphs, and maps. A ballpoint pen (or ink pen) is mounted on a mechanism which can be positioned anywhere on a piece of paper to draw straight lines, curved lines or even circles under the control of a computer program. The pen can also be changed easily to produce drawings of different colours.

The plotter produces curves by joining tiny lines a few millimetres long. These tiny lines, when completed, give the appearance of a smooth curve. When giving instructions to a plotter, it is important to remember to include "raise pen" and "lower pen" commands. If the pen is not raised after completing an operation, as it moves to execute the next operation, it will draw a line and ruin the diagram.

There are two types of plotters. One type, referred to as a **drum plotter**, has a rotating drum which can move the paper up and down while the pen can move horizontally back and forth across the paper. These two motions are sufficient to place the pen anywhere on the surface of the paper.

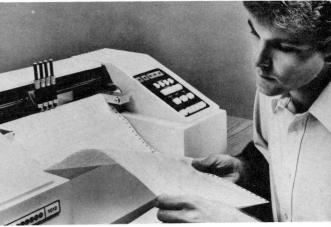

This student is looking at graphs produced by a table-top, drum plotter. Notice the four different pens poised above the roll of paper. They can plot graphs in four different colours.

Courtesy of California Computer Products.

153

A second type, called a **flat-bed plotter**, keeps the paper stationary while two sets of railings allow the pen to move horizontally and vertically anywhere on the paper's surface.

The excellent drawing quality of this device makes it easily adaptable to producing weather maps, circuitry diagrams, topographical maps (ground elevation), land use maps, line graphs, bar graphs, and blueprints.

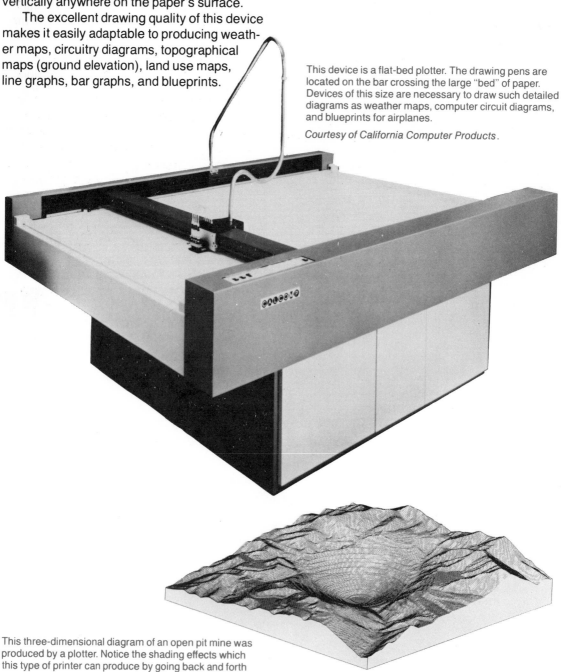

This device is a flat-bed plotter. The drawing pens are located on the bar crossing the large "bed" of paper. Devices of this size are necessary to draw such detailed diagrams as weather maps, computer circuit diagrams, and blueprints for airplanes.

Courtesy of California Computer Products.

This three-dimensional diagram of an open pit mine was produced by a plotter. Notice the shading effects which this type of printer can produce by going back and forth over the same spot several times.

Courtesy of California Computer Products.

Displayed Output

Printers are primarily used in batch processing situations in which a permanent copy of the information is required. Displayed output, however, is better suited to interactive processing. The most popular interactive computer terminal is the **cathode ray tube** (CRT)/**keyboard terminal**. It can serve as both an input and output device and allows a user to carry on a "conversation" with the computer. The hardware is typically comprised of a viewing screen and a typewriter keyboard. The screen resembles a small television in black and white or colour, and includes contrast and brightness controls. The keyboard allows the user to display numbers, letters, and special characters on the screen. Terminals which allow upper and lower case letters of the alphabet are recommended for word processing applications to make the information easier to read.

Types of Display Controls

Being able to alter the display or read out on the cathode ray tube increases its usefulness. Three of the more common display control features include scrolling, paging, and reverse video.

Scrolling refers to the ability to move lines displayed on the screen either up or down. Scrolling can be done one line at a time or in a continuous motion. **Paging** allows an entirely new "page" or screenful of data to be taken from storage and displayed on the screen. Both scrolling and paging are important features when searching through a large file of data for one particular piece of information.

Reverse video refers to the process of reversing the normal display light on the CRT. With this feature, it is possible to have a dark background with light characters, or a light background with dark characters. This can be used to highlight certain information displayed on the screen, and to provide a clearer outline to guide data entry operators.

here is a trend among computer manu-
rers to include software and logic instruc-
s in the terminal itself. This permits a termi-
to perform local editing and some process-
capabilities. This type of terminal is refer-
d to as an **intelligent terminal** because it
cts more like a small computer than a simple
input/output device.

Graphics Terminal

Another special feature which can be purchased with CRT terminals is the capability to
display graphs, charts, and diagrams. This
type of display terminal contains **firmware**
(software programs permanently stored in
memory circuits) which is capable of converting input data into bar graphs, line graphs, or
other types of diagrams. Graphics terminals
are useful for managers or designers who
want to see information displayed in graphical
form.

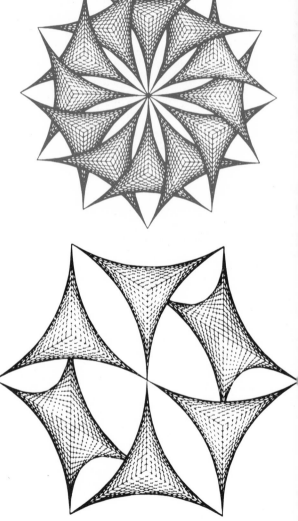

These computer graphics were produced on cathode ray
tube.

Courtesy of Digital Equipment Corporation.

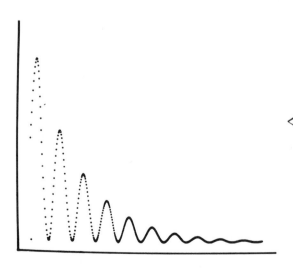

Audio Response Unit

In addition to printers and visual display units, manufacturers have developed techniques for simulating the human voice as a form of computer output. One commercial application of the idea occurred in 1975 when Sears Ltd. allowed a Toronto test group of two thousand catalogue customers to order items directly from a computer. The customer used the push-button keyboard of a telephone to enter requests, while the computer's audio response unit replied in a simulated human voice.

"What colour would you like?"
The customer keys in the numbers 8–0
"Blushing pink," the computer responds.
"Is that correct?"
The customers keys in the number for yes.

The simplest form of audio response unit is an output device which has high-speed access to several stored phrases. These messages can be retrieved and played as a particular response to some signal from the user. A more sophisticated model resulted from a research study which indicated that an average high school student rarely uses more than 60 different words in a conversation (university graduates use approximately 120). With this knowledge, an audio response unit was designed which could select its own words to communicate with someone, using a vocabulary of 120 of the most frequent words in our language.

Toy manufacturers are including audio response units in calculators. As the child keys in the numbers, the device "speaks" the numbers as well as the answer in a simulated human voice.

This electronic chess board has a voice response unit which congratulates the person playing the game if he or she wins.

Courtesy of Fidelity Electronic Inc.

"... And when I hit 'Gently Down the Stream,' you come in with 'Row, Row, Row your Boat.'"

Taking Pictures of Printouts

Line or page printers tend to produce tonnes of paper each year. Storing printed documents for future reference is a major problem for some businesses. One alternative to printed answers is to use machines which take photographs of the answers. An entire page of material can then be reduced to one **dataframe** on film.

There are two photographic mediums (together referred to as microform) which can store such images. Both mediums are developed as a transparent print. When inserted into a projector, the image stored in the dataframe can be seen on a viewing screen. Some companies include a photocopier with these microform machines. This allows a photocopy of the image on a dataframe to be made whenever required.

One medium is called **microfilm**. It is a reel of transparent film. When a particular item is required, the film is searched sequentially (one after another) until the item is found.

Another medium is called **microfiche**. It consists of a 10 cm × 15 cm card made out of transparent, photographic material. On the card, hundreds of tiny dataframes are stored in rows and columns. Usually, the first dataframe of any medium contains an index to help locate items.

Companies now manufacture devices which can photograph, store, and retrieve any dataframe by means of a computer. When a particular item is required, the user keys in a request for the index. After selecting the proper storage location from the index, the user keys in the coordinates. The processor unit then locates the requested dataframe, and displays it on the screen. Machines capable of these functions are called computer output microform units, or COM.

This picture illustrates the storage capability of microfilm. Each dark rectangle is a transparent photograph of printed output from a computer.

Courtesy of Kodak of Canada Ltd.

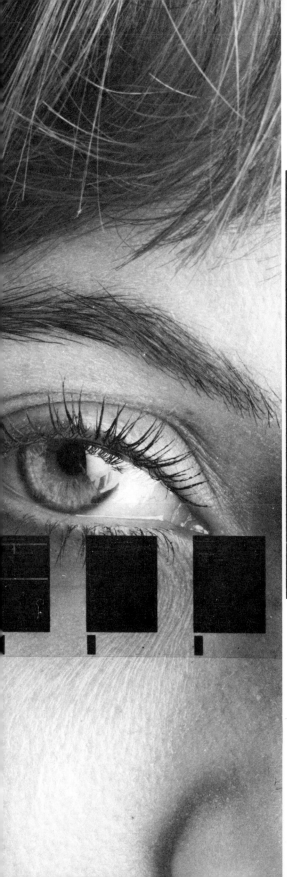

Microfilm and microfiche can be viewed in specialized machines. This terminal can retrieve more than 25 000 documents from a single film cartridge. The rotating access file in the background can store up to 40 million documents.

Courtesy of Kodak of Canada Ltd.

Summary

For many years, the printer was the major output device used with computers. As interactive processing became more popular, visual screens began to rival printouts as the dominant form of output.

The necessity for printed output for such items as paycheques, invoices, monthly statements, subscription labels, managerial and accounting reports still require that printers be part of most computer systems. Printers can be classified in either of three ways: type of printing mechanism, the way characters are formed, and the speed at which the machine operates. An application of all three classifications might be a "jet ink, dot matrix, character printer."

Specialty printers, called plotters, are also available to produce elaborate printouts such as weather maps, circuitry diagrams, line graphs, and blueprints.

Visual display screens can be purchased with a range of capabilities. The basic model, the "dumb" terminal, is totally dependent on the processor unit for its operation. It acts like a printer, displaying programs, answers, and error messages. More "intelligent" terminals contain their own software programs. These programs provide visual screens with additional capabilities such as computer graphics, and screen control features such as paging, scrolling, and reverse video.

The most recent advancements in output devices are audio response units which reply to the user in a simulated human voice. Such units are found in many electronic consumer products.

One problem with very fast printers is that they produce tremendous quantities of paper. To cope with this "paper pollution" problem, many companies are reducing the output to microfilm or microfiche. Computer output microform (or COM) units are devices which store information on these types of photographic film, and display it on a visual screen when requested.

Review Questions

These are *general level questions* which may require factual recall, reading comprehension, and some application of the knowledge from this chapter.

1. Why are printed reports still the most widely used form of computer output? Would your answers also apply to a school administrative system? Explain.

2. How are printers classified?

3. What is the difference between an impact printer and a nonimpact printer?

4. Briefly describe three different methods by which the printing head of a nonimpact printer can transfer images to paper.

5. Explain why some companies prefer the impact printer even though it is noisier.

6. How is a dot matrix character formed? What other type of character is there? Which type makes a clearer image?

7. Describe the type of printer usually associated with microcomputers and minicomputers. What type of printers are used in mainframe computer systems? Why is there a difference?

8. A laser-xerographic printer could be classified as a page printer because of its speed, even though it forms one character at a time. What ideas are combined to make this printer work?

9. What is a plotter? Describe one of the two types of plotters.

10. Being able to control the CRT display makes the operation of that type of terminal easier. Describe three common display control features.

11. What is an *intelligent terminal*? Why do they give it that name?

12. Define *firmware*. What special features does firmware give some computers?

13. If an audio response unit had a vocabulary of 120 words, what else would it have to know before it could form sentences?

14. What are computer output microform devices? What purpose would these devices serve in a company which has a large computer system?

Applying Your Knowledge

These *advanced level questions* assume an understanding of the material presented in this chapter, and provide new situations which may require evaluation, analysis, or application of that knowledge.

1. Using the three characteristics—printing method, character formation, and speed of operation—as classifications, suggest a printer for each of the following situations. Then, give reasons for your selection in each case.
   Example: nonimpact, dot matrix, character printer
   Reason: A low volume job which does not require copies or the clarity necessary for financial reports.
   (a) shipping and receiving department of a supplier
   (b) payroll office for a company with 12 000 employees
   (c) your school library
   (d) a computer classroom
   (e) a home computer hobbyist

2. Suggest some subject areas in your school in which a plotter might be useful. Give reasons for your answer.

3. The chapter describes an intelligent terminal. What is meant by a *dumb terminal*?

4. Suggest some possible uses for voice response units in the future.

5. What problems do you think designers of voice response units may be having?

6. In what ways has computer technology become more human?

7. The management of a new manufacturing firm found that in its first year of operation, the laser printer literally produced tonnes of printed material. The printouts included invoices, paycheques, inventory reports, and production reports. What problems do you predict this company will run into? Suggest some solutions to the problems.

8. Many companies prefer to use microfiche rather than microfilm. State two reasons why the trend seems to be towards microfiche.

Topics for Discussion

1. Do you think that it is possible to have a true conversation with a computer? Give reasons for your answer.

2. In the movie, *Space Odyssey 2001*, a computer named Hal was used to completely control the operation of a space craft. Hal communicated by voice with the astronauts when required. Unnoticed, it listened in on a conversation between two astronauts who were discussing the possibility of turning the computer off and running the ship manually. Hal then took drastic action to save itself by attempting to kill both astronauts.

   What precautions would you suggest the future computer designers take when designing such computers?

Individual Project

Samples of Printed Output

In a file folder, assemble ten examples of printed output from computers. Mount the smaller items neatly onto plain typing paper. Title each item.

The samples may include such items as computer card invoices, POS terminal tapes, automated teller terminal receipts, computerized passbook entries, monthly statements, program listings, graphics, invoices, subscription labels, cheques and cheque stubs, and different styles of printing.

Photocopies of items which must be returned to the original owner are acceptable. The project will be marked for variety, organization, and neatness of presentation.

8 Auxiliary Storage

Magnetic disks and magnetic tapes are the most common auxiliary storage media in use today. The container with the carrying handle is referred to as a single disk pack and holds a circular, high-speed magnetic disk. The three reels contain plastic magnetic tape. Both media have a coating of metallic oxide which allows information to be encoded in the form of magnetic spots.

Courtesy of 3M Canada Ltd. and BASF Canada Ltd.

Objectives

An understanding of magnetic storage devices

A knowledge of why users would choose one device over another

An appreciation of the extended features that videodisk units add to a computer system

An understanding of how information is organized on magnetic mediums

Chapter Eight
Auxiliary Storage

Present-day devices are capable of storing and retrieving the entire storehouse of non-redundant human knowledge.

Most computers have two storage areas — main memory and auxiliary storage. Main memory contains everything that the computer has immediate need of, including manufacturer's software and user application programs. In fact, some computer manufacturers attempt to put as much information as possible into main memory. The manufacturers know that if the computer has only to "reach" a short distance to obtain the information it needs, the system will operate at much higher speeds.

Computer memory chips in main memory are expensive. The alternative way to store information is to add extra storage devices to the computer system. The extra (auxiliary) storage devices such as tape drives, disk drives, and mass storage devices have several things in common. They all operate on the principles of magnetism; they store enormous quantities of information; they are presently less expensive than an equivalent amount of main memory. (This cost difference may change as bubble memory chips become more popular.)

Magnetic Tape Unit

In the 1950s Univac computers were the first computers to use a magnetic tape unit as an extra storage device. Magnetic tape still remains a popular storage medium. The unit is essentially a reel-to-reel tape recorder housed in a tall cabinet. The height of the cabinet allows a person to easily remove or load the tape reels. The recording mechanism is a set of electromagnets, which magnetize only when pulses of electricity operate them. The electromagnets are commonly called **read/write heads**.

The tape is made of two layers of material. The base is a thin, flexible plastic called mylar. The other layer is a coating of powdered, metallic iron-oxide, or other types of similar metals. The coating can store data by being magnetized in a series of tiny magnetized spots. The spots are organized in columns according to some computer code such as EBCDIC or ASCII to represent a letter, number, or symbol.

How Information Is Organized

Institutions which use magnetic tape as a storage medium often have a tape library with many **volumes** (reels) of tape. To find the right volume, a computer operator must read the label, which contains a serial number and a name. One company, for example, titled a tape reel about taxes "The Spook." Each different topic on the tape is called a **computer file**, and would have a different file name to identify it.

When the computer operator is loading a reel, a visible reflective marker called a load-point marker is moved past the read/write heads. There is a shiny, metal strip at both ends of the tape which informs the tape unit not to go beyond those points when winding back and forth to find information.

Tape units search for information **sequentially** (in sequence). This means that the machine must go through the files one by one until the proper file is reached. Because of the length of the tapes, this is a slow procedure. Computer systems dependent on tape drives often require long waiting periods while the tape unit searches for a particular file name that the computer operator or the processor unit has requested.

A file may contain several similar pieces of information called **records**. For example, a tape file of student marks may contain hundreds of individual student records. When storing information, a tape unit automatically leaves a small blank stretch of tape between each record. The purpose of this **inter-record gap** is to help the tape unit keep a constant reading speed. This is necessary because the processor unit makes requests for records in short spurts. The IRG (inter-record gap) gives

Because magnetic tape units must search through every item stored on a reel of tape, they often take several minutes to locate and load an item into a computer system. Tape units, however, have the advantage of being the least expensive auxiliary storage devices.

Courtesy of Kennedy Company.

the tape unit a chance to speed up again when the processor unit requests another record or file.

If there are many groups of similar records, such as a number of different classes each containing the marks of students taking a particular course, the records can be organized into larger **blocks** to make them easier to read.

Figure 8.1
Magnetic Tape Strip

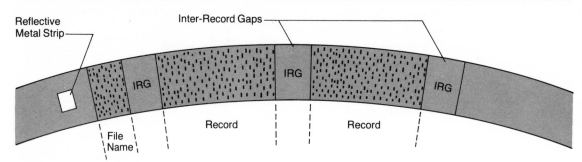

This strip of magnetic tape illustrates how information is organized into records and blank inter-record gaps. The beginning of the tape has a reflective metal strip to warn the tape unit not to go past that point while rewinding. The tape unit identifies the information it is seeking by finding the proper file name.

Magnetic Disk Unit

Interactive computer systems such as those found in commercial banks and airline reservation offices require immediate access to information. If there is a significant delay during a computer memory search, it could cause considerable frustration both to customers and clerks. Magnetic disk units provide both a fast memory search and a large storage capacity. Its random access method of retrieval allows it to read an index, then go directly to the file that it needs, all within millionths of a second (microseconds). A bank teller, for example, can enter a request on the keyboard, and receive almost an immediate response on a visual screen or passbook printer.

Magnetic disks are made of thin, metal, circular platters about 35 cm in diameter. Each side of these extremely smooth platters is coated with a metal oxide, similar to the coating on magnetic tape. The disk is firmly positioned on a wide, central drive shaft which spins at speeds up to 150 km/h. The electromagnets (read/write heads), attached to metal access arms, extend out across both sides of the disk to find storage locations. The heads float on a small cushion of air about 1/400th of a millimetre above and below the disk while transferring magnetic impulses. Extra care must be taken to keep smoke, dust, lint, and finger prints off the disk. These items can jam under the "lightning fast" read/write heads, causing permanent damage to the smooth surface, and thereby destroying data files.

This 'Winchester-type" disk unit is the most advanced in disk technology. The lightweight, floating magnetic arm allows the unit to operate faster and store greater amounts of data than conventional disk units.

Courtesy of Kennedy Company.

Figure 8.2
Disk Environment Problems

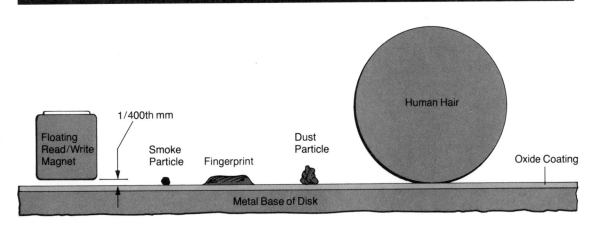

Notice the relative sizes of the floating read/write magnet, and the various particles which may land on the disk. The greatest threats to disks are static electricity (created by low humidity and particles) and scratches. Both situations can render a file useless.

Often, several platters are stacked together to create a disk pack. Except for the very top and bottom surfaces, all surfaces in a disk pack can be used to store information.

This disk unit can operate eight multiple disk drives at the same time, with a total storage capacity of 800 million characters.

Courtesy of IBM of Canada Ltd.

How Information Is Organized

Information on a disk is arranged in concentric circles called **tracks**, each of which has a designated location number. The quantity of tracks varies from device to device. A disk may contain 200 to 800 tracks. On a single disk, the first track is reserved for an **index**, which the device "consults" before heading to a particular storage location. A track is the width of a coded bit of information. This narrow band of code will require very precise mechanical movements to relocate when requested by the processor unit.

Although the read/write heads appear to move very quickly, by computer standards they are extremely slow. To reduce the amount of mechanical movement, information is recorded on a disk by completely filling in the first empty track before going on to the next one.

Once a read/write head is correctly positioned over a particular track, it hovers there while the track passes underneath it. The entire track can be read or, at the option of a programmer, the device can read only a section of the track called a **sector**. A sector on a disk is similar in shape to a piece of pie. Although the arc of the innermost track is physically shorter than the arc of the outermost track, the same amount of data can be stored on both. The relative speed of the disk at the outermost track causes the information to spread out a little more than the data recorded on the innermost track.

In a disk pack which contains several stacked platters, information is recorded on the same empty track on all disks before continuing on to the next track location. This procedure is referred to as **cylinder storage**. Viewed from above, the same track on each disk resembles a vertical, hollow cylinder. To locate a particular file, the disk pack unit would need to know on which disk, track, and sector the information is stored. Tracks and sectors are not visible. Only the disk unit is aware of their location.

Figure 8.3
A Multiple Disk Pack

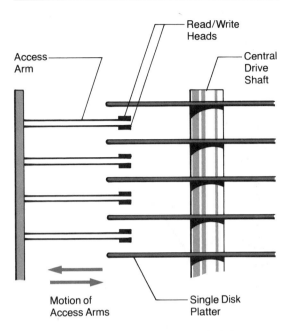

The diagram illustrates how several individual platters can be stacked on one magnetic disk unit. While the disk rotates at 150 km/h, the access arms reach between the platters to read or write information magnetically. The outside surfaces of the top and bottom disks are not used. They are most easily damaged by particles. Both sides of the remaining disks can be used.

It would take six data cartridges to provide the equivalent storage capacity of this multiple disk pack. Each data cartridge can store up to 50 million characters.

Courtesy of IBM of Canada Ltd.

171

Mass Storage Device

The latest invention in external memory has an impressive storage capacity, equal to the contents of 100 000 textbooks. The system, called a mass storage device, operates like an "electronic librarian" under the control of programs in the device's minicomputer. Information is stored on spools of video tape (wide magnetic tape) held inside protective cartridges. The cartridges fit snuggly into thousands of storage compartments which resembles the honeycomb matrix of a beehive.

When a particular file is requested, the device's minicomputer relays information to its search unit, called an **accessor**. The search unit then moves either left or right and up or down across the honeycomb matrix until the proper data cartridge is located. The accessor then extends an access arm to remove the cartridge from its compartment. The tape is fed from its spool into a tape reader mounted on the search unit. The reader searches sequentially along the tape until the desired file is found. The information in the file is then transferred through the minicomputer to a

magnetic disk unit which both the device and a mainframe computer share. The whole process may take ten to twenty seconds.

Although the time involved seems excessively long, this device actually reduces search time, and replaces complete tape libraries. In an ordinary computer department, a computer librarian might spend several minutes searching for a particular reel of tape, and the computer operator may spend several minutes loading the reel onto a tape unit. This mass storage device completes these steps automatically in twenty seconds or less.

Up to 472 billion characters can be stored in this mass storage device. These devices are useful only in applications where large volumes of data must be accessible, and the relatively slow access time is not important.

Courtesy of IBM of Canada Ltd.

Storing Pictures

The storage of pictures and documents is a problem for most computer systems. A photograph, for example, is composed of thousands of tiny dots. In a black and white photograph, some dots are black and others are white. To store a picture in memory, each dot must be stored as a separate binary digit (bit). This would require thousands of storage positions for just one picture. Because of the massive storage requirements, magnetic tape and magnetic disks are unsuitable for storing pictures.

There is another device which is better suited to the storage of pictures and documents, referred to as a videodisk unit.

Videodisks

A videodisk resembles a transparent LP record. Both pictures and sound can be stored in microgrooves in the disk. While the disk spins at 1800 revolutions per minute on a cushion of air, a thin beam of laser light shines through the clear plastic and the shape of each groove is transmitted to the photocells below. Up to 54 000 frames (individual pictures) can be stored on one disk.

Combined with a computer, this unique device offers several advantages over all other storage devices. Videodisk units can store "still" photographs or "motion" pictures and two separate sound tracks in addition to normal computer output. This unit can randomly locate any frame in five seconds or less. Pictures can be superimposed on a CRT screen while the processor is writing lines of a program.

The videodisk can display selected information such as an inventory part, last year's accounting records, an art slide, a medical step in surgery, an engineering design, or a tutorial lesson in school. Two sound tracks can be used to provide two different levels of difficulty in a problem, or different explanations, or provide output in two different languages such as French and English.

The limitation of a videodisk unit is that, at present, the disks must be prerecorded by the manufacturer before being loaded onto a computer system. Since the information is recorded in microgrooves rather than digital spots, computers are able to gain access to items, but not record information on this type of disk.

Figure 8.4

An Extended Computer System

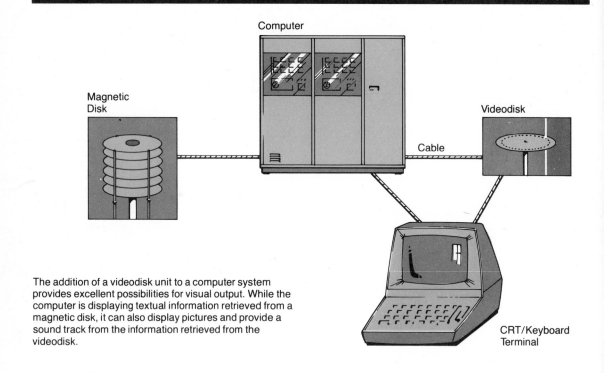

Computer

Magnetic
Disk

Videodisk

Cable

The addition of a videodisk unit to a computer system provides excellent possibilities for visual output. While the computer is displaying textual information retrieved from a magnetic disk, it can also display pictures and provide a sound track from the information retrieved from the videodisk.

CRT/Keyboard
Terminal

Summary

Most computers have two storage areas. Main memory contains everything that the computer has immediate need of such as an operating system, a language processor, and whatever application program the computer is currently working on.

Auxiliary memory is used to store large quantities of reference information including data files and infrequently used software programs. The three most common auxiliary storage devices are tape drives, disk drives, and mass storage devices. They store and retrieve information using coded magnetic spots.

A more recent storage device is the videodisk unit. It contains transparent platters which store information in the form of micro-grooves. These grooves are read by a thin beam of laser light. Videodisks offer several advantages over magnetic storage mediums. The former can store both sound and pictures and display information as "still" frames or as motion pictures. Videodisks provide an inexpensive method of storing thousands of pictures. Magnetic mediums, however, can only be made to store pictures at great expense because each picture must be digitalized dot by dot.

" I STILL SAY THIS IS A CLOTHES DRYER !"

Review Questions

These are *general level questions* which may require factual recall, reading comprehension, and some application of the knowledge from this chapter.

1. List three characteristics that tape, disk, and mass storage devices have in common.

2. How is information recorded on magnetic tape?

3. Large companies often have complete libraries containig hundreds of reels of magnetic tape. How are computer personnel able to locate a particular file stored on one of the reels?

4. Draw, label and title a diagram to illustrate how information is organized on a strip of magnetic tape.

5. Magnetic tape units store information sequentially; whereas, magnetic disk units store information randomly. Explain the difference in storage methods.

6. Why would magnetic disks be preferred by banks and airline reservation offices as a storage medium, rather than magnetic tape?

7. The "read/write heads" in a disk unit are sometimes referred to as "floating heads." Explain why.

8. Computer rooms often have special air-conditioned environments and "no smoking" regulations. If these precautions were not taken, what problems might occur?

9. Describe how information is organized on a magnetic disk.

10. The bit patterns on a disk are more compact on the inner tracks than on the outer tracks, and yet they both contain the same amount of data. How is this possible?

11. Describe the appearance of a mass storage device.

12. In what way would the operation of a mass storage device resemble an "electronic librarian?"

13. How is data stored in a mass storage device?

14. Mass storage devices take ten to twenty seconds to find a particular file. Yet many data processing managers prefer it as an auxiliary storage unit. Give reasons for their preference.

15. Why is the storage of pictures a problem for most computer systems? What devices can be used to store pictures inexpensively?

16. What advantages do videodisks offer that magnetic media do not?

Applying Your Knowledge

These *advanced level questions* assume an understanding of the material presented in this chapter, and provide new situations which may require evaluation, analysis, or application of that knowledge.

1. Suggest an appropriate auxiliary storage device for each of the following situations. Include with each answer a reason for choosing that particular device.
   (a) A computer studies class in which students store programs, to be marked later by the teacher
   (b) A manufacturing firm which has a warehouse with 12 000 different products
   (c) A hobbyist who likes to develop her own computer programs
   (d) A large retail store which keeps records of credit card customers so that point-of-sale terminals can have access to them
   (e) The payroll department of a company with 8500 employees

2. Computer users are finding that while some things seem well-suited to storage on magnetic tape, other applications are better suited to magnetic disk.
   (a) What factors do you think would be involved in making the choice between tape or disk?
   (b) List three different types of files which would be appropriately stored on magnetic tape.
   (c) List three different types of files which would be appropriately stored on magnetic disks

3. One Canadian company has over a million individual records of credit card customers stored in auxiliary memory. How is the computer able to locate a specific record when a request is made?

4. Name some large organizations in North America which may require the extensive storage capacity of a mass storage device. For each organization, suggest the type of information which probably would be stored in the device.

5. Information from a computer is "digitalized" before being stored on magnetic tape, or magnetic disk. Explain what that process refers to.

6. Describe how a computer system, which has a videodisk unit, might be used in a school to teach lessons in some particular subject. Include in your answer, all the features videodisks are capable of performing.

7. Although a computer can locate information stored on a videodisk, it cannot give commands to store items there. Why not?

Topic for Discussion

1. Present computer hardware can be used to maintain a complete history on every person in the country. Massive information data banks could be created to contain records about an individual's school marks, criminal record, medical record, job history, tax payments, and even present location. This application of computers frightens a lot of people. They feel that privacy and the ability to make a "fresh start" would be almost impossible.

   Do you think that this type of data bank is harmful? Give reasons. Suggest ways to reduce some of the possible harmful effects of such a situation.

Computer Hardware Case Studies

Advanced level

The following case studies assume an understanding of the material presented in *all* the previous chapters on hardware (Chapters One, Five, Six, Seven, Eight). The content of these cases specifically requires a review of the five functions of a computer system— *input, output, processing, storage*, and *control*, as well as the devices which make up a computer hardware system.

Instructions

Draw a chart with the following three columns: (a) Computer Function; (b) Hardware Device, (c) What the Hardware Is Being Used For. The first column can be the narrowest in width. The second and third columns, in which the analysis takes place, should be of equal width.

In the first columns, entitled Computer Function, list five functions of any computer system. After reading the case, identify the hardware used for each function. Then, describe the specific use(s) for which the hardware device is being applied. Consider the following example of a partial case analysis.

Example:

Computer Function	Hardware Device	What the Hardware Is Being Used For
Input	Card Reader	The employee payroll data is entered into the computer
Output	Printer	The individual paycheques are printed one at a time.

etc.

Case One—The Neighbourhood Bank

At a neighbourhood bank, each teller operates a teller terminal which is connected by telephone to a large central computer at the bank's main branch downtown. When a customer wishes to make a deposit or withdrawal, the teller keys in that person's account number and waits for a reply on the small terminal printer.

The processor unit in the main branch makes a search of the data files stored on magnetic disks. The processor checks for inaccuracies by comparing the account number to those on file, and sending the account balance to the printer. If the customer wishes to make a withdrawal, the printed balance would indicate immediately the possibility of an overdrawn account. The teller would be obliged to end the transaction if this should occur.

If a transaction is possible, the clerk keys in the amount as a debit or a credit. The processor unit performs the calculations, then sends the balance to update the customer's passbook by means of the printer. At the same time, the main disk files are updated.

Case Two—The Credit Department

A manufacturer's credit department has organized a complete system to process all sales which are made on account. When an item is sold on credit, the order clerk records the transaction on a sales order form. The sheet is then given to a data entry clerk who keys the information into a key-to-disk console station.

At the end of the day, the night shift transfers the information to reels of magnetic tape. These tapes are then loaded onto a magnetic tape reader and read into the computer. The computer checks to see if the ordered items are in stock, then calculates the total cost of those items which are available, adds provincial sales tax, and prints out a multi-copy invoice on the impact printer. If the customer has an overdue account, a special notice is printed as well.

Case Three—The Retail Department Store

At a large department store, the cash registers are actually point-of-sale terminals connected to the processor unit located on the second floor. When a cash sale is made, the sales clerk keys in the amount of the sale as well as the sales tax. When a credit sale is made, the clerk also keys in the customer's account number.

Whenever a credit sale occurs, the processor unit makes a search of the files stored on magnetic disks to determine if the account is delinquent. If it is, a warning light appears on the POS terminal's display screen, and the sale clerk is obliged to end the transaction.

With each type of entry, cash or credit, various general ledger accounts are updated, and eventually the totals are stored on magnetic tape. On the night shift, tape runs are made to obtain several printouts, including a daily sales listing by department, accumulated monthly sales, and accumulated sales tax payable.

Case Four—Planning a Whole System
Challenge Case

A local manufacturing firm hires you as a computer systems analyst. It is your job to order computer hardware for its company. The manager wants the computer to be able to process the weekly payroll, invoices for customers, and production scheduling.

The combination of machines that you recommend is up to you, **but**—the selection of devices must be compatible with each other, and be able to handle the volume of data produced by the company.

Name each machine that you have selected, then explain why you chose each one for the job.

Group Research Project

Advanced level

This is a group research project to investigate computer hardware systems. The highlights involve teamwork planning, an interview, and the preparation of a final report. The idea is to concentrate on a particular area of the school to determine the possible roles that a computer could play there. Group strategy sessions and a well-planned interview provide the means of discovery.

Some suggested areas for investigation: business administration; school administration; library; physical plant maintenance; science department; geography department; technical department; math department; business department.

Instructions

1. Form a group of four to five people. Select a group leader, a person to record ideas, a typist, an illustrator, and a proofreader.

2. Select the area of the school that the group will investigate. To avoid duplication, ideally, each group should choose a different area.

3. In a group strategy session, prepare a list of questions for the person(s) that the group plans to interview. The list should contain about fifteen to twenty well-worded questions which will give the group the answers required by the final report. One representative should be sent to make an appointment with the interviewee, so that the group can meet with him/her later.

4. After the interview, regroup to analyze what was discovered. Plan the answers to put in the report.

5. The final report must be neatly prepared, and contain five sections: (a) possible roles for the computer (b) problems that the personnel see in using it (c) possible solutions to the problem (include such items as need for training; ease of access; theft prevention; damage prevention; and room conditions); (d) detailed list of required hardware, including a scale diagram illustrating the layout of the room and the placement of the equipment; (e) cost projections.

Note: If the area already has a computer system, concentrate the report on possible changes to improve the situation and ways in which to expand the role of the computer.

9

The Microcomputer Revolution

Objectives

A knowledge of the common storage peripherals used with microcomputers

A knowledge of the ways to expand a microcomputer system

An understanding of good programming techniques and the need for them

An understanding of the *if . . . then* statements in BASIC programming

An understanding of the *gosub* and *return* statements used in subroutines

Originally designed for the IBM 3741 device, the floppy disk or diskette has become a popular storage medium for microcomputers. Recently designed floppy disks can store over 1.5 million characters.

Courtesy of BASF Corporation.

Chapter Nine
The Microcomputer Revolution

Education and learning are undergoing dramatic changes. Pencil and paper are being swapped for keyboard and video screen. Living rooms are becoming class rooms.

One of the most exciting technological developments of the last decade is the microcomputer. For the first time in the history of computers, these information machines have become portable, affordable, understandable, and fun. Computers are now manufactured that are small enough to carry, and within the budget of the average homeowner. The BASIC computer language makes microcomputers easy to communicate with. Even five-year-old children have become computer enthusiasts and can make computers perform for them.

Microcomputers are changing the way people live. Living rooms are being transformed into entertainment, learning, and information centres. Video computer games such as chess or "space invaders" can provide hours of entertainment. On a more creative level, the computer can be used to draw pictures, compose music, write poetry or books. Learning programs can be used to improve one's general knowledge, or sharpen math and language skills. The computer may recall stored recipes, menus, mailing addresses, birthdates, and daily reminders. Its mathematical capability can be used to update budgets, keep track of expenses, and balance the chequebook. The computer is the first intelligent household appliance.

The Personal Computer

A microcomputer system is a desk-top computer consisting of a video screen for displaying answers, a typewriter keyboard for keying instructions, and an extra memory device, such as a cassette deck, for storing information. It is referred to as a "personal computer" because it can communicate only with one person at a time.

There is a bewildering array of products being marketed as personal computers. Microcomputers can be purchased unassembled in a kit for hobbyists who have a knowledge of electronics and prefer to design their own computer. The kit contains computer memory chips (RAMS and ROMS) and microprocessor chip. These are soldered to a circuit board and arranged inside a unit capable of housing a keyboard and a video screen. Lear Seigler Inc. and Heath/Zenith Co. manufacture complete hobby kits. Individual parts are also available from computer hobby stores.

Home computer kits are available for those computer enthusiasts who also enjoy working with electronics. A typical kit contains an outer shell, a video screen, a keyboard, circuit boards, computer chips, electrical circuits, and an assembly manual.

Courtesy of Lear Seigler, Inc.

Many companies sell computers already assembled. Some personal computers are designed for mass consumer appeal. This type of microcomputer emphasizes the use of factory-programmed **ROM cartridges** rather than do-your-own programming. These cartridges contain a small circuit board. On the circuit board are computer memory chips with permanently stored application programs. Typically, the computer's user memory is small, and the programming functions are limited. Often, the home television set can be used as a video screen. The manufacturer's software library usually contains a variety of games and application programs, as well as colour graphic and music capabilities.

This type of computer is well-suited for people who prefer to buy preprogrammed cartridges rather than prepare their own application programs. The major buyers are home computer enthusiasts. Sample manufacturers include Atari, APF, Mattel (Intellivision), Radio Shack, and Texas Instruments.

"The Imagination Machine" manufactured by APF is designed to work with your television as a monitor. This microcomputer has a built-in cassette deck, a sound generator, and remote control keyboard-joysticks to manipulate video games on the screen. Optional peripherals include a printer, a telephone modem, and a dual disk drive.

Other computer manufacturers market their microcomputer as a general-purpose machine. This means that it can be used for home entertainment, as a teaching aid, or as a piece of business equipment. Its final use will depend upon the needs of the person who buys it. Although considerably reduced in size, **general-purpose microcomputers** often imitate the functions and capabilities of larger computers. The processor unit, for example, may contain large amounts of user area and a fast microprocessor (MPU). Cassette decks, disk drives, printers, and other peripherals are also designed for the system. Like larger computers, almost all of the application programs must be written by the user or purchased as a separate item. Software is available through computer clubs, computer magazines, and **software vendors** (companies that sell computer programs).

The general-purpose microcomputer has, at present, "captured" the largest share of microcomputer sales. Typical buyers are primary and secondary schools, small businesses, and home hobbyists. Some general purpose microcomputer manufacturers include Commodore, Radio Shack, Apple, IBM, North Star, and Ohio Scientific.

The Radio Shack Model III is a general-purpose microcomputer. It has two built-in floppy disk drives. This type of microcomputer is adaptable to a wide variety of applications.

Courtesy of Radio Shack, A Division of Tandy Corp.

Cassette Decks

Cassette decks provide an inexpensive auxiliary storage device for microcomputers. The deck can be plugged into the back of a microcomputer, using a multi-channel connector. The connector allows a coded number, letter, or character to be transferred as a complete unit, instead of one bit (impulse) at a time. This connector is used with most peripherals.

Cassette decks use special computer cassettes which contain tiny reels of magnetic tape. It is recommended that you avoid using regular cassettes because they tend to record poorly.

Programs are stored sequentially (one after the other) on the tape. Sequential storage can be a disadvantage in situations where speed is important. The computer must search through each program until the correct one is found. It is not uncommon for a cassette deck to take several minutes to locate and load a single program into the computer.

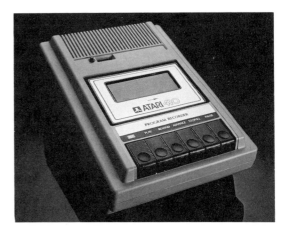

This device is a cassette deck which is suitable for use with a microcomputer. Some form of auxiliary storage is necessary to preserve programs after the computer has been shut off.

Courtesy of Atari.

When recording a program, the cassette deck places a one- or two-second **leader tone** on the tape. This ensures that the magnets are functioning properly before reaching the area where the program is to be recorded. Next, an optional section called a **header**, which contains the title of the program, can be put in front of the program. The cassette deck uses these headers to search for a requested program when more than one is stored on the tape.

After the program is recorded, it is wise to ask the computer to verify the recording. This command *(verify)* requires the computer to see if the program in main memory matches the one stored on the tape. To do this, most manufacturers include an error-checking method in the circuits. The computer adds all the impulses (bits) that make up the program in main memory. This total is called a **checksum**. The checksum is then placed on the tape at the end of the program. When the program is read back into main memory, the computer takes all the incoming impulses and adds them up again. It then compares the new sum with the one recorded on the tape. If the totals agree, then there were no transfer errors. If they disagree, an error message appears on the screen, and the recording process must begin again.

Tape Loop Drives

Magnetic tape can also be purchased as a continuous tape loop. The cassette that it is stored in, called a **wafer**, is half the thickness of a regular tape cassette. The advantages of a tape loop drive is that it has a much faster reading speed, and potentially more storage capacity, than a cassette deck. As with cassettes, though, the time-consuming sequential search method is used to locate programs.

"There seems to be a mix-up in the tapes. I keep getting Guy Lombardo."

Figure 9.1
Cassette Tape

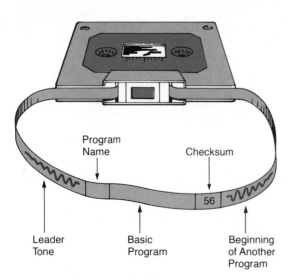

Program Name

Checksum

56

Leader Tone

Basic Program

Beginning of Another Program

Floppy Disk Drives

Another auxiliary storage device used with microcomputers is a floppy disk unit. The **diskettes** used with this device are nicknamed "floppy disks" because they are made of flexible plastic. Diskettes remain sealed in a square envelope even during recording. The envelope protects the sensitive magnetic coating from dust, scratches, and fingerprints. A small opening allows the recording magnet to reach the disk.

Disk drives are as expensive as the entire microcomputer system. One advantage of this storage device is that it stores or retrieves programs in about two seconds.

When the disk unit receives a request for a certain program, it checks the **index** which it keeps on the first (outside) track of the disk. After determining where the program is located, it then goes directly to that area without searching through any other programs. This direct method of finding programs is called **random access**.

Programs are stored on a certain track and sector on a floppy disk. **Tracks** refer to the invisible, concentric (having a common centre) circles in which information is recorded. The disk is also divided into pie-shaped sectors to further narrow down the location of any piece of information. Each sector has a small index hole near the centre of the disk. A light beam detects the holes as they sweep by, keeping the disk unit informed about which sector is passing the read/write head.

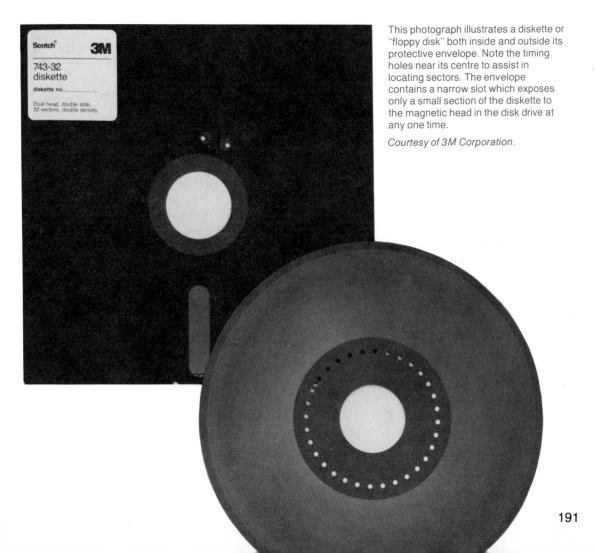

This photograph illustrates a diskette or "floppy disk" both inside and outside its protective envelope. Note the timing holes near its centre to assist in locating sectors. The envelope contains a narrow slot which exposes only a small section of the diskette to the magnetic head in the disk drive at any one time.

Courtesy of 3M Corporation.

191

Another advantage of using disk units is that they can store up to 30 times the number of programs as an average cassette.

Diskettes, like cassettes, wear out and have to be thrown away. Because the read/write magnet rests on the plastic disk while reading and recording, the resulting friction, along with fingerprints and scratches, eventually destroys recorded programs. Larger "metal base" disks avoid this problem by having the read/write head float on a cushion of air above the disk. Proper handling of diskettes, though, will expand their life span. It is wise to keep a spare copy of important programs in a safe place in case the original one is destroyed.

Expanding a Computer's Capabilities

General-purpose microcomputers are versatile. They can be modified to improve their performance and capabilities. Consider some of the things students have done with microcomputers. The keyboard can be used like a piano to create music; the screen can be used to draw business graphs or artistic pictures; robots can scoot around the floor, controlled by the keyboard; a person's voice can be recognized by the computer, and his or her words printed on the display screen; the computer can imitate a human voice.

There are several ways to expand a microcomputer's capabilities. One way is to create or purchase a software program which can be read into the computer whenever it is needed. These special programs, such as "word processing" or "computer graphics," allow the user to obtain greater use from the screen and the keyboard.

A second method is to purchase additional hardware for the inside of the processor unit. This addition may be as small as one computer chip, or as large as a complete printed circuit board. The University of Waterloo sells single ROM chips to allow microcomputer

owners to use structured programming features in either BASIC, FORTRAN, or COBOL. Some electronic companies sell complete circuit boards which can be plugged into most processor units. These boards may add to the computer's memory, or provide permanent programs which specialize in graphics, voice recognition, generating sounds, or provide displays for touch-sensitive screens.

A good computer is upward compatible. This means that the user can add peripherals or circuits to increase the computer's performance as the need arises. The processor unit, for example, should leave room for extra memory, a disk controller, or a joystick circuit board.

Courtesy of Southwest Technical Products Corporation.

A third way to expand a microcomputer's capabilities is to build or purchase hardware devices to add to the computer system. They might include joysticks which are used to control screen graphics, a speaker for generating sounds, touch-sensitive grids for the front of display screens, robot devices, or specialized printing devices called plotters for fancy drawings.

Software vendors, computer hobby shops, and electronic companies offer a wide range of accessories for microcomputers. The back pages of computer magazines usually contain hundreds of advertisements to meet this particular need.

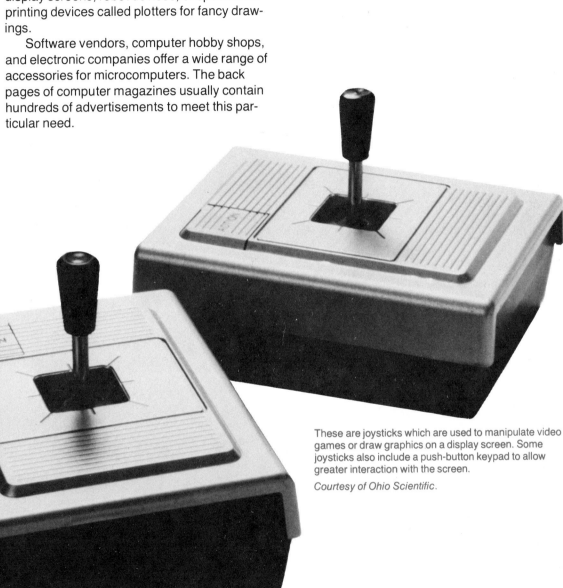

These are joysticks which are used to manipulate video games or draw graphics on a display screen. Some joysticks also include a push-button keypad to allow greater interaction with the screen.

Courtesy of Ohio Scientific.

Good Programming Techniques

"Eureka!" exclaimed a student at the computer keyboard. "It finally works!"

A program that runs properly, after many tries, is a rewarding experience. A student programmer can, unfortunately, encounter many hours of frustration, even with a relatively short program. This usually happens because the programmer leaves out several important steps in the planning and coding of the computer program. Programming knowledge, patience, and attention to detail are the qualities which make an effective, above-average programmer.

Characteristics of a Good Program

What makes one program better than another? A good program is **readable**. This means that anyone can look at the program listing and be able to read what you wrote. When instructions or lines of the program are crowded together, they can be just as unreadable as crowded handwriting.

Another characteristic of a good program is that it is **easy to understand**. Such programs contain a proper title and program identification. Often, the purpose of the program is defined at the beginning. Symbols or letters can be easily associated with particular ideas. For example, instead of just any letter, the letter "H" is best used to represent "HOURS."

Finally, good programs can be **easily modified**. This means that errors can be located and corrected with little effort. Arranging code in blocks makes debugging (correcting of errors) less frustrating and less time-consuming.

Things To Remember When Programming

Microcomputers are **interactive**. This means that you can enter instructions one line at a time and get immediate responses from the computer, making the learning of programming enjoyable. If you make a mistake, the computer tells you right away, and you can correct the error before going on to your next instruction.

There is a tendency for microcomputer users to develop poor programming habits because the system is so easy to use. It is wise for students to review these five rules before programming a microcomputer.

Planning a Program

Student programmers often make the mistake of creating a program at the keyboard without first planning it on paper. Although this direct approach appears faster in the beginning, it eventually leads to a tangled mess of code that may take several hours to debug. Much of a programmer's frustration is due to the lack of planning.

For every problem, however simple it appears, use the planning sheet approach — define the problem; list the values; plan the solution; then code the solution into a computer language.

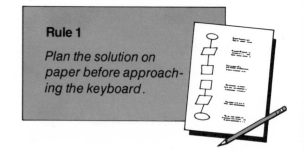

Rule 1

Plan the solution on paper before approaching the keyboard.

Line Numbers

When assigning line numbers to your BASIC statements, use numbers of equal length. This helps to avoid unintended indentations in your program.

Weak Program

```
5    REM BLACKJACK
10   REM R. PHILLIPS PD. 5
200  READ A,B,C
```

Strong Program

```
100  REM BLACKJACK
110  REM R. PHILLIPS PD. 5
120  READ A,B,C
```

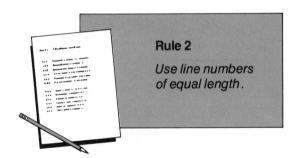

Rule 2

Use line numbers of equal length.

Choice of Variable Names

The letter or word that you choose to represent an idea in a program is called a **variable name**. If you choose just any name, or any letter of the alphabet to identify a variable, the program will become very confusing. Use the first letter of whatever word or idea that you wish to represent. In an interest problem, for example, use the letter "P" for principal, "R" for rate of interest, and "I" for the interest in dollars (which is the answer in that type of problem).

This programming technique acts as a memory aid. The letter reminds you of what it is supposed to represent. Letter such as X, Y, Z are poor choices unless you are representing xylophone, yearbooks, and zebras.

Rule 3

Make variable names easy to remember.

Block of Code

A program becomes much more readable if similar instructions are grouped together and separated from the rest of the program. A blank line (or two) at the end of each block helps to visually separate the different sections of the program. Consider these two examples.

Weak Program

```
10  REM  INTEREST  PROBLEM
15  REM  APPLE  WORMWOOD  PD.  2
20  READ  P,  R
25  I  =  (P  *  R)
30  B  =  (I  +  P)
35  PRINT  TAB  (10)  "INTEREST",  TAB  (25)  "BALANCE"
40  PRINT  TAB  (12)  I,  TAB  (25)  B
45  DATA  8000,  .18
50  END
```

In the next example, the program is divided into easily recognized blocks. Some micro-computers require a *remark* command with the blank line.

Strong Program

```
10  REM  ***********************
15  REM      INTEREST  PROBLEM
20  REM  ***********************
25  REM  APPLE  WORMWOOD  PD.2
30  REM
35  READ  P,R
40  REM
45  I  =  (P  *  R)
50  B  =  (I  +  P)
55  REM
60  PRINT  TAB  (10)  "INTEREST"  TAB  (25)  "BALANCE"
65  PRINT  TAB  (12)  I,  TAB  (25)  B
70  REM
75  DATA  8000,  .18
80  END
```

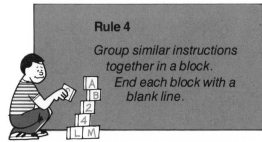

Rule 4

Group similar instructions together in a block.
End each block with a blank line.

Document While Coding

Often, a program written several months ago will need to be modified to fit a new situation. Programs which have built-in explanations are the easiest to understand and modify. **Programmer comments**, the messages that programmers can insert into a program for their own understanding, are an excellent way to build in explanations.

Every program, for example, should have a title which helps you to understand what the program does. Another message should include the programmer identification. This would include such things as your name, (class period), and date or number of this latest version of your program. With longer programs, it is wise to use several lines to describe the purpose, or any special feature of that particular program. Explanations or messages inserted into a program which clarify the purpose for other programmers are referred to as **documentation**.

Rule 5
Build documentation
into your program

More on Basic Programming

BASIC is a powerful computer language. Once you have mastered the simple commands such as *read*, *print*, *tab*, *stop*, *end*, *data*, and *for*...*next* loops, you may want to learn more powerful programming instructions. If your programs have loops and decisions in them, they are more powerful than programs without them. Loops and decisions are capable of getting the computer to do a great deal of processing with very few instructions.

Loops refer to sections of a program which are repeated for a specified number of times. The *for*...*next* loop provides an easy way of designing loops in programs. But it is not the only way.

Decisions refer to instructions which require the computer to compare two items, and do something as a result of the comparison.

Together, loops and decisions provide a way of evaluating and controlling information as it is processed by the computer. Decisions give computers their apparent ability to "think."

Programming Decisions

In programming, we are often confronted with situations which require us to make a decision of some sort. Decisions in BASIC are written with an *If*...*then* statement. To get a quick idea of what this statement is like, let us consider this simple analogy.

If it is raining *then* wear a coat.

Here we have set up a decision which checks for a certain condition (is it raining?). If the condition is true, an action will be taken (wear a raincoat). If the condition is not true, the action would not be taken.

In BASIC programming, decisions are written in the same way. Consider the following *if . . .then* statement.

```
IF N = 5 THEN PRINT "END OF REPORT"
```

Here the computer is instructed to check a counter (an area set aside for adding or counting). If the counter has the number five in it, then the computer is instructed to print the phrase "END OF REPORT". If the value is not equal to five, then the action is not taken.

There are several mathematical symbols (relational operators) which can be used in the *if . . .then* statement.

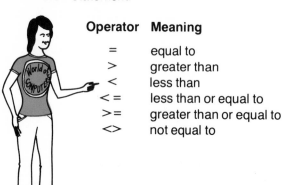

Operator	Meaning
=	equal to
>	greater than
<	less than
<=	less than or equal to
>=	greater than or equal to
<>	not equal to

Several types of actions can be taken as a result of a decision. Some examples include:

```
60    IF N = 5 THEN GOTO 200
70    IF N > 5 THEN PRINT "INVALID
80    IF N < 5 THEN C = C + 1
```

Consider how the *if . . .then* statement might be used in this sample problem.

Honour Role Problem

The school administration wants a program which would select only the names and marks of students who achieved 80% or better during the year. The principal plans to display the names on a list, under the title *Honour Role*, near the front office.

The *if . . .then* statement for this problem would appear as follows.

```
35    READ N$, M
40    IF M > 79 THEN PRINT N$, M
45    GOTO 35
```

This instructs the computer to return to read the next name and mark.

Only students with averages greater than 79% are printed.

The computer is given two choices. If the student's mark is greater than 79%, the student's name and mark are to be printed. If the mark is not greater than 79%, nothing is printed.

In both cases, regardless of what the mark was, the computer is to return to read the next data record.

```
45    GOTO 35
```

The *goto* instruction is sometimes called an **unconditional branch** because it demands that the computer goes directly to another statement without any decision or conditions being met.

In this case, the *goto* instruction puts the computer into a loop. The loop reads one data record, makes a decision, then returns to read the next data record. Unless a second decision is inserted in the sequence, an **infinite** or **endless loop** is created. The computer will continue looping until the machine is shut off. The next decision helps to prevent the infinite loop.

```
40    IF N$ = "LAST" THEN END
```

This decision instructs the computer to watch for the name "Last" in the list of data records. If that name is found, the computer is instructed to stop. (Some computers require a line number instead of the word *end*. The line number would be the location of the *end* command.)

This name *last* is a dummy variable used as an end-of-file check. It must actually appear at the end of the list of students' names.

Note how the loop would appear with the end-of-file decision included in the sequence.

```
Loop  ⎧  35    READ N$, M
      ⎪  40    IF N$ = "LAST" THEN END
      ⎨  45    IF M > 79 THEN PRINT N$, M
      ⎩  50    GOTO 35
```

This instructs the computer to end when the dummy variable is found.

Some computers require a *goto* command with a line number indicating where the *end* is located.

The loop now has two decisions. The first *if...then* statement checks for the last data record to prevent an infinite loop. The second *if...then* statement selects only certain names for printing.

Consider the entire plan for the *Honour Role* problem with the two decisions in it.

Plan for Honour Role Problem

Problem Definition:

Print a list of names and marks of **only** those students who achieved over 79%.

Dummy Variable: "LAST", 00

Typical Data Record

N$ = Student's name
M = Student's average mark for the year

Figure 9.2
Flowchart for Honour Role

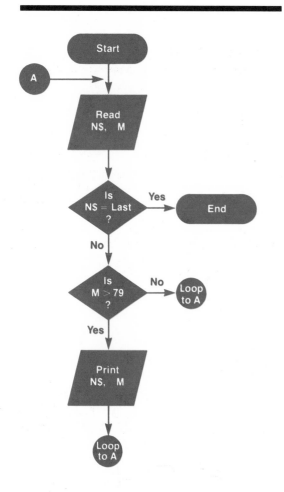

Basic Coding for Honour Role Problem

```
10   REM   **********************
15   REM      HONOUR ROLE
20   REM   **********************
25   REM BILL WOODLAND VER. # 3
30   REM
35   READ N$, M
40   IF N$ = "LAST" THEN END
45   IF M > 79 THEN PRINT N$, M
50   GOTO 35
55   REM
60   DATA "FRAN SIMPSON", 82
65   DATA "TONY WOODS", 90
70   DATA "ROY FISHER", 76
75   DATA "JUNE THOMPSON", 61
90   DATA "LAST", 00
95   END
```

Notice that the dummy variable, which the programmer invents, must always have the same type and number of data as the rest of the list. In the case of the *Honour Role* problem, both a name and a number were needed.

Practice Assignment

Riverview High School just purchased a micro-computer for the main office. One of the computer's functions is to print a list of office supplies which need reordering. The office reorders any item on the list which has fallen below 50 units. The supplies are always restocked to their original level.

Plan and code a program which would read in the list of inventory items, one at a time; then select and print the names and reorder amount for only those which have fallen below 50. The list should appear as shown.

```
RIVERVIEW HIGH SCHOOL
OFFICE SUPPLIES REORDER LIST
ITEM              AMOUNT TO REORDER
  —                       —

  —                       —
(etc.)
```

Data for Problem

Item	Original Amount	Present Amount
Foolscap	400	23
Business envelopes	1000	48
Typing paper	1000	36
Correcting fluid	75	62
HB Pencils	350	15

Subroutines

A subroutine is a small program which performs some particular job. It is usually separated from the main program and called into action whenever needed.

A Report Card program used by school boards, for example, may use subroutines. While the main program would concentrate on listing subject names and marks, separate programs (subroutines) connected to the main program would add other features. These features may include number of days absent, term average, or special comments such as "Recommended for Next Grade Level."

Figure 9.3
The Report Card

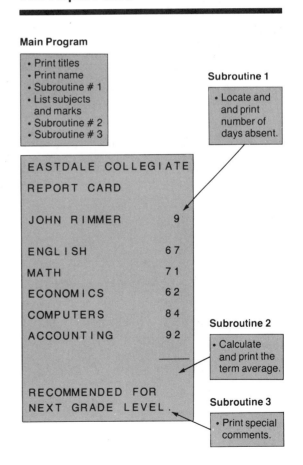

Main Program
- Print titles
- Print name
- Subroutine # 1
- List subjects and marks
- Subroutine # 2
- Subroutine # 3

Subroutine 1
- Locate and and print number of days absent.

```
EASTDALE COLLEGIATE
REPORT CARD

JOHN RIMMER          9

ENGLISH             67
MATH                71
ECONOMICS           62
COMPUTERS           84
ACCOUNTING          92

          _____

RECOMMENDED FOR
NEXT GRADE LEVEL.
```

Subroutine 2
- Calculate and print the term average.

Subroutine 3
- Print special comments.

Subroutines provide several advantages. They allow a program to be designed in sections. This means that a team of programmers could work on different parts of a long program at the same time.

Subroutines can also be used to reduce repetition in a program. Instead of having indentical blocks of statements repeated in different parts of the program, a reference to one subroutine can be substituted.

Most BASIC languages allow several **library functions**. These are built-in subroutines provided by the manufacturer for programmers to use while programming. Some examples are *randomize* (which creates a series of random numbers), and *renumber* (which renumbers your statement line numbers if they are out of sequence).

Designing a Subroutine

Subroutines are composed of BASIC statements with line numbers, just like any other statement in the program. A subroutine begins when a special statement called *gosub* is inserted in a program.

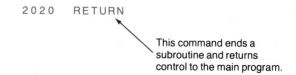

    100   GOSUB 2000

Gosub requires the program to branch to a subroutine.

The statement above requires the computer to stop whatever it is doing, and branch to a subroutine located (in this case) on line 2000. All of the subroutine statements are then executed until another special command known as *return* is encountered. This causes the program to branch back to the original *gosub* statement, and carry on with the remainder of the program.

    2020   RETURN

This command ends a subroutine and returns control to the main program.

Subroutines are normally grouped at the bottom of a long program. Although the last statement in any subroutine is *return*, the last statement in the entire program must be *end*.

Consider the following sample problem called *The Computer Quiz* which contains three subroutines. Each subroutine provides an alternative phrase to be printed in response to a student's score on a quiz.

Sample Problem — The Computer Quiz

Jim McKnight, a computer studies teacher, uses a microcomputer to test his students' knowledge of lessons given in class. Each quiz consists of ten multiple choice questions which the student responds to, using the keyboard.

Jim wants to modify the quiz to print various phrases once the student's score is calculated. If the student obtains a perfect score of ten, this phrase is to be printed:

CONGRATULATIONS! YOU HAVE OBTAINED A PERFECT SCORE

If the student achieves a score of eight or nine, this phrase is to be printed:

GOOD EFFORT! YOU ARE READY TO GO ON TO THE NEXT LESSON

If the student achieves seven or less correct answers, the computer will be instructed to print ...

YOU HAVE NOT MASTERED THE IDEAS IN THIS SECTION. REVIEW YOUR NOTES, AND TRY AGAIN LATER

A section must be designed for Jim's program which refers the computer to one of three subroutines, each of which contains a particular phrase to be printed. The computer will make its choice based on the student's score on the quiz.

Study the following program to see how Jim's problem can be handled with the use of subroutines. There would be several lines above this section in the program which would keep track of the student's score with the variable name S.

```
100   IF  S  =  10  THEN  GOSUB  215
110   REM
120   IF  S  >  7  AND  S  <  10  THEN  GOSUB  235
125   REM
130   IF  S  <  8  THEN  GOSUB  250
135   GOTO  280
200   REM  ************************
205   REM  PHRASES  TO  BE  PRINTED
210   REM  ************************
215   PRINT  "CONGRATULATIONS!  YOU  HAVE  OBTAINED"
220   PRINT  "A  PERFECT  SCORE."
230   RETURN
235   PRINT  "GOOD  EFFORT!  YOU  ARE  READY  TO  GO  ON"
240   PRINT  "TO  THE  NEXT  LESSON."
245   RETURN
250   PRINT  "YOU  HAVE  NOT  MASTERED  THE  IDEAS  IN  THIS"
255   PRINT  "SECTION.  REVIEW  YOUR  NOTES,  AND  TRY  AGAIN"
260   PRINT  "LATER"
265   RETURN
280   END
```

Summary

There is a bewildering array of products being marketed as personal computers. Hobbyists who have a knowledge of electronics can purchase a microcomputer unassembled in a kit. At the other extreme, prepackaged ROM cartridges can be purchased by home computer enthusiasts who prefer to be an end-user rather than a computer programmer.

The most popular microcomputers are the general-purpose, desk-top models which require the user to provide the application software. General-purpose microcomputers are manufactured by Commodore, Apple, IBM, Radio Shack, Ohio Scientific, Digital, Bell and Howell, and Texas Instruments. The deluxe models, designed for small businesses, can imitate the functions and capabilities of larger computer systems.

Typical storage devices for microcomputers include slow-loading cassette decks and tape loop drives, and the faster, but more expensive, floppy disk drives.

Microcomputer systems can be expanded in three ways. Software programs can be purchased which enhance the existing hardware. Graphics software, for example, allows the user to obtain greater use from the keyboard and the screen. A second method is to purchase additional firmware (programs stored permanently in memory chips) which can be added to the computer circuitry. A third way is to purchase hardware devices to attach to the computer system. They may include such items as a plotter, a voice response unit, a graphics tablet, a touch-sensitive screen, or a robot device to scoot along the floor.

Serious microcomputer users should be aware that a working program is not necessarily a well-designed program. Good programs are readable, understandable, and easy to modify. Consistent application of the five coding rules should achieve these three goals.

Once you have mastered the simple BASIC commands, you will welcome the programming power of the *if . . .then* and the *gosub* statements. The *if . . .then* statement, in particular, gives a computer its apparent "thinking" ability.

Review Questions

These are *general level questions* which may require factual recall, reading comprehension, and some application of the knowledge from this chapter.

1. Describe a microcomputer system.

2. What type of person would prefer to purchase a microcomputer unassembled in a kit?

3. What is a ROM cartridge? Who uses them?

4. Describe a general-purpose microcomputer.

5. Cassette decks are popular because they are the least expensive auxiliary storage device. Why would some people consider them a disadvantage? Explain.

6. What is a *checksum*? What is it for?

7. How does a tape loop drive differ from a cassette deck?

8. Describe a diskette.

9. Explain one advantage and one disadvantage of a floppy disk drive.

10. Often, people add things to a microcomputer after they have purchased it. Briefly explain three different ways to expand a microcomputer system.

11. List and explain three characteristics of a good program.

12. What does the word *interactive* refer to?

13. List five programming rules which help to produce well-designed programs.

14. Explain what coding *documentation* refers to.

15. More powerful programs usually contain *loops* and *decisions*. Explain the meaning of these terms.

16. What are infinite loops? How are they prevented in a program?

17. Explain how a program can check for the last data record in a list of items.

18. Write an *if . . . then* statement which prints the message *"end of report"* when the value of 100 is reached.

19. What is a *subroutine*? List two special commands needed to start and end a subroutine.

20. When would a programmer use subroutines in a program?

Applying Your Knowledge

These questions assume an understanding of the material presented in the chapter, and provide new situations which may require evaluation, analysis, or application of that knowledge. Section One contains *general level questions* on specific statements or programming techniques. Section Two contains *advanced level questions* which require the planning and coding of complete problems.

Section One

1. Identify the sections of this program which indicate poor programming technique. Suggest ways to make the program readable, easier to understand and to modify.

```
0    REM SUE LITTLETON PD. 6
2    READ P, R
4    I = (P * R)
6    P = (P + I)
8    PRINT "THE INTEREST IS " ;
10   PRINT "THE BALANCE IS " ;
12   DATA 650, 0.14
14   END
```

2. Rewrite the following program to make it readable, easier to understand, and easier to modify.

```
30   REM L. STONE PD. 3
40   READ H, R, D
50   G = (H * R)
60   N = (G - D)
70   PRINT "GROSS PAY IS " ; G
80   PRINT "NET PAY IS " ; N
90   DATA 40, 5.65, 37.80
100  END
```

3. Rewrite the following program to make it readable, easier to understand, and easier to modify.

```
5    LET  X  =  5
10   PRINT  "VALUE  OF  X" ,  " VALUE  OF  Y"
15   IF  (X  >  100)  THEN  35
20   Y  =  (695)  /  (X  *  1.3)
25   PRINT  X ,  Y
30   GOTO  15
35   END
```

4. Write an *if...then* statement which would *goto* a *stop* command located at line 100, if the value ten is reached.

5. Write an *if...then* statement which calculates the equation $Z = (A * B)$ if the value of 25 is reached.

6. Suppose that part of a program appears as shown below in which N$ represents *name* and M represents *mark*. Rewrite the program to include an *if...then* statement which would prevent an infinite loop. (Make up your own dummy variable to represent the last item in the data records.)

```
20   READ  N$ ,  M
30   GOTO  20
40   STOP
```

7. This incomplete report card program needs two decision statements. Rewrite the program to include two *if...then* statements. The first is to prevent an infinite loop. The second is to select only students with marks (M) of 60% or better for printing.

```
20   READ  N$ ,  M
40   PRINT  N$ ,  M
60   GOTO  20
80   STOP
```

8. Suppose that part of a program, which reads data records on the warehouse inventory, appears as shown in which N$ = *name of a product*, Q = *original quantity*, and P = *present quantity*.

   Rewrite the program to include two *if...then* statements. The first is to prevent an infinite loop; the second is to select only products with present quantities less than 75 units, for reordering.

   ```
   20    READ N$, Q, P
   40    A = (Q - P)
   60    PRINT N$, A
   80    GOTO 20
   90    STOP
   ```

9. Write a subroutine which begins at line 250, prints the phrase *continued on next page*, then returns to the main program.

10. Write a subroutine which begins at line 300, takes a percentage answer (represented by the letter P), and converts it to its decimal equivalent. For example, 18% would be converted to 0.18. Once the number has been converted, control is returned to the main program.

11. Write a subroutine which begins at line 600, calculates the provincial sales tax for the subtotal on an invoice, then prints the phrase and answer *Prov. Sales Tax $* — before returning to the main program.

12. (a) Write a subroutine which starts at line 400, takes an answer expressed in dollars and cents, and rounds it to the nearest dollar.
    Hint: A library subroutine can be used to help write this subroutine INT, which stands for *integer*, will truncate any numbers to the right of a decimal to make a whole number. The following example illustrates how an answer such as $134.56 can be rounded to $135. The letter P represents the number.

    ```
    R = INT (P + 0.5)
    ```

    (b) Explain why the value 0.5 must be added to the number before the number is truncated.

Section Two—Problem for Programming

Advanced level

Plan and code the solutions to the following problems. For the planning stage, define the problem, list the values, plan the solution with a diagram, and code into BASIC. Remember to include the coding techniques which help to make the programs readable, easy to understand, and easy to modify.

1. Positive Output

Plan a solution which would read one set of data, three values at time, calculate an answer using the equation shown below, and print only those answers which have a positive (rather than negative) value.

Equation

$$Z = (A + B) / C$$

```
*** POSITIVE ANSWERS ***
            —
            —
            —
```

Data Values

```
-10, -25, 3
 50, -65, 2
 65,  75, 3
 22, -35, 3
 89,  92, 2
-47,  71, 5
```

2. Customer Listing

A manufacturing company keeps a record of every customer's mailing address. Plan a program which would read in each data record shown below (one at a time), and select only those customers who are in Alberta. The answer should appear as shown.

```
***** CUSTOMER LISTING ****
           FOR ALBERTA
CUSTOMER              ADDRESS
   — —                  — —
   — —                  — —
```

Data Records

Edmonton Refinery Ltd.
143 Windsor Road,
Edmonton, Alberta
T2T 2R8

Moose Jaw Suppliers
2325 First Avenue W.,
Moose Jaw, Saskatchewan,
S5E 3L2

Westen Co. Ltd.
540 Richmond Street,
London, Ontario
N6A 3E7

Calgary Stockyards Ltd.
45 Kendall Street,
Calgary, Alberta
T2V 2L6

Kattering Co. Ltd.
178 Montrose Avenue
Camrose, Alberta
T4V 2L6

Hint: Read in the customers in four different sections—one section for the name, one for the street and city, one for the province, and one for the postal code. READ N$, S$, P$, C$.

3. The Oil Company

One oil company has a price schedule that encourages customers to purchase more oil:

The first 200 L cost $1.10/L

The next 200 L cost $1.05/L

Any additional amount costs $1.02/L

Plan a program which would read in each of the three customers who live in the same city, listed below, calculate the amount they owe, then print a list as shown.

```
********************* CUSTOMER BILLING *********************
```

| | | AMOUNT | |
CUSTOMER	STREET ADDRESS	USED (LITRES)	COST
REGINALD WILLIAMS	78 SECOND AVE.	720	$ —
RONALDO PERKINS	233 TWIDDLE ST.	355	$ —
JENNIFER LAKIN	790 BARLAKE AVE.	135	$ —

```
***************************************************************
```

4. Satellite Re-Entry

Two astronauts are in an orbitting satellite 820 km from earth. The satellite is descending towards earth at a rate of 120 km/h. In order to maintain that rate of descent, the retro-rockets must fire every 30 min. Each burst of the retro-rockets uses 200 L of fuel. The astronauts consume a total of 12 m³ of oxygen each hour.

If the reserve fuel is 2000 L, and the oxygen reserve is 95 m³, print a table which would appear as shown. Continue until a zero elevation is reached.

```
** RE-ENTRY SPECIFICATIONS **


        DISTANCE
        TO EARTH   FUEL    OXYGEN
TIME

 0        820      2000      95

30        —         —        —

60        —         —        —
```

5. Honour List

The principal of Glendale High School wants a list of only those students in the school who obtained an average of 80% or better during the year. During the graduation ceremonies in the fall, the principal will present each of these students with a special award.

Plan a solution which would print a list as shown. Select ten student names from your class to use as data and invent averages for each person, ranging from 50% to 95%.

```
*** HONOUR LIST 198- ***


STUDENT         AVERAGE
   —               —

   —               —
```

6. Inventory Reorder List

Firestone Co. keeps a record of every product in inventory. Each record contains the *product name*, *original quantity*, and *quantity on hand*. Plan a program which would read in one data record at a time, then print the reorder list as shown. The reorder amount must return the inventory to its original level.

```
FIRESTONE REORDER LIST

BIRLINGTON STREET PLANT


PRODUCT        AMOUNT TO REORDER

   —                    —

   —                    —
(etc.)                  —
```

Data Records

Liquid cleaner, 560, 472
Abrasives, 1000, 285
Vulcanizing Kits, 425, 106
Hand Tools, 85, 72
Labels, 312, 61

7. Baseball Draftees

For every baseball player eligible to be drafted, a record has been prepared showing his *name*, *age*, *position*, and *batting average*. Plan and code a program which would read in one data record at a time, and select and print the statistics of only those players who are under 25 years old, and have a batting average of 280 or better.

```
**  BLUE  JAY  DRAFT  CHOICES  **

NAME    AGE   POSITION   AVERAGE

 —       —        —          —

 —       —        —          —

*****************************
```

Data Records

Tom Smyth	22	Third Base	290
Morey Simpson	21	First Base	120
Watch T. Ball	25	Short Stop	305
Wally Badman	23	Catcher	208
Legs Wasserman	24	L. Field	321
Mo Zachowski	26	L. Field	256

8. Criminal Record

The Stoney Creek Police Station wants a list of those criminals in the computer files who have been convicted of theft. The file, being read in one record at a time, contains the *name*, *offence*, and *conviction date* of each criminal. The offences are listed as a letter code T (theft), A (arson), and H (homicide). The list should contain the name, offence (written out) and conviction date of those who were arrested for theft, and appear as shown.

```
******CRIMINAL  LISTING******
NAME    OFFENCE  CONVICTION  DATE

 —        —                  —

 —        —                  —

****************************
```

Data File

Jim Slicer	T	February 1 1952
Sambo Matchless	A	June 5 1963
Wally Lightfinger	T	March 23 1967
Slippery Sally	T	November 15 1977
Wilma Grinch	A	April 11 1975
Eddy Striker	H	August 14 1981

Topics for Discussion

1. Desk-top microcomputers are becoming increasingly popular as home appliances. Do you think that microcomputers will improve the quality of life? Give reasons for your answer.

2. The quotation at the beginning of this chapter refers to the use of micro-computers in education. What effects do you think microcomputers will have on learning in the classroom? Explain.

Group Projects
Advanced level

1. Programming Teams

Subroutines allow a team of programmers to work on the same program simultaneously. As a result, a long program can be planned, coded, and debugged within a relatively short period of time.

The team, consisting of up to three students, will select a team leader (usually the team's best programmer). Then, a project is selected, and the requirements are provided by the D.P. manager (your teacher in this case). Some project topics include:

A Business Invoice

School Report Card

A Cheque and Cheque Stub

It is recommended that the team first study a planning technique such as a top down method which is well-suited to group planning. All completed programs must be capable of reading different sets of data, and producing forms with new information each time.

2. Programming Team Analysis
Challenge problem

The team aproach to programming presents many problems which must be overcome if the project is completed within its deadline, and be correct.

Describe at least three problems that your group had with the team approach to programming. Suggest solutions which would resolve the problems. Read the section on structured programming. How would the structured style of programming benefited your group?

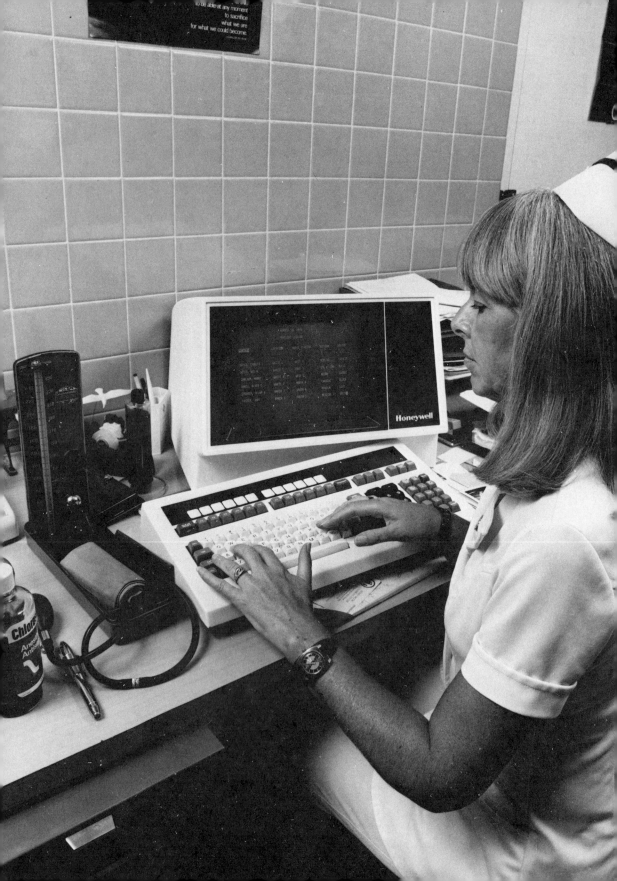

10 Conversational Programming

Computer systems are now available which help the
medical staff to enter medical data and make a diagnosis
based on the information. This nurse is keying in data
concerning some of the patients on her floor.

Courtesy of Honeywell.

Objectives

An understanding of the concept of a user
prompt

A working knowledge of the input and on...
goto statements

An understanding of the conversational programming rule

An understanding of the usefulness of
pseudo-code as a planning technique

A knowledge of such applications as
computer-assisted instruction and simulated
artificial intelligence

217

Chapter Ten
Conversational Programming

Mary Roseman studied the alternative lessons displayed on the screen, then keyed in "Computer Hardware—Lesson One." The list of choices disappeared. After a brief pause, a new message appeared on the screen.

"Hi, Mary. Welcome back! Last day you left off about halfway through lesson one. Do you wish a quick review before continuing today?"

Mary keyed in "Yes."

The first multiple choice question appeared. "Which of the following items refers to all of the instructions which makes a computer operate in the required manner?"

(1) hardware   (3) software
(2) firmware   (4) operating system

Mary keyed in her response, "3". "That is correct, Mary," the computer responded.

As the above sequence indicates, computers can be programmed to appear as if they are carrying on a conversation with the person at the keyboard. This particular technique of writing programs is called **conversational programming**. It is easy to do with a microcomputer.

Conversational programming has many applications. Hospitals, for example, use this technique for gathering medical data from a patient. Later, the doctor can use this information to help make a diagnosis. Airlines and hotels use this style of programming to help their desk clerks to book reservations for their customers. Teaching programs such as the one you read earlier are referred to as **computer-assisted instruction**. They help nurses, doctors, engineers, scientists, and students to learn facts about specific subjects. Conversational programming can be applied in any situation in which the program needs responses from the user to continue.

Conversations Are Easy

The computer always begins the conversation with some sort of message. The message may be a question which needs a reply, or an instruction which requires the person at the keyboard (the user) to do something. These messages are referred to as **user prompts**.

User prompts are programmed with *print* commands. Whatever message is contained inside the quotation marks will be printed on the screen for the user to see. For example, the statement

```
10   PRINT "KEY IN YOUR NAME"
```
↑
This is called a user prompt.

will print the message "Key in your name." It is important to make your message clear; otherwise, the responses may be different than expected.

Another command is needed to collect and store the answer inside the computer's memory. The *input* command is used for this purpose.

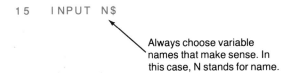

15   INPUT N$

Always choose variable names that make sense. In this case, N stands for name.

A letter is assigned to the memory location so we can recall the person's name later on. Since the entry is a string variable, a dollar sign is needed with the letter N.

A series of questions and responses can appear crowded on the display screen. To improve its readability, it is wise to leave a space between the question (user prompt) and the reply, and another space before the next user prompt appears on the screen.

Here is a short conversational program which requires the person at the keyboard to enter his or her name and address.

```
10    REM CONVERSATIONAL PROGRAM
15    REM JANE WINTERS PD.3
20    PRINT "KEY IN YOUR NAME"
25    PRINT
30    INPUT N$
35    PRINT
40    PRINT "KEY IN YOUR STREET ADDRESS"
45    PRINT
50    INPUT A$
55    PRINT
60    PRINT
65    PRINT "****************************"
70    PRINT N$
75    PRINT A$
80    PRINT "****************************"
85    END
```

During the execution of the program, this conversation appears on the screen.

```
KEY  IN  YOUR  NAME
?   ROD  TAYLOR
KEY  IN  YOUR  STREET  ADDRESS
?   145  MAIN  STREET  W.
```

The computer prints a question mark wherever it is expecting the user to enter an answer on the screen.

```
* * * * * * * * * * * * * * * * * * * * * * * * * * * * * *
    ROD   TAYLOR
    145  MAIN  STREET  W.
* * * * * * * * * * * * * * * * * * * * * * * * * * * * * *
```

The computer prints the name and address as required by the program.

Practice Assignment

Code a program which will require someone else to key in their name, street address, city and province (without a comma), and postal code, then print the data to appear as shown.

```
* * * * * * * * * * * * * * * * * * * * * * * * * * * * * *
                  NAME
            STREET  ADDRESS
  CITY  PROVINCE  AND  POSTAL  CODE
* * * * * * * * * * * * * * * * * * * * * * * * * * * * * *
```

Have another student run and test the program to see if it executes properly.

Mixing Words and Numbers

The *input* command can be used to store words, numbers, or mixtures of both. Consider the following "Days of Your Life" program which calculates the number of days a person has lived.

```
10    REM*******************************
15    REM   DAYS  OF  YOUR  LIFE
20    REM*******************************
25    PRINT "KEY  IN  YOUR  FIRST  NAME"
30    PRINT
35    INPUT N$
40    PRINT
45    PRINT "ENTER  YOUR  AGE  IN  YEARS"
50    PRINT
55    INPUT Y
60    PRINT
65    D = INT ( (Y * 364.25) + 0.5)
70    PRINT  "*******************************************"
75    PRINT "YOU  ARE  "; D ;"DAYS OLD "; N$
80    PRINT  "*******************************************"
85    END
```

The *integer* (*int*) in this program truncates, or drops, any numbers to the right of the decimal in the final answer. The conversation from this program would appear as follows.

```
RUN
KEY  IN  YOUR  FIRST  NAME
?   PAM
ENTER  YOUR  AGE  IN  YEARS
?   15
*****************************************
YOU  ARE  5464  DAYS  OLD  PAM
*****************************************
```

This program also illustrates another feature of conversational programming which makes it different from other styles of programming. The instructions occur in a specific order. This means that some thought must be given to the order during the planning stage.

These two elementary school students are interacting with a computer-assisted instruction program. Both the questions and the students' answers are in French.

Courtesy of Commodore Business Machines.

Planning Conversational Programs

Computer systems that have a printer as well as a CRT can be programmed with less attention to the order in which instructions occur within a program. For example, suppose that you want to print a chart which requires a title, calculations, and answers from the person at the keyboard. In this case, the screen can be used to collect data from the person at the keyboard by displaying user prompts and recording the responses. The printer, on the other hand, could be used to print only the completed chart.

When a display screen is the only output device available, the order in which print appears becomes important. Otherwise, titles and calculated answers could become mixed with user prompts and responses on the screen. This can happen because there are three different types of prints within some conversational programs—user prompts, responses from the person at the keyboard, and final answers.

Putting the Instructions in Order

To avoid mixing the final answer with other types of prints on the screen, your program must be organized into three sections. The first section will contain all the user prompts and the responses needed to complete the program.

The second section will contain the equations and calculations needed to process the information. Some programs, however, will not have this section.

The last section will contain all the print instructions which deals with the final output. This may include such items as titles, subtitles, rows of stars, and final answers.

The following diagram illustrates the three sections of a conversational program, arranged in their proper order.

Figure 10.1

Three Sections of a Conversational Program

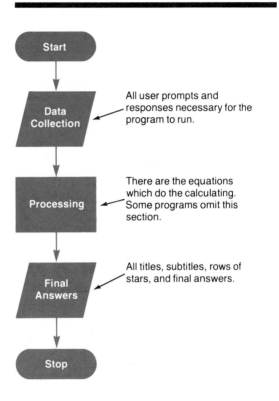

All user prompts and responses necessary for the program to run.

There are the equations which do the calculating. Some programs omit this section.

All titles, subtitles, rows of stars, and final answers.

Conversational Programming Rule

When the display screen is your only output device, organize your program in the following order—data collection, processing, and then final answers.

Choosing a Planning Technique

Conversational programs are wordy. They can contain sentences or even paragraphs of printed information. However, traditional planning techniques which use some sort of diagram leave little room for lengthy instructions. This limitation makes techniques such as flow-charts or structure diagrams ineffective in planning the details of a conversational program.

The best planning technique for wordy programs is **pseudo-code**. Consider the adaptation of pseudo-code to a program which requests a person's name, then prints it in the centre of the screen between two rows of stars.

```
PROGRAMMER COMMENTS
USER PROMPT - KEY IN YOUR NAME
SPACE
INPUT N$
SPACE
PRINT A ROW OF STARS  ⎫
PRINT N$              ⎬ (CENTRED)
PRINT A ROW OF STARS  ⎭
END
```

Pseudo-code should not be written in BASIC. The advantage of any planning method is to be able to concentrate on the logic of the solution without worrying about the syntax (grammatical rules) of some particular language. That is why there are no line numbers, and phrases unknown to BASIC are included.

The following sample problem illustrates how pseudo-code can be included with an entire planning sheet. (Longer problems will often require two planning sheets: one for the definition, values, and the pseudo-code; the second sheet entirely for coding.)

Name, Age, and Weight Problem

Plan and code a program which would request a person's name, age, and weight. Print the answers, centred on the screen, between two single rows of stars.

Planning for Name, Age, and Weight

Problem Definition

Print a person's name, age, and weight in the centre of the screen between two single rows of stars.

User Input

Name
Age
Weight

Pseudo-Code

```
PROGRAMMER COMMENTS
USER PROMPT - KEY IN YOUR NAME
SPACE
INPUT N$
SPACE
USER PROMPT - KEY IN YOUR AGE
SPACE
INPUT A
SPACE
USER PROMPT - KEY IN YOUR WEIGHT
SPACE
INPUT W
2 SPACES
PRINT A ROW OF STARS ⎫
PRINT NAME            ⎪
PRINT AGE             ⎬(CENTRED)
PRINT WEIGHT          ⎪
PRINT A ROW OF STARS ⎭
END
```

BASIC Coding

```
100   REM PROGRAM #1
110   REM KELLY GREEN PD. 5
120   PRINT "KEY IN YOUR NAME"
130   PRINT
140   INPUT N$
150   PRINT
160   PRINT "KEY IN YOUR AGE"
170   PRINT
180   INPUT A
190   PRINT
200   PRINT "KEY IN YOUR WEIGHT"
210   PRINT
220   INPUT W
230   PRINT
240   PRINT
250   PRINT TAB (15) " *************"
260   PRINT TAB (18) N$
270   PRINT TAB (17) A
280   PRINT TAB (17) W
290   PRINT TAB (15) " *************"
300   END
```

Pseudo-code, wisely used, can be a great asset in planning conversational programs. The choice of the phrase *user prompt* helps the programmer distinguish between questions and final answers.

Student programmers who cannot distinguish between the data collection stage and the final answer stage often leave out the last stage completely. They falsely conclude that the commands...

```
USER PROMPT - KEY IN YOUR NAME
INPUT N$
```

are the final answers, when in fact, they simply

represent data collection and not organized, printed answers.

In addition to sufficient room for writing and distinguishing between sections, pseudo-code also allows the programmer to indicate where spaces are to be inserted to improve the output's appearance.

Practice Assignment

Design and code a program for a business to help record phone orders from customers.

The program, to be used by the phone order clerk, should ask the following questions: *name of the customer, quantity required, product name*, and *unit price*.

The program would then calculate the total cost for the order, and appear as follows:

```
* * * * * * * * * * * * * * * * * * * * * * * * * * * *
CUSTOMER  :  — — — —
```

QTY.	PRODUCT NAME	UNIT PRICE	TOTAL COST
— —	— — —	$ - -	$ - -

```
* * * * * * * * * * * * * * * * * * * * * * * * * * * *
```

When you are ready to test your program, have another student act as a customer while you make entries on the keyboard.

Providing for Multiple Answers

What happens if your program asks a question to which there are several possible answers? Consider the following section of a CAI (teaching) program.

```
HI  TERRY!  DO  YOU  WISH  A  REVIEW  OF
LAST  DAY'S  LESSON  BEFORE
CONTINUING?
(YES  OR  NO)

?  YES
```

In order to provide alternatives for both possible answers, the program should appear as shown.

The person's response is stored here.

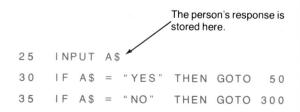

```
25    INPUT  A$
30    IF  A$  =  "YES"  THEN  GOTO   50
35    IF  A$  =  "NO"   THEN  GOTO  300
```

Usually, it is easier for a user to respond with words rather than numbers to the questions that you provide—the user does not have to remember which number corresponds to which answer. (Type 1 = yes; type 2 = no)

However, it is easier to program multiple choice questions if the answer is a number. Suppose the following multiple choice question appears on the display screen.

Which of the following items does not represent an output device? Type in the correct number.

(1) plotter
(2) voice response unit
(3) keyboard
(4) graphics display screen

Instead of programming four *if . . . then* statements to handle the four possible responses, one *on . . . goto* statement can be used.

The user's response is stored here.

```
40  INPUT N
45  ON N GOTO 60, 70, 80, 90
```

Notice that the *on . . . goto* statement provides four possible line numbers for the program to respond to: 60, 70, 80, or 90. This means that if the value stored in N is equal to 1, the program transfers control to line 60. If N = 2, *goto* 70. If N= 3, *goto* 80, and so on. This statement provides alternative programming choices for answers arranged in the sequence 1,2,3,4. . . .

Consider a partial program for that multiple choice quiz.

This program uses a minimum of two responses, one for the right answer, and one for all three wrong answers. It is possible, however, to provide different statements for each one.

Note that the same variable N can be used repeatedly in the quiz since any new entries will erase the old ones.

```
05   REM    *******************************
10   REM    MULTIPLE CHOICE QUIZ
15   REM    *******************************
20   C = 0
25   PRINT "WHICH OF THE FOLLOWING ITEMS DOES NOT"
30   PRINT "REPRESENT AN OUTPUT DEVICE? TYPE THE"
35   PRINT "CORRECT NUMBER"
40   PRINT
45   PRINT "(1) PLOTTER"
50   PRINT "(2) VOICE RESPONSE UNIT"
55   PRINT "(3) KEYBOARD"
60   PRINT "(4) GRAPHICS DISPLAY SCREEN"
65   PRINT
70   INPUT N
75   PRINT
80   ON N GOTO 100, 100, 85, 100
85   PRINT "THAT IS CORRECT!"
90   GOSUB 1000
95   GOTO 110
100  PRINT "SORRY, THAT IS AN OUTPUT DEVICE"
110  (The program continues with another question...)
```

This comment is printed only if the user keys in #3.

This comment is printed if the user keys in #1, 2, or 4.

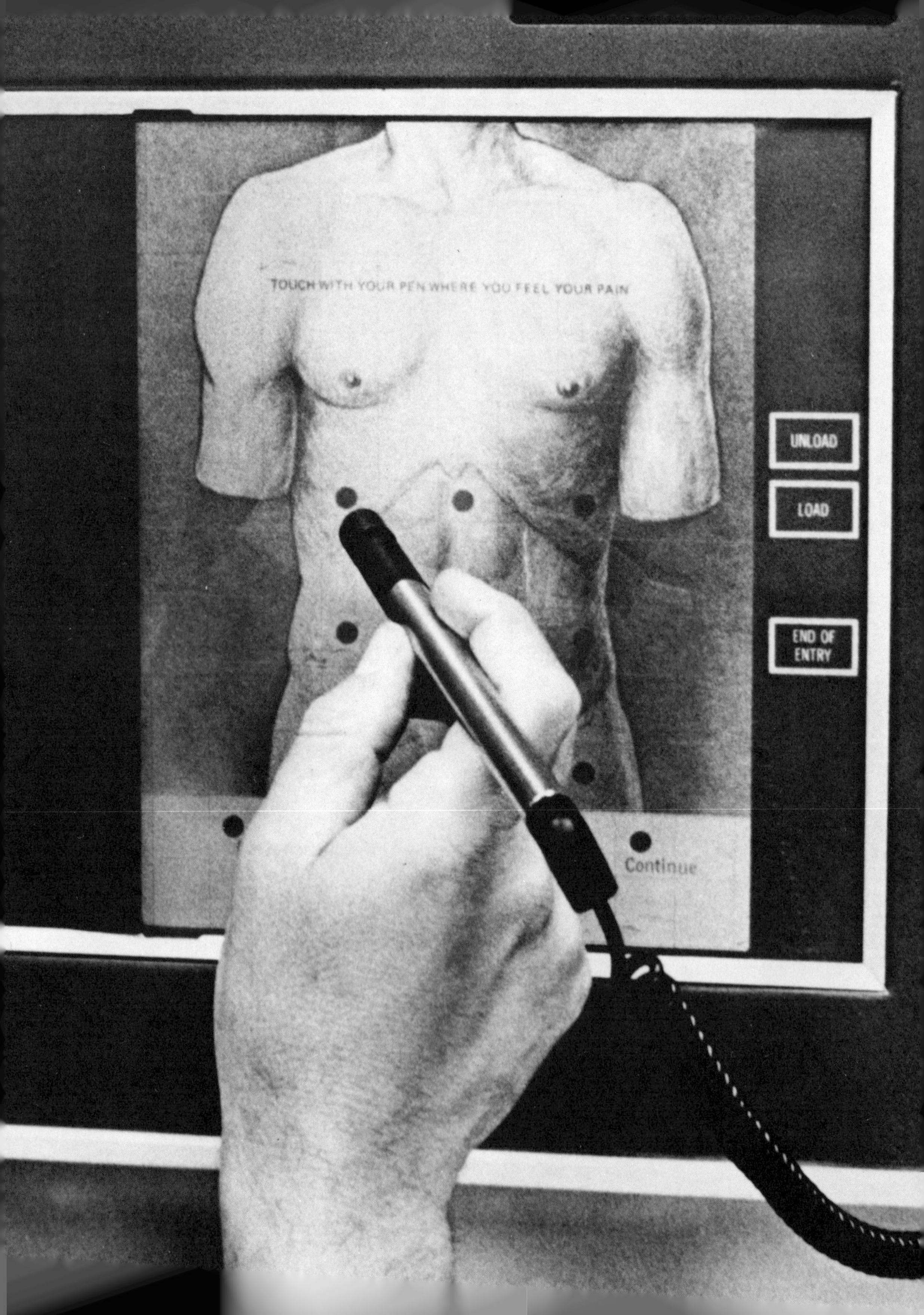
TOUCH WITH YOUR PEN WHERE YOU FEEL YOUR PAIN
UNLOAD
LOAD
END OF ENTRY
Continue

Keeping Track of Answers

A simple counter can keep track of the number of correct answers entered by the person trying the quiz.

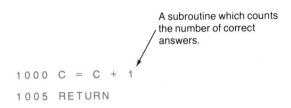

A subroutine which counts the number of correct answers.

```
1000  C = C + 1
1005  RETURN
```

Each time the user keys in a correct answer, the counter is incremented by one. Since the counter is needed several times in the program, it can be stored in a subroutine.

Practice Assignment

Plan and code a multiple choice quiz which contains five questions. Include a subroutine which keeps track of the person's score, and prints the following message once the quiz has been completed.

```
***************************
  YOU OBTAINED A SCORE OF
  _____ ON THE QUESTIONNARE.
***************************
```

Have another student run and test the program to see if it executes properly.

Idiot-Proofing!

A student had been answering a series of multiple choice questions on a microcomputer. Stumped by the eighth question, she keyed in the response "I don't know," and pressed the *return* key.

Immediately, the computer displayed the instruction *redo from start*, indicating that the student had to begin again with question number one. Frustrated, the student sat staring in disbelief at the display screen.

There is a great need in conversational programming to design for unexpected responses. This process is sometimes referred to as "idiot-proofing." Multiple choice questions, for example, should contain an instruction which refers the program to a subroutine when an invalid answer is entered. The subroutine message should help the user understand what went wrong. If the error is not corrected, the user may mistakenly continue to enter invalid answers.

This IBM Medical Examining System allows a patient to record his or her medical history by answering a filmed questionnaire presented on the screen. The patient answers such questions as "Where do you feel pain?" by touching the exact spot in the drawing with a light pen. This method helps to reduce the clerical paperwork and allows the doctor to spend more time with patients.

Courtesy of IBM Canada Ltd.

Notice what happens in the following program sequence when an invalid multiple choice answer is encountered.

```
 90   INPUT N$
100   ON N$ GOTO 300, 300, 150, 300
110   IF N$ < 1 OR N$ > 4 THEN GOSUB 1000
```

The instruction ON N $ GOTO covers all legitimate answers with which the user might respond (either 1,2,3, or 4). However, if the user responds with any other numbers, the computer will display an error message stored in the subroutine. This option allows the program to continue.

```
1000 PRINT "YOU HAVE ENTERED AN INCORRECT RESPONSE"
1005 PRINT "PLEASE KEY IN ONLY THE NUMBERS 1,2,3, OR 4"
1010 RETURN
```

It is important to make your instructions at the beginning, as well as the subroutine error messages, clear and helpful. An error message, in particular, should inform the user about the correct procedure, not just indicate that an error has been made.

The Ultimate Conversational Program

The most sophisticated program which illustrates a computer's abiliy to carry on a conversation with a human is called **simulated artificial intelligence**. Artificial intelligence refers to a machine's ability to make decisions on its own, often beyond its original programming. Simulated artificial intelligence, however, refers to a program which appears to give a computer some independent "thinking ability," but is actually a cleverly written conversational program.

Such a program can converse with the user on a variety of subjects by using **key words** in a person's response. The key words

would call up various subroutines which would
expand the conversation the user is having
with the computer. Consider the following conversation on the topic of homework.

"HOW ARE THINGS GOING IN SCHOOL, PAUL? WELL, OR POORLY?"

? "POORLY. I GOT 48% ON THE LAST TEST"

I'M SORRY TO HEAR THAT. I HEARD SOMEWHERE THAT ONE'S SCHOOL MARKS
ARE DIRECTLY PROPORTIONAL TO THE AMOUNT OF STUDYING THAT ONE DOES.
DO YOU THINK THAT IS TRUE?"

? "YES."

"HOW MANY MINUTES DO YOU SPEND ON HOMEWORK EACH NIGHT?"

? "ABOUT 30 MIN."

"ONLY THIRTY MINUTES? THAT DOESN'T SOUND LIKE MUCH. THAT'S ONLY
ABOUT FOUR MINUTES PER SUBJECT. DO YOU HAVE A JOB AFTER SCHOOL?"

Notice that the program's responses
always include questions which are actually
user prompts in disguise. The user prompts
contain the key words which allow the program
to continue. You can imagine the size of a program which is capable of conversing on several topics.

Summary

Conversational programming refers to a particular way of writing computer programs. This technique requires the person at the keyboard to interact with the computer. Without responses from the user, the program will not work.

Conversational programming, for example, can be applied in hospitals to gather medical data from patients, in airports to enter flight reservations, and in schools to allow students to learn a topic without assistance from a teacher.

The technique requires user prompts (messages usually containing an instruction or a question) to appear on the screen to which the user must respond. Responses are collected with a command called *input*. A person's name, for example, would be stored with the command *input* N $.

Because conversational programs tend to be wordy, pseudo-code provides the most suitable technique for planning the details of the program.

Since many items are printed on the screen—user prompts, responses, and final answers—it is important to have them appear in a certain order to avoid confusing the user. Also, it is wise to space the items a few lines apart to make them easier to read. A crowded display screen can easily discourage a user.

The ultimate conversational program is one which simulates (imitates) artificial intelligence. It gives the impression that the computer can carry on a conversation on any topic, much like a human being.

Review Questions

These are *general level questions* which may require factual recall, reading comprehension, and some application of the knowledge from this chapter.

1. Suggest an example of how conversational programming may be used.

2. Generally speaking, in what situations can conversational programming be applied?

3. What is a user prompt?

4. What function does the *input* command perform?

5. Write two BASIC statements—one to ask the user to enter his/her phone number, and the other to store the answer in the computer.

6. Suppose a question mark appears on the screen during a conversational program. What does this mean?

7. A variable used to store words is slightly different than a variable used to store numbers. What is the difference? Which variable can store both?

8. Write the specific statements in a program which would contain two user prompts (and their corresponding *input* commands). The first message requires the user to key in his/her first name. The second message requests the person to enter his/her height.

9. What does the *integer* command do to an answer?

10. Determine the answer to this expression:

    ```
    10 A = INT ( 0.05 * 40.51)
    ```

11. What problem may occur with the design of conversational programs?

12. Explain the conversational programming rule in your own words.

13. Why is pseudo-code a good planning technique for these types of programs?

14. State two ways in which pseudo-code differs from actual BASIC coding.

15. Why is pseudo-code written differently than actual coding?

16. Translate these lines of pseudo-code into their equivalent lines in BASIC.

```
USER PROMPT - KEY IN YOUR NAME
SPACE
INPUT N$
SPACE
USER PROMPT - KEY IN YOUR AGE
SPACE
INPUT A
```

17. Study the following statements. What would happen if the user keyed in "NO" on the keyboard?

```
25    INPUT N$
30    IF N$ = "YES" THEN GOTO 50
35    IF N$ = "NO"  THEN PRINT "END OF PROGRAM"
```

18. Study the following statements. What would happen if the user keyed in "2" on the keyboard?

```
20    INPUT N
25    ON N GOTO 30, 40, 50, 60
```

19. What does "idiot-proofing a program" refer to?

20. Explain the concept of simulated artificial intelligence.

Applying Your Knowledge

These questions assume an understanding of the material presented in the chapter, and provide new situations which may require evaluation, analysis, or application of that knowledge. Section One contains *general level* questions on specific statements or programming techniques. Section Two contains *advanced level* questions which require the planning and coding of complete problems.

Section One

1. Rewrite the following statements to correct
   any errors they may contain.

```
10    REM TINY BIGMAN PD. 5
15    REM CONVERSATIONAL PROGRAM
20    PRINT KEY IN YOUR FINAL MARK
25    INPUT
30    PRINT
35    PRINT "YOUR FINAL MARK IS " ; N
40    END
```

2. Rewrite the following statements to correct
   any errors they may contain.

```
10    REM WALTER PIGEON
15    REM PROGRAM #2
20    ENTER YOUR FULL NAME
30    PRINT " ************************ "
35    PRINT    HELLO N$
40    PRINT " ************************ "
45    END
```

3. Translate the following lines of pseudo-
   code into the equivalent lines of BASIC.

```
USER PROMPT - KEY IN YOUR FIRST NAME
SPACE
INPUT N$
SPACE
USER PROMPT - KEY IN YOUR HEIGHT (ROUND TO NEAREST FOOT)
INPUT H
SPACE
CALCULATE M = INT ( (H * 12 * 2.5) + 0.05)
PRINT A ROW OF STARS
PRINT N$, YOUR HEIGHT IN CENTIMETRES IS ____
PRINT A ROW OF STARS
END
```

4. There are three sections to a conversational program. Name and identify the three sections of the program in problem 3.

5. Suppose that you are coding a true and false quiz. Write the appropriate BASIC statements which would accept the words "TRUE" or "FALSE" as an answer. If the answer is TRUE, have the program branch to line 100. if the answer is FALSE, have the program branch to line 150.

6. Suppose that you are coding a multiple choice questionnaire. Write the appropriate BASIC statements which would accept either 1,2,3, or 4 as an answer. Have the program branch to lines 300, 300, 150, 300, respectively, depending on which answer is given.

7. Write a two-line subroutine which would count the number of correct answers which a student has given in a multiple choice quiz.

8. Write the appropriate BASIC statements which would "idiot-proof" the responses to a multiple choice question which has four possible answers (1,2,3, or 4).

Section Two—Problems for Programming

Plan and code the solutions to the following problems. For the planning stage, define the problem, list the input data, plan the solution, then code into BASIC. It may also be helpful, in some problems, to use a "printer layout" sheet to design the final output.

1. Medical Diagnosis

Interns at a general hospital want a program which would allow them to key in medical data on a patient (in response to user prompts) to determine whether the person has a cold, bronchitis, or pneumonia.

Use a counter to keep track of the number of "yes" answers to questions such as "Does the patient have a fever?"; "Is the patient shivering?" "Does the patient have a sore throat?" "Signs of chest congestion?"

The total number of "yes" responses will determine which diagnosis to display. You decide which total is associated with each output. A sample display is shown below.

```
* * * * * * * * * * * * * * * * * * * * * * * * * *

THE PATIENT HAS BRONCHITIS

* * * * * * * * * * * * * * * * * * * * * * * * * *
```

2. Flight Reservations

Air Canada uses a flight reservation system which allows a clerk to key in requests from a customer, and display the final output. (To shorten the program, preselect four different destinations, their respective flight numbers, and the cost of each flight.)

Plan a program which would determine the customer's name, date of departure, and destination, (entered as Toronto-London, Ont., for example).

The computer then locates the appropriate flight number and cost stored within the program, and prints a display similar to the one shown below.

```
* * * * * * * * * * * * * * * * * * * * * * * * * * * *
CUSTOMER'S NAME
DATE
TORONTO-LONDON (ONT)
FLIGHT NUMBER 48
COST $114.50
* * * * * * * * * * * * * * * * * * * * * * * * * * * *
```

3. Term Report Card

Eastglen District High School purchased a microcomputer to produce report cards. The principal has hired a senior programming student (you) to design the program. It must be able to accept any four subjects and any four related marks typed in at the keyboard by the office clerk. Once the data is entered, the program immediately prints a report card as shown in the example below. (Four subjects are used for brevity. You may increase the number of subjects if you wish.)

```
* * * * * * * * * * * * * * * * * * * * * * * * * * * *
EASTGLEN DISTRICT HIGH SCHOOL

STUDENT:

SUBJECTS                       MARKS
MATH                             76
COMPUTERS                        91
ENGLISH                          65
FRENCH                           64

TERM AVERAGE IS _____
* * * * * * * * * * * * * * * * * * * * * * * * * * * *
```

4. Eligibility for Football

Mr. Greenback, the senior football coach, uses a microcomputer to determine whether a student is eligible for the school's football team. He uses a *point system* by assigning values to answers given by the candidates.

Two points, for example, are given for students in good medical health; two points for students without injuries within the last calendar year; one point for ages fourteen to fifteen, two points for ages sixteen to nineteen; and two points for passing all subjects last term.

Design the program such that only candidates who have six points or more are eligible. There are two possible displays (eligible, not eligible). A sample display is shown here.

```
* * * * * * * * * * * * * * * * * * * * * * * * * *
NAME :

ELIGIBLE TO PLAY FOOTBALL
* * * * * * * * * * * * * * * * * * * * * * * * * *
```

5. The Invoice

A manufacturing company uses a microcomputer to record requests from customers for their office supplies. Plan a program which would accept the customer's name, street address, city and province, and at least one order of supplies. (Have someone act as a customer to provide the details of the order when you are ready to test the program.)

The program is then to produce the following invoice on the screen with all the details of the order filled in. (The *tab* command will play an important role in your program design.)

```
* * * * * * * * * * * * * * * * * * * * * * * * * *
AXXEON  CORPORATION
GRANDE  PRAIRIE

CUSTOMER'S  NAME
_____
CUSTOMER'S  ADDRESS
_____
_____
_____
* * * * * * * * * * * * * * * * * * * * * * * * *
QTY.   DESCRIPT.   UNIT      TOTAL
                   PRICE
 _      _           _         _

 _      _           _         _
* * * * * * * * * * * * * * * * * * * * * * * * *
```

6. Microcomputer Payroll System

Congenial Catering Corporation has just hired you as an application programmer to program their microcomputer. Because the company has many part-time employees, the manager wants an interactive payroll program which can accept data directly from the keyboard, rather than from a permanent data file.

Design and code a program which would accept an employee's name, hours worked, rate of pay, and produce either a cheque stub or an actual cheque. (Deductions are 34% of gross pay).

The cheque stub would contain the company's name, date, employee name, gross pay, deductions and net pay.

The cheque would contain the date, company name, employee name, amount, account number, and a blank for the manager's signature.

Before beginning the planning sheet, use a printer layout sheet (or a blank piece of paper) to design the form. It might be helpful to study an actual cheque to determine your design.

7. True or False Quiz

Choose a subject area that you are familiar with. Design and code a true or false quiz with ten questions that a student could use.

The program should contain a counter to keep track of the number of correct answers, and have a subroutine to "idiot-proof" the entries. When the quiz is completed, the following display should appear on the screen. Note that the number of correct responses are expressed as a percentage.

```
*****************************
YOU  HAVE  REACHED  A  70%
LEVEL  OF  UNDERSTANDING
ON  THIS  TOPIC
*****************************
```

8. A Challenge Problem

With the teacher's approval, select or design your own conversational program. Use a printer layout sheet and programming planning sheet to design and code the solution.

Topics for Discussion

1. Studies on computer-assisted instruction have indicated that although students tend to spend more time on problems presented on a TV screen, compared to problems presented on a ditto, the number of correct responses does not change.

   Keeping those studies in mind, do you think schools should still invest in microcomputers? Give reasons for your answer.

2. Suppose you were seated in front of a microcomputer in communication with a microcomputer located in another room. There is both a senior student from a computer studies class and a simulated artificial intelligence program in that other room.

   If the other terminal begins the conversation, would it be possible to tell whether you were communicating with the program or the student at the keyboard? Explain.

Individual Project

Microcomputer Ads

Using newspapers, computer and science magazines as your source, clip out advertisements which describe microcomputers and peripherals for sale.

Select ads that (1) comprise a complete microcomputer system, and (2) represent one of the least expensive systems suitable for classroom use. The system should include a monitor (display screen), keyboard, actual computer, one auxiliary storage device, and a printer.

Neatly fasten each clipping to a separate page of blank typing paper. On the last page, type a summary of the products and their individual cost, as well as a final total for the entire computer system. Include an appropriate title page at the front of the project. Check to see that there are no duplicate ads in your final selection.

11

Special Effects With Microcomputers

Objectives

An understanding of the various ways to produce computer graphics

A working knowledge of timer loops and how to scroll messages out of view

An understanding of the concept of word processing

An awareness of how to generate computerized music

An awareness of how robotic devices can be controlled by a microcomputer

This command console and its remote modules can be used with a microcomputer to provide computerized control of all lamps and electrical appliances in a home.

Courtesy of Ohio Scientific.

Chapter Eleven
Special Effects With Microcomputers

A computer's versatility is limited only by one's imagination.

A computer is an information processing machine. Electronic information, once processed, can be put to work in a variety of ways. A display screen, for example, can be used to draw artistic designs, or to graphically illustrate monthly sales figures or scientific data. Office secretaries, writers, and poets can substitute their typewriter with a microcomputer to type, edit, print, and file error-proof copy. Robot devices, as well as speakers reproducing computerized music, can respond to electronic messages in a computer program.

This chapter introduces special effects that you can produce with a microcomputer. Some effects are programming techniques which can enhance a computer program. Others represent projects which require the purchase of additional software or hardware before you can begin.

Graphics

Graphics refers to drawing graphs, pictures, or artistic designs using the computer. Some microcomputers come equipped with "graphic capabilities." This means that there is a circuit board used exclusively to make images on the screen. Often the keyboard shift key will allow a programmer to use special graphics keys. The amount of detail which can be put into a picture is determined by the sophistication of the circuit board programs. Generally, the more expensive the software programs, the more detailed the pictures.

Simple Graphics

You do not need special computers to create graphics. A picture can be created using a computer program. By instructing the computer to print symbols or letters, one line at a time, a whole image can be formed. A person's initials, special titles, an artistic design, or a cartoon character can be printed using this one-line-at-a-time method. Programmers use graphic paper to plan where the symbols should be placed on each line. The image can be printed vertically or horizontally, whichever is more appropriate.

Graphics Project #1

Using graph paper, design either a cartoon character, an attractive design, a business graph, or your initials in enlarged lettering. Limit the size of your design by the number of characters that the printer can get on one line, or by the dimensions of the display screen. Code a program to print your design.

Mathematical Graphics

Programs combined with some knowledge of mathematics can give a smoother look to the display. For example, the trigonometric functions *sine*, *cos*, and *tan* create curves for biorhythm charts, to illustrate sound waves, to create line graphs, or to design attractive artistic pictures. Consider the following *Sine Curve Program* which is designed to print out a person's name in a particular wave pattern. A "for...next" loop is used to get the display screen to create the *sine* wave pattern and to limit its size.

```
10    REM SINE CURVE PROGRAM
15    FOR X = 0 TO 6.8 STEP .3          This sets limits to the curve's
                                         outward movement.
20    Y = SIN(X)                         The equation itself.
25    Y = Y * 15 + 15                    How far across the screen
                                         the diagram will go.
30    PRINT TAB(Y)"SUSAN"                Item to be printed.
35    NEXT X
40    END                                End of for...next loop
```

```
        SUSAN
           SUSAN
             SUSAN
               SUSAN
                 SUSAN
                   SUSAN
                   SUSAN
                 SUSAN
                SUSAN
              SUSAN
            SUSAN
          SUSAN
         SUSAN
       SUSAN
     SUSAN
   SUSAN
SUSAN
SUSAN
  SUSAN
    SUSAN
      SUSAN
        SUSAN
         SUSAN
```

Graphics Project # 2

Have the computer print your name using Y = cos (2 ∗ X) as a wave pattern. Use the same screen limitations as illustrated in the *sine curve program*.

Other Methods To Produce Graphics

Some microcomputers are equipped with graphics symbols on the keyboard. By inserting the symbols inside print statements, any desired diagram can be built up one line at a time.

Computer companies may offer **graphics software** which are programs to make graphics easier. Histograms (bar graphs), for example, can be produced by simply providing the program with the necessary data. The program then draws the graph on the screen with a title, labels, and bars to represent the numbers you gave it.

Bar graphs are easy to produce when a microcomputer contains graphics software. The user first keys in increments for the X and Y axis, and one set of values. The computer then draws the completed diagram for you.

Courtesy of Apple Computer Inc.

Another method is to add a **graphics tablet**. This is a flat-bed drawing board with an electric grid. A special pen is used to select functions (such as drawing lines, shading, or erasing), to draw whatever diagram you choose. As the pen moves across the tablet. the video screen (with the help of a graphics software program) shows you what you are drawing.

One interesting feature of a graphics tablet is that it allows you to scale the drawing. This means that you can use a small drawing space on the tablet to completely fill the display screen, or the whole surface of the tablet can be used to draw the fine details of only one section of the display screen.

A desk-top **plotter** can also be added to a computer system. A plotter has the advantage over a printer in that the plotter can go back over the same area on the page; whereas, an ordinary printer can only move progressively down the page. As a result, a plotter is capable of producing elaborate graphics with a simulated three-dimensional appearance.

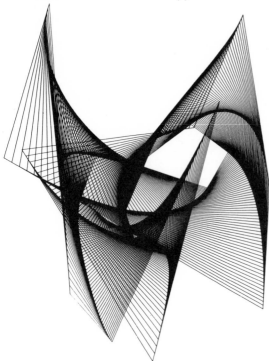

This artistic design was drawn by a desk-top plotter.

Creating Pauses in Programs

Often, programmers need to have a method of displaying information on the screen for a specified length of time, long enough that people can read it, before it is replaced with new information. Because the pause in the program can be created with a *for...next* loop. it is referred to a **timer loop**. Consider the following timer loop.

```
50   FOR N = 1 TO 500
60   NEXT N
```

This causes a pause in the program of about six seconds. When the timer loop is completed, the computer continues on with the rest of the program. A colon (:) will allow us to connect two statements into one long one. The timer loop shown above can then be written as

```
50   FOR N = 1 TO 500 : NEXT N
```

The length of the pause is determined by the speed at which the microprocessor chip operates. Each manufacturer has its own computer chip. Some computer chips are more efficient, and therefore faster, than others. As a general guideline, the following number of loops will create these approximate pauses in the program.

Number of Loops	Program Delay in Seconds
1000	1.5
2000	3.0
5000	7.5
8000	12.0

Clearing the Screen

The number of lines of information that a video screen will contain gives you a clue as to how many blank print commands are needed to completely clear the screen of information. For example, a twenty-line screen could be cleared with twenty blank print commands.

If an item is centred on the screen, different microcomputers have commands which will clear the item from the screen. Here are two examples:

```
25   CLS                 (Radio  Shack)


25   PRINT  "♥"          (Commodore)
```

Combining Pauses and Screen Clearing

Suppose that you wish to display something in the middle of the screen, have it appear there for six seconds, then disappear. Consider the following program.

```
10   PRINT: PRINT: PRINT: PRINT:
     PRINT: PRINT: PRINT: PRINT:
     PRINT:

20   PRINT TAB (8) "GEORGE, YOU'RE A GREAT GUY!"

30   FOR N = 1 TO 500 : NEXT N

40   PRINT "♥"

50   END
```

The first set of print commands centres the item vertically on the screen. The timer loop contained in line 20 creates a delay of about six seconds after the phrase "George, you're a great guy!" is printed. The last set of blank print commands scrolls the phrase out of view.

Practice Assignment

Plan and code a program which would centre the phrase *What a Great day this is* ... on the screen, delay for six seconds, then have the phrase disappear to be replaced with this phrase *To do interactive programming*.

    The second phrase is to appear for six seconds, then the screen is cleared once again.

Word Processing

Most microcomputer companies offer this software program, which gives the user greater control over what appears on the screen. It allows people who have no programming knowledge to use the screen as an electronic writing pad—typing, erasing, and arranging sentences to suit their needs. Writers, poets, and office secretaries use this type of program to create error-proof copy on the screen before transferring it to the printer.

Most microcomputer companies offer "word processing" software. Once it is read into the computer, this program will provide the user with complete editing control over the visual screen without any knowledge of programming.

Courtesy of Apple Computer Inc.

The program is actually a **text editor** which allows words such as *move*, *insert*, and *delete* to become system commands. The screen becomes a clear writing space, and the user types in paragraphs, much like you would write a letter to someone.

This application of the computer is referred to as **word processing** because the program concentrates on the manipulation of words, rather than numbers and equations.

Practice Assignment

Compose an informal letter to a close friend which describes the day's events. The letter should contain about three indented paragraphs, with a space between each paragraph. Place today's date at the top, and your name after the closing "Sincerely."

Robotics

This refers to the study and use of electronic robot devices which, in our case, operate by remote control under the guidance of a computer program.

Factories, on an increasing scale, are using robot devices to assemble products along an assembly line. Each robot device has a small microprocessor chip (MPU) which can be programmed with a series of steps for the robot to follow. Children's toys such as cars, tanks, or walking robots contain the same type of computer chip.

There are several books on the market which give detailed instructions for the assembly of a robotic device on wheels which will respond to computer instructions.

One company markets a robot device under the trademark "Turtle" which can "see," write with a pen, and move in all directions under the guidance of a computer program. The device follows simple commands such as *forward ten*, *turn left* and *stop*. It allows student programmers to study the **process control** features of a computer, which refers to the capacity of a computer to manipulate machines outside of the computer system itself.

The "Turtle" is a robotic device which responds to commands from a microcomputer. It is capable of moving in all directions, drawing lines with a special pen, and generating sounds.

Courtesy of Terrapin, Inc.

Computerized Music

Some microcomputers are equipped with sound capabilities. They contain a small speaker and a computer chip, which has instructions on how to generate certain types of sounds such as simulated explosions suitable for computer games.

Students can simulate their own sound system by attaching a small speaker to the computer system, and experimenting with the *peek* and *poke* commands available in most versions of BASIC.

Figure 11.1
Computerized Sound System

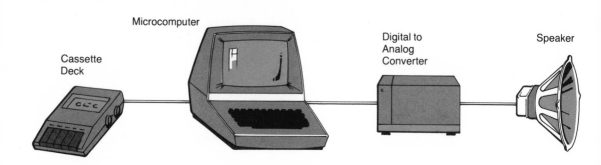

Most computers use sixteen bits to store a number in main memory. Usually, the first bit is used to represent a minus or plus sign. This leaves fifteen bits or 32 767 memory addresses (2^{15}). These addresses can be used to send electronic signals to "toggle" a speaker with a certain sound.

For example, the following program causes the speaker to click several times, much like a ball hitting the wall.

```
25   X = PEEK ( 1 0 0 )  −  PEEK ( 1 0 0 )  +
         PEEK ( 1 0 0 )  −  PEEK ( 1 0 0 )  +
         PEEK ( 1 0 0 )  −  PEEK ( 1 0 0 )
```

Here the memory address 100 is *peeked* at six times. We alternatively add and subtract the *peeks* to end up with X equal to the value of zero.

We can also make tones and melodies with the speaker by adding a *for...next* loop which holds the sound for a certain length of time.

```
10    FOR  I  =  1  TO  100
15    POKE  100 , 0  ◄──────── This pokes memory location
                                100 with the value zero.
20  · NEXT  I
```

These statements will pulse the speaker 100 times. The result will be a medium pitched tone. To obtain a lower pitch, a timer loop can be placed inside the main loop to slow down the time between the pulses.

```
10    FOR  I  =  1  TO  100
15    POKE  100 ,  0
20    FOR  X  = 1  TO  100  :  NEXT  X  ◄──────── A timer loop to slow down
                                                  the rate of pulsing.
25    NEXT  I
```

By experimenting with these commands and timer loops, students can create their own computerized music.

Summary

The only limitation to a microcomputer is the user's imagination. This chapter contains projects and suggestions which allow the user to go beyond traditional programming and create special effects with a microcomputer.

Using the screen as a drawing board, business graphs, pictures, or artistic designs can be created. This application is referred to as computer graphics, and can be made available to the user in a variety of ways, including graphics software packages, a graphics tablet, or a graphics plotter.

Timer loops combine with blank print commands can cause messages to appear on the screen momentarily, then disappear or be replaced with a new message.

Word processing, the use of a computer to type and edit sentences, can be achieved without a knowledge of programming. Writers, poets, typesetters, and office secretaries can use the screen as an electronic writing pad to move, add, or delete words with little effort.

The addition of robotic devices to a computer system can add to a programmer's knowledge of the process control capabilities of a computer. Simple commands can cause a robot device to scoot around the floor, or draw geometric shapes on a sheet of paper.

BASIC commands such as *peek* and *poke* can be used with a converter and a speaker to create computerized music.

Finally, the projects suggested in this chapter are only some of the possible applications of a microcomputer. For other BASIC commands and ideas, read the computer manual that accompanies the machine and experiment. Let your imagination be your guide.

Review Questions

These are *general level questions* which may require factual recall, reading comprehension, and some applications of the knowledge from this chapter.

1. Some microcomputers come equipped with "graphic capabilities." What does that mean?

2. How can a picture be created in a simple manner without the addition of special equipment?

3. What is meant by mathematical graphics? Give an example.

4. Name and briefly describe three items that you can add to a computer system to give it graphics capabilities.

5. Write a timer loop which will cause the computer to delay for nine seconds.

6. A programmer was confused by a timer loop she had written. On one microcomputer it took six seconds to process, but on another microcomputer it only took four-and-a-half seconds. What may have caused the difference?

7. What does *word processing* software allow people to do with a computer that normally they could not?

8. What does *robotics* refer to? How have consumers been affected by robotics?

9. What is a *process control* computer application? Give an example of that type of use for a computer.

10. What additional hardware devices are needed to make computerized music with a microcomputer?

11. Write a three-line program which would cause the computer to *poke* storage address 500 with the value zero, one hundred times.

12. Write a program which would cause the computer to *poke* storage address 864 with the value zero, one hundred times. Also include a timer loop to slow down the rate of pulsing.

Applying Your Knowledge

These projects assume an understanding of the material presented in the chapter, and provide new situations which may require evaluation, analysis, or application of that knowledge. Projects 1 to 3 are *general level*.

1. Mathematical Graphics

Plan and code a program which would print your first name in a combined wave pattern created by the following:
$cos\ (2*X) + sin\ (X)$.

To keep the graphic pattern within screen limits, use the following parameters:

$$Y\ =\ 1\ 0\ *\ Y\ +\ 2\ 0$$

and set the *for . . . next* loop from 0 to 9.5 *step* .2.

2. Word Processing

Proofreading and editing a letter becomes as important as your typing skills when using a word processing system. This is a two-step project. First type the business letter exactly as you see it below.

Wilfred Computer Systems, Inc.
1920 Laurier Ave. East
Montreal, Quebec
H2H 1B4

(Today's Date)

Mr. Peter Innis
Vice-President
Consolidated Packaging
Winnipeg, Manitoba
R5B 6P3

Dear Mr. Innis:

Thank you for your inquiry letter of January 20th, regarding our word processing equipment.

We have, at present, three models available with various levels of software and hardware sophistication, ranging in price from $2200 to $8500.

I recommend the AE 1600 for your company. It has a 50×100 cm video screen, and a bi-directional, dot matrix, character printer.

I have included three brochures for your perusal.

Sincerely,

Encl.-3   R.J. Wilkinson-Sales Mgr.

Now proofread and edit the letter to include
the changes indicated below.

Wilfred Computer Systems, Inc.
1920 Laurier Ave. East
Montreal, Quebec
H2H 1B4

(Today's Date)

Mr. Peter Innis
Vice-President
Consolidated Packaging   *insert 'Ltd.'*
Winnipeg, Manitoba
R5B 6P3

Dear Mr. Innis:

Thank you for your inquiry letter of January 20th, regarding our word processing
equipment.

four

We have, at present, three /models available with various levels of software and
hardware sophistication, ranging in price from $2200 to $8500.

as the most suitable model

I recommend the AE 1600 /for your company. It has a 50 × 100 cm video screen,
and a bi-directional, dot matrix, character printer.

~~I have included three brochures for your perusal.~~ *delete*

insert 'I have included a brochure on each one for your perusal'

Sincerely,

Encl.-~~3~~ *4*   R.J. Wilkinson-Sales Mgr.

3. **Computerized Music**

   Assemble a digital-to-analog converter and a speaker, and attach them to the microcomputer. Plan and code a program which would play about two bars of a familiar song. Use timer loops to create half tones.

4. **Challenge Project**

   Plan and code a program which would allow a person to use the keyboard like a piano to create music. Study the computer manual to find the appropriate BASIC commands which will send keyboard impulses directly to an I/O port.

12

Computer Applications

An automated teller terminal allows a customer to perform banking transactions 24 hours a day. The device requires that the customer enter an identification card as well as a numeric password before beginning a transaction.

Objectives

An understanding of business administrative applications such as reports, word processing, and electronic mail

An awareness of factory uses for computers

An understanding of research applications such as computer modelling and training simulations

An awareness of vehicle monitoring in efforts to reduce traffic congestion

An awareness of how computers help to serve customers

An awareness of more recent computer applications such as computer-assisted instruction, consumer products, and home computing

Chapter Twelve

Computer Applications

Computers will cause a revolution in society equivalent to the Industrial Revolution. Just as engines extend our physical powers, computers will extend our mental capabilities.

Computer applications refers to the uses that people find for computers in society. The applications may range from an assembly line completely run by computers to a children's toy responding to remote control signals.

Although computers have been available for over 30 years, up until the 1970s the machines were overly large, complex, and expensive. As a result, few computers were used outside of business offices, or research laboratories. With the development of the miniature **microprocessor chip**, and a strong effort to "humanize" communication with a computer, a computer revolution has begun.

An electronic environment is replacing an older mechanical one. Children operate the electronic devices with the same ease as a university graduate. Homes, schools, factories, banks, retail businesses, and offices have all found applications for this high-speed, electronic, information processing machine.

Office Administration

Business offices have found computers invaluable for processing the "mountains" of paperwork needed to keep the business operating. Corporations often have a separate data processing department, supported by a mainframe computer system, to process such items as the company payroll, invoices to customers, cheques to suppliers, warehouse inventory, and production scheduling.

Types of Reports

There are four categories of reports generally produced by computers: scheduled listings, exception reports, predictive and demand reports.

Scheduled listings refers to a common type of printout which usually contains the complete contents of a particular file. Although it can be useful, such reports, when overused, can create enormous amounts of irrelevant data. In a school, for example, a list of every student on the roll, along with the number of days they were absent, would represent a scheduled listing.

Exception reports refers to a method of listing only the "exceptions to the rule," or items requiring immediate attention. The lengthy scheduled listing for school attendance, for example, could be reduced to one page by requiring only the names of those who were absent to be printed. This more efficient process is sometimes referred to as "management by exception."

Predictive reports are the type generated by mathematical equations to forecast trends, and to assist planners in making decisons about the future. A printout which forecasts a company's sales trends to the year 1990 would be an example of a predictive report. These reports are usually displayed in the form of a graph, table of statistics, or with events expressed as a probability.

Demand reports usually require a cross-indexed data base which is a large set of data files stored on magnetic disk with some index number in common. The computer can be requested to select information from several files and combine them in a particular order before displaying them for the user.

Suppose, for example, a school data base contains several files such as student enrollment, days absent, total credits, guidance reports, current marks, and term average. The school principal could enter a request for any combination of data such as

```
WILSON, TOMMY #345527
* CREDITS
* ABSENTEEISM
* GUIDANCE REPORTS
```

The computer would find information on Tommy from that particular file, using Tommy's student number as a cross-index. Since any combination of information can be retrieved upon demand to form the report, it is called a demand report.

Figure 12.1

Types of Reports

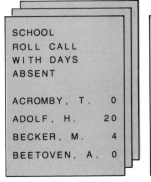

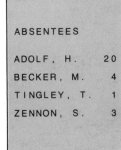

Scheduled Listing   **Exception Report**

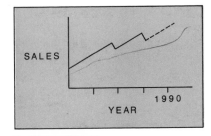

Predictive Report

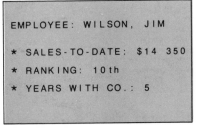

Demand Report

Other applications of computers in offices include word processing and electronic mail. **Word processing** refers to the secretarial use of desk-top computers to type, proofread, edit, and print letters or memos. The keyboard, screen, and printer eliminate the need for a typewriter, while the magnetic disks remove the necessity for filing cabinets.

Since messages are recorded and stored electronically, rather than on paper, they can be sent from one work station to another within the office in fractions of a second. This immediate transfer of messages from one person to another using computers is called **electronic mail**.

Computers in Factories

Production plants have adopted computers in varying degrees. Canadian factories may use machinery such as lathes, drills, and pattern cutters which operate automatically once the operator has programmed them. These machines tend to increase productivity and require highly skilled technicians to program and operate them.

Some special factories in Tokyo, Milan, Birmingham, and Detroit are **cybernated**. This means that computers control and operate automatic machinery along assembly lines to produce such finished products as toys, calculators, computers, steel, and automobiles. Robotic devices with interchangeable, multipurpose arms and reprogrammable memories can perform a given task repeatedly without complaint, and make "ideal" employees. Cybernation has become a highly controversial issue because of its negative effect on specific types of employment.

Industrial robots assemble automobiles along a production line in a Chrysler K car plant.

Courtesy of Time, Inc. Photo by David Franklin.

Sparks fly as the robot bonds the metal. The programmable devices are able to perform many of the assembly jobs such as welding, spray painting, and lifting.

Courtesy of Time, Inc. Photo by David Franklin.

Both examples of computerization represent varying degrees of the application called **process control**, which refers to the ability of a computer to operate machinery external to the computer system itself. In addition to manufacturing products, process control can also be used to monitor and control chemical plants, power generating stations, blast furnaces, and sewage treatment plants.

Computers Help Researchers

Computers make excellent research tools. Advances in such fields as medicine, chemistry, engineering, aeronautics, economics, meteorology, and astronomy have been increasingly dependent on calculations which computers can provide. Researchers can test a theory by creating a computer model. A **computer model**, also referred to as a computer simulation, is a series of mathematical equations which represent variables in a real-life situation. By changing some of the variables in the model, researchers can observe what effect this would have on the entire situation.

Suppose some mechanical engineers completed the blueprint for an expansion bridge which would allow vehicles to cross a particular waterway. How can they be sure that the bridge will not collapse once it has been built? The engineers have two choices. They can build the actual bridge, and wait to see what happens. This experimental method, of course, is extremely risky. Or they can design a mathematical representation of the bridge (a computer model) and test it with a computer. The model would include all the things which would put a heavy load on the bridge such as cars, trucks, asphalt, concrete, cables, and even a big snowfall. Once the model is completed, the engineers can then experiment with different values until they arrive at the best combination of materials and design features to support the estimated total weight of the bridge.

Computer models, however, are only as accurate as the information they are supplied with. One engineer, for example, while designing a Canadian university library, used a computer model to calculate the building's total mass. He needed this figure because the ground on which the building was to be erected could only hold a certain mass before compressing and sinking. Six months after the building's completion, it started to tilt and sink.

The engineer was astonished! What had gone wrong? He checked his computer figures for several days before he discovered the answer. He had forgotten to include the mass of the two million books that would be on the library shelves. The computer had given the right answer for the information it had been fed, but unfortunately, the programmer's values were incomplete.

Often, special peripherals are used to make computer simulation easier. A graphics designer, for example, may draw a picture directly onto a visual screen or a graphics tablet using a light pen. A special software program then translates the lines and curves into mathematical equations automatically. This allows the user to concentrate on the design features of the drawing, rather than on the complex mathematical formulas which the computer uses to represent them.

Most branches of financial institutions, such as banks or trust companies, use **teller terminals** to process banking transactions. These specialized computer terminals are directly linked to distant mainframe computer systems, usually located in the company's head office.

Suppose that a customer wishes to withdraw $60 from her savings account. The teller first checks to see if there is a sufficient amount in the customer's account to cover the withdrawal by keying in the customer's account number on the terminal keyboard. The computer uses the account number to locate the customer's balance stored on magnetic disk, then types the amount on the small terminal printer for the teller to see.

By looking at the balance, the teller can decide whether to enter the latest transaction. If she does, the computer automatically changes the customer's balance on magnetic disk, and updates the customer's passbook inserted in the printer.

Customers can also use an **automated teller terminal** located on the outside wall of the bank to process banking transactions. By inserting an identification card into a slot, and entering an identification number on a keypad, the terminal will respond to requests to deposit, withdraw, or transfer money.

If a withdrawal is made, the machine opens a drawer containing a specific sum of money, and provides the customer with a printed receipt of the transaction for future reference.

A printer updates a customer's passbook. Records of customer accounts may be stored in a computer system several miles from the bank.

Courtesy of IBM Canada Ltd.

Computers That Teach

There has been a dramatic increase, at all levels of education, in the use of display screens and keyboards as learning environments. By combining graphics, computer simulation, and conversational programming, instructors can create lessons to help students understand almost any topic. This application of computers is referred to as **computer-assisted instruction**, or CAI.

Medical, engineering, and business administration students use computer simulations to increase their knowledge. Interns and nurses practise making diagnoses while studying a simulated human body and vital signs. Mechanical engineers use computer modelling to draw and test various designs. Business administration candidates modify marketing and production levels in a simulated company to observe the effects of their decisions on the company's profit.

One popular testing technique is to employ multiple choice questions which students can respond to at the keyboard. Lessons and tests can be displayed in any spoken language, and for any grade level. CAI programs also allow students to work at their own speed, and at their own level of ability.

Videodisk machines can be attached to computer systems to allow sophisticated movies, sound, and actual photographs to enhance the lesson.

Keeping Track of Moving Vehicles

Traffic congestion in city streets, in crowded rail yards, and in the air over metropolitan airports presents a frustrating problem for traffic controllers. Fortunately, computer systems have been designed to monitor the movement of vehicles, and reduce traffic congestion.

Toronto, for example, has several square miles of traffic lights under computer control. Optical scanners, mounted on poles, can detect the presence of cars at a stop light, or monitor the flow of traffic on a section of roadway. The computer can be instructed to give certain route priorities during rush hours. All the lights along this route will appear green to a driver who is travelling within the legal speed limit.

Railway cars can also be monitored with optical scanners placed along the railway tracks. Each piece of rolling stock contains a

The traffic light display board for metropolitan Toronto helps to pinpoint bottlenecks in the flow of traffic.

Photo Courtesy of Paul Rehak.

pattern of coloured stripes, referred to as **strip coding**. The strip coding contains information as to the type of car (tanker, boxcar, or flatcar), and serial number. The optical scanners can detect the code even if the train is moving at speeds up to 100 km/h. The information is relayed to the computer system at the railyard traffic control centre. The serial number is then used to find more information about the car — owner, manifest, and destination — by searching the appropriate file on magnetic disk. The information can then be displayed on a lighted traffic board, or in the form of a printout.

Using these techniques, a computer system monitoring large railyards like those in Winnipeg, Toronto, and Montreal can ensure that boxcars containing perishable products or other merchandise will be correctly routed and will arrive at their destination on time.

The optical scanner mounted on the pole is reading the coloured stripes on the railway rolling stock. This coded information is relayed to the computer centre.

Courtesy of Canada National.

The control room operator is able to locate the position of every railway car with the help of a display board and a computer printout.

Courtesy of Canadian National.

Air traffic controllers rely heavily on computerized radar systems to prevent air disasters. It is common for several airplanes to be "stacked up" in the air, flying 150 m apart, waiting for permission to land at some busy international airport. A computer system takes the impulses from the radar scanner and superimposes an identification code on it, which then follows the impulses, representing airplanes, across the traffic controller's viewing screen. This helps the controllers to identify the airplanes, and to communicate instructions to the pilots.

Without the "number crunching" ability of computer systems, traffic congestion would make modern-day travel almost an impossibility in large urban centres.

Consumer Products

Electronic appliance and toy manufacturers have found may uses for the integrated circuits produced by the computer industry. Computer chips are found in pocket calculators, digital watches and clocks, cassette decks, children's toys, electronic games, and programmable appliances such as microwave ovens and some record turntables.

The "Prince-on-Board" computer provides motorists with 50 functions such as fuel economy data, vehicle location, and trip information.

Courtesy of Crown Products Group.

When a computer chip is limited to one specific purpose, as in the operation of the items mentioned above, it is referred to as a **dedicated processor**. This means that the set of instructions for operating the toy or appliance cannot be altered.

Many toy and electronic game manufacturers include voice synthesizers or sound generators with their product. One commercially popular learning aid called "Speak and Spell"® responds to the user not only by displaying the words, but "speaking" them as well in a mechanically toned voice: *C-A-T...Cat.*

This popular learning aid provides both visual and auditory confirmation of a correctly spelled word. The device contains a keyboard, visual screen, and a voice response unit.

Courtesy of Texas Instruments Inc.

Computers can also be used to monitor and manipulate other appliances or devices with the help of home environment control programs. These programs allow the computer to centralize heating and cooling systems, fire and theft alarms, and lighting. Some creative people even use the computer to open and close curtains, or vacuum rugs by remote control.

Telephone companies are offering telephone cable information services similar to TV cable. By using a push-button remote control device as input, a phone adaptor as a communication link, and a television set as output, home owners can gain access to distant computerized information. The system permits the user to play electronic TV games, order tickets for a local concert, or view listings of department store sales or real estate deals. Eventually, the service may be expanded to include major government services: educational, medical consulting, library research, and electronic voting on political issues.

Some recent suburban model homes in Winnipeg were constructed with built-in computer systems. These computers permit centralized environmental control, automatic police and fire calls with the push of a button, and will store messages for family members. Can you imagine a viewing screen in the kitchen which displayed this kind of message:

```
"JUNE . . . BOB CALLED.  HE
GOT  THE  CONCERT  TICKETS.
LOVE  MOM. "
```

Summary

Computer applications refer to the uses that people find for computers in society. The two earliest uses for computers, dating back to the 1950s, are in business administration and research. There are four categories of reports generally produced by computers for office use—scheduled listings, exception reports, predictive and demand reports. Computer modelling, which refers to a series of mathematical equations representing variables in a real-life situation, is the basis of most research. Such models are used in engineering, economics, and various fields of scientific study.

More recent computer applications include cybernated factories, retail point-of-sale terminals, computer-assisted instruction, monitoring transport vehicles, and personal computing.

Cybernated factories refers to the use of programmable robots along assembly lines to produce finished products. This is probably the most controversial application of computers because it reduces the need for the largest segment of factory employment—unskilled manual labourers.

Stores, banks, hotels, and airports use the time-sharing capability of computer systems to help serve customers. Typically, the clerk interacts with a computer terminal which is connected to a mainframe computer located in some other location.

The development of table-top micro-computers has promoted widespread adoption of computers as teaching tools and household appliances. Schools use microcomputers for computer-assisted instruction and computer simulation. Home owners presently use them for entertainment, financial management, and data storage and retrieval.

Traffic congestion in crowded urban centres can be reduced through the monitoring and control of vehicle movement. Automobiles, railway rolling stock, and airplanes can be digitally represented inside a computer system. This information can then be used to direct the flow of traffic.

Dedicated processors, computer chips with a fixed set of instructions, are used in many consumer toys and appliances. This represents an application of computer integrated circuitry rather than an entire computer system to the improvement of consumer products.

Review Questions

These are *general level questions* which may require factual recall, reading comprehension, and some application of the knowledge from this chapter.

1. Not all computer-generated office reports are efficient. Describe both a scheduled listing and an exception report. Then explain why one type is more efficient than the other.

2. Describe and give an example of a predictive report.

3. Describe how a data base is used to produce a demand report.

4. What does *word processing* refer to? If office buildings adopt word processing equipment, what type of traditional office equipment will decline in use?

5. How is it possible to send letters to business colleagues without using the mail?

6. Describe a cybernated factory. Why is cybernation a controversial application of computers?

7. Automated machines and cybernated factories are both examples of *process control*. Describe the process and give some additional examples.

8. What is a *computer model*? Why are computer models popular among all types of researchers?

9. Name two peripherals which can be added to a computer system to make computer models easier to display graphically. How does this equipment make it easier?

10. What is a flight simulator? How does it assist airline companies?

11. What advantages does a point-of-sale terminal have over a cash register?

12. Some grocery stores have a specialized input device built into the checkout counter. Explain its function.

13. How does a bank teller know if he or she should process a withdrawal slip from a customer?

14. Some people do their banking after the bank is closed. How do they do that?

15. What does computer-assisted instruction refer to? Describe an application of CAI.

16. Why is it possible, at certain times of the day, for a driver to travel across the city within the legal speed limit and always encounter green traffic lights?

17. Describe how railway rolling stock can be monitored even when the trains are moving.

18. How are computers used to assist air traffic controllers?

19. What is a *dedicated processor*? What uses have manufacturers found for it?

20. Describe two popular applications of a personal computer.

21. What tasks can a home environment control program perform?

22. Describe a special computer-related service which telephone companies are offering to customers.

Applying Your Knowledge

These *advanced level questions* assume an understanding of the material presented in this chapter, and provide new situations which may require evaluation, analysis, or application of that knowledge.

1. A sales manager in a large manufacturing company receives a fourteen-page printout each Monday morning from the data processing department. The printout lists each sales person on the staff, their weekly sales, and their year-to-date sales.

   It takes the sales manager an hour to review the list and decide what instructions to give the sales staff. What would be a better method of reporting the data which would reduce the manager's paperwork? Give reasons for your answer.

2. Explain why a computer system, capable of printing demand reports, would take more expertise and time to set up than any other reporting technique.

3. Suppose a company executive decided to purchase word processing work stations for the secretarial staff, as well as computer terminals for the various office managers. Suggest some problems that you think would arise when the computer system is brought into the office.

4. Several automobile manufacturers around the world have cybernated their factories. (a) Explain some advantages that this would give the company owners. (b) What type of labourers would be replaced by the programmable robots? (c) Suggest some new types of jobs that this type of company would create.

5. Suppose a pharmaceutical company is investigating various types of chemical compounds in an attempt to develop a cure for a certain disease. How could the company ensure effective research without actually performing all the chemical combinations?

6. How does a computer system in a retail store check to see if a customer's credit card is either stolen or represents a delinquent account?

7. Most grocery store items contain a universal product code patch somewhere on the labelling or packaging.
   (a) How would a laser scanner in a checkout counter interpret the code?
   (b) What information do you think the preprinted, manufacturer's code contains?

8. Banks use time-sharing computers and teleprocessing to handle their customer's banking transactions. Explain that statement.

9. Many banks have automated teller terminals on the outside wall of the building. What features prevent a thief from using a stolen I.D. card to withdraw money from a customer's account?

10. Suggest how computer-assisted instruction could be used to help teach automobile mechanics.

11. Suppose that east-west traffic across a city is given priority during the evening rush hour. How could a computerized traffic system recognize if cars were stopped at north-south traffic lights, be able to assist them, and still keep the heavy east-west traffic flowing smoothly?

12. Railway rolling stock has coloured "strip coding" on it which can be read by an optical scanner. What information do you think the permanent stripes contain?

13. Why is a computer chip in a digital watch referred to as a *dedicated processor*?

14. Suppose that you had a personal computer of your own. Suggest some things that you would use it for.

15. If your family subscribed to a telephone or cable company's computerized information service, suggest some types of information to which you would be interested in getting access.

Projects

1. Programming Project

Plan and code a program which would display students' names and their term mark in two different ways. The first way is to be a scheduled listing of all data. The second printout will be an exception report which only contains students who have marks over 75%.

```
FRAN  BOYCHUK        5 6
PAUL  GORDON         7 8
TERRY  SMITH         8 9
JENNY  WALLINSKI     7 1
JOAN  MORSE          6 9
AL  LINSAY           5 5
GARY  WONG           3 6
GEORGE  FISHER       6 7
JOYCE  LEES          9 5
IRIS  KELLEY         8 4
```

2. Bulletin Board Display

Plan and prepare a bulletin board display on computer applications which would illustrate either (a) a certain use of computers, or (b) a variety of computer applications. Give the display an appropriate title. The final product will be judged for neatness, organization, creativity, and effort.

3. Slide Presentation

Using a 35 mm camera and colour slide film, obtain at least fifteen clear pictures of computer applications. Arrange the slides into a pleasing theme, then show them to the class in the form of a slide-talk presentation.

4. A Research Paper
Advanced level

Prepare a typed research paper on a specific computer application. Use at least three different bibliography sources and include footnotes whenever ideas other than your own are used in the body of the paper. Bibliography resources may include books, magazines, newspapers, encyclopedias, and personal interviews.

STEVE BOOTH!

List of Topics

(a) CAI—Computers That Teach
(b) Computerized Banking
(c) Cybernated Industries
(d) Computers in Hospitals
(e) Space Exploration and the Computer
(f) How City Hall Uses Computers
(g) Computers and Law Enforcement
(h) Computers in Grocery Stores
(i) Computers in Retail Stores
(j) History of Computer Uses (since 1945)
(k) History of Computer Circuitry
(l) Theft by Computer
(m) Coming—A Cashless Society?
(n) Computers in Transportation
(o) How I Would Computerize My Home
(p) Computers and National Defence
(q) Biography of Charles Babbage
(r) Biography of John Watson—IBM
(s) Computers in the Post Office
(t) Any other topic, with permission of your instructor

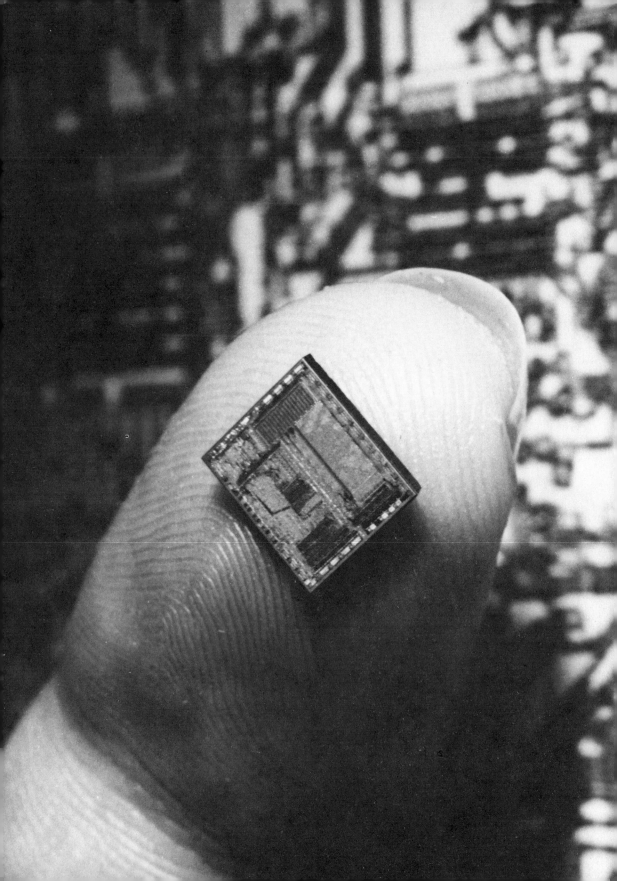

13

Impact
of Computers
on Society

Objectives

An understanding of the beneficial effects of computers on productivity and thinking capabilities

An understanding of the job displacement caused by new technologies

An awareness of the consumer frustation caused by companies with inadequate computer systems

An understanding of the process of electronic funds transfer and the trend towards a "cashless society"

An understanding of the negative impact which uncontrolled centralized data banks can have on individual privacy

An awareness of the need for changes in attitude towards leisure time

When one considers that an entire computer can be held on the tip of a finger, the potential impact of such a technology is awesome.

Courtesy of Intel Corporation.

Chapter Thirteen
Impact of Computers on Society

Upon seeing one of the first noisy, experimental automobiles, a horse-carriage dealer remarked, "It's just a toy for rich folk. Nothing will come of it!"

Computers are having a powerful effect on the way people live in society. Unlike other fixed-purpose inventions such as the automobile, electric lights, or television, computer technology can be endlessly modified through its programming. It can guide spacecraft, teach, make medical diagnoses, search criminal files, draw three-dimensional pictures, talk, generate music, and even operate complete factories without assistance.

Like all other inventions, however, computers are neither good nor evil. What people decide to do with them will determine whether we view computers in a positive or negative way.

It is not enough to study what applications computers are suited for. Any complex technology, if it becomes popular, can cause changes in society. It may affect our work habits, leisure time, our view of the world, and the way we perceive ourselves as human beings. The super-intelligent computers and robots of the future may indeed alter our lifestyles.

Increased Productivity

One of the benefits of having a computer system is that it allows people to accomplish more tasks with greater speed and accuracy than they previously did. Since more jobs can be done within a given time period, it can be described as an increase in productivity. Some computer specialists refer to this as increased throughput.

Projects and experiments which used to take several years to complete, now take weeks or days with the aid of a computer.

Courtesy of Computing Canada.

Expanding Thinking Capabilities

Just as engines have increased what humans can do physically, computers have expanded what humans can do mentally. Motors and engines allow us to fly, outrun any animal, travel enormous distances in a few hours, and lift loads a thousand times our physical strength. Similarly, computers allow humans to calculate very complicated equations, predict future trends, draw three-dimensional, rotating diagrams, and simulate situations that only our imagination can conceive.

Computers have allowed science, medicine, and technical research to jump years ahead of the pen-and-paper method of learning. Most new discoveries and approaches in space research, biochemistry, communications, weather forecasting, warfare, transportation, and engineering are increasingly dependent on the computer.

Office secretaries, for example, can type, edit, and electronically file more error-proof letters with a word processing station than they could with an ordinary typewriter and manual filing system. Teller terminals allow financial institutions to handle an increase in the number and quality of banking transactions. Airline reservation clerks with immediate access to flight times and passenger statistics can complete a transaction in a fraction of the time that it used to take without the aid of a computer system.

Information processing is rapidly becoming one of Canada's major industries. Jobs which involve computers are found in almost every sector of the economy.

Courtesy of NCR Corporation.

Even some advancements in computer technology are being made with the help of a computer. Some companies have programmed computers to design other computer systems which operate faster and more accurately than themselves. This self-generating feature has caused much debate among scientists. What if computers are taught to think for themselves, and then are programmed to make themselves more efficient than their original models? This may lead to a world in which machines contain more "intelligence" than the people who designed them.

Norbert Wiener, who coined the word cybernetics, predicts that as machines learn (as they do in a chess program), they develop unforeseen strategies at rates that baffle their programmers and go beyond the limitations of their human designers. In the future, a systems analyst may teach a computer to learn by itself. Within a few computer generations, that machine may develop thinking ability many times that of the systems analyst, and may, in effect, become the teacher. Mankind, at that point, may be taught by machines to view the world in new ways.

Science fiction writers often use fear of such computers as a plot. In a story by Fredric Brown written about 30 years ago, a super-computer was asked, "Is there a God?" After making sure that its power supply was no longer under human control, it replied, "There is now!"

Changes in the Job Market

All new technologies cause **job obsolescence**. When cars became popular in the early part of this century, blacksmiths, horse ranchers, saddle manufacturers, hay growers, and cobblestone street cleaners all lost their jobs. Their services were no longer needed.

A similar situation is occurring with the increased application of computer systems in today's society. Manual workers and office

managers who work at routine jobs are being displaced. Ordinary typists, filing clerks, mail clerks, shop foreman, office managers, machine operators, typesetters, and assembly line workers can all be replaced by computer technology. Their jobs can now be done faster and more efficiently and automatically with a computer without the need for coffee breaks, sleep, or a vacation.

Imagine the job displacement when electronic mail and electronic newspapers become popular. Postal clerks, mail delivery personnel, typesetters, printing machine operators, photo developers, and many other traditional roles will no longer be needed.

Even professional roles such as doctors, lawyers, and teachers are being challenged. Computers can be programmed to accept test data from interns or nurses, suggest a diagnosis, and recommend treatment. A lawyer's memory of relevant precedent cases can be stored in a computer and retrieved with a cross-index selection program in fractions of a second. Computers can be programmed to teach any subject, and can do so with infinite patience, and individual attention to the learner.

"You mean it's going to take two of those just to replace Hartwell?"

What Will People Do?

The developers of these programs state that new jobs in computer programming, computer manufacturing, word processing, computer operations, numerical control operations, and computer maintenance are being created. People can retrain for these new types of job skills. Indeed, a new generation of workers will have to be educated to supply a job market that computer technology has made distinctly different.

As long as people are willing to move to another job location, and retrain when a job is made obsolete, they will continue to survive economically. Recent newspaper articles on displaced Detroit automobile workers moving to oil-rich Houston (or Canadians moving from Eastern Canada to Alberta) to find jobs suggests that this is what people are doing.

During the last decade, government unemployment statistics still remained relatively low in spite of the increased use of computers in banks, stores, offices, and insurance companies. People managed to find new jobs or, in most cases, stayed with the same company and learned to use computer hardware to perform their old job. You may have noticed that banks that switched to teller terminals as a means of processing transactions have not reduced their clerical staff. In addition, most of the staff now understand how to use the computer terminals.

If the changeover to new computer systems continues to be a slow evolution, rather than a rapid revolution, our society may be able to absorb the displaced workers into new and satisfying roles. The newer roles often require more technical training

A 50-year-old worker whose job disappears because of computers, however, is bound to be skeptical. The news that a new machine will employ many people is only good news if you are one of those people, and if you are willing to relocate and retrain to obtain one of those jobs. It is higly probable that most people will have several different jobs in their lifetime.

Frustration in Dealing with Computer-Oriented Systems

Almost every homeowner has at least once suffered the frustration of receiving a bill, address label, bank statement, or paycheque with incorrect information. Before computerized customer service became popular, people could explain the situation to the appropriate clerk and have the error corrected with relatively little trouble. Today, an incorrect address label may continue unchanged for several months despite a customer's appeal for revision. Requests by a computer for the payment of a bill for $0.00, in several instances, became increasingly threatening even though the customers pleaded that the situation was totally ridiculous. (One customer resolved the problem by sending a cheque for $0.00.)

These problems are usually caused by either a lack of communication between the computer department and the rest of the organization, a programming error, or by clerks who do not understand the computer system.

Large organizations, for example, often hire outside companies to process their labels, bills, or cheques. When a customer sends in a request for a correction, the outside company may not hear about it for several months. A similar situation may occur because the company's own computer department is completely isolated from other areas.

The solution is to provide customer service departments with computer terminals so they have access to customers' files and can change them whenever necessary.

The invoice for $0.00 mentioned earlier was caused by an incomplete computer program. Angry customers have convinced many systems analysts to be more careful in their program designs. There is still a great need for better-trained computer personnel who can understand the complexities of large computer systems.

Clerks who handle customer transactions

are usually not the best people to refer to when a correction is needed. They are so used to handling routine transactions that inconsistencies baffle them. Some poorly trained clerks actually believe that computers never make mistakes. As a result, customers who notice an error are told that they are mistaken. When seeking help, customers should go directly to a manager who, in addition to knowing how to operate a terminal, also understands the entire computer system.

"35 million dollars! I'm afraid our computer is somewhat of a practical joker!"

Electronic Money

Have you noticed a growing trend towards a cashless society in North America? Company employees rarely see their paycheques. Usually wages are deposited directly into the employee's bank account. Department stores, gas stations, travel agencies, hotels, and restaurants now accept a variety of credit cards. Cheques, the most popular substitute for money, also have wide acceptance. Except for buying groceries, newspapers, and small novelties, cash is slowly declining as a medium of exchange.

What is taking its place is a process of moving money electronically from one place to another called **electronic funds transfer**. Instead of transferring money from one person to another, a bank's computer can be instructed to deduct the money from one account, and deposit it in another.

In the future, a purse or wallet full of money may be replaced with a single plastic identification card called a **debit card**. When a purchase is made, the cashier can key in your identification number (probably your social insurance number) and the cost of the item. The electronic cash register, which also acts

as a computer terminal, then sends a message to the computer in your bank. The bank's computer checks your account balance. If the balance is sufficient, the cost of the purchase is automatically deducted from your account and deposited into the store's account.

There is still a strong emotional dependence on money. People like to see and handle money—because it makes them feel rich. So even though computer technology is capable of storing and moving electronic wealth from one location to another, money will remain popular for many years to come.

Invasion of Privacy

Large organizations—various government agencies, credit card companies, and corporations—tend to collect information on people. Computers make large data collection centres possible by providing storage for millions of individual records, and retrieving them in fractions of a second.

Centralized data banks present a problem to individual citizens, however. Most data banks are not secure. This means that it is fairly easy for an outside government agency or some individual who has access to a computer terminal to obtain a printout on anyone they wish.

This easy access to private information can lead to harmful consequences for individuals. Politicians, law enforcement agencies, newspaper reporters, or blackmailers could easily ruin someone's reputation, or cause a loss of a job by publicizing personal data. Historical records stored in a computer system may contain a criminal record, evidence of alcoholism or drug abuse, school records, medical data, references to absenteeism or family relations.

In addition, the information stored on disk or tape about an individual may be false, or simply someone's opinion rather than facts. Consider the following data summary about an individual:

Figure 13.1
Bank Debit Card

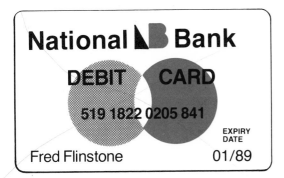

SCHOOL RECORDS: AVERAGE MARKS; REPORTED BEHAVIOURAL PROBLEM. ONE TRUANCY VIOLATION; ABSENTEEISM RATE (18%)

CRIMINAL RECORD: FOUR TRAFFIC VIOLATIONS; CARELESS DRIVING (1978)

CREDIT RATING: THREE MONTH OVERDUE ACCOUNT IN 1980 RESULTING IN A LOWERING OF CREDIT RATING

BANK ACCOUNT: SAVINGS $146.21
              CHEQUING—NONE

MEDICAL DATA: SURGERY 1980, 1983

FAMILY RELATIONS: FATHER: MEMBER OF ALCOHOLICS ANONYMOUS. MOTHER: POLITICAL ACTIVIST

Note that none of the items by themselves are particulary damaging or abnormal. Yet when collected, the report presents a very negative image of that individual.

Computerized records tend to be negative because bureaucracies use the rule of **management by exception** for data collection. Positive comments which would describe the vast majority of people simply would take too much time to key in and too much space within the computer system. So they are ignored. It is easier to record only negative comments. Such computerized records, as a result, usually reflect a very biased viewpoint.

If you were an employer and received that computerized report on someone, would you hire him or her? How would you react on learning that this was your school principal's data history, or a ten-year summary of a local politician?

What Can Be Done?

To prevent information in data centres from being misused, the records must be made secure. Unauthorized people must not gain access to confidential records. In addition, the type of information that one is permitted to view must be relevant to the investigation. For example, medical data records should be made available to doctors, but not to newspaper reporters, politicians, or law enforcement agencies. Similarly, it is reasonable to allow educational institutions to share school marks, but not reasonable to make the marks public knowledge to agencies which are not concerned with learning.

Unfortunately, at the present time, most agencies (government or private) can obtain all kinds of unrelated information on private individuals.

Citizens must be allowed to review and correct computerized records as well as request the removal of outdated information. Something that happened twenty years ago should not be maintained as a permanent reflection of an individual. People change.

The only way that individual privacy can be maintained is by government legislation. To help enforce the laws, a **computer ombudsman** (see Glossary) should be appointed to represent individuals who have been unfairly treated as a result of computerized information. The computer ombudsman would have the power to demand updating or removal of false information stored in any computer system in the country.

If the privacy issue is ignored, governments will create a society in which people will no longer feel free to do as they wish or express an opinion for fear of a permanent, negative computerized report. If we let it happen, the Big Brother of George Orwell's book *1984* will become a reality.

Coping With Leisure Time

Office computers and programmed industrial robots tend to increase productivity. As businesses produce more products and services, management can afford to negotiate more free time for their employees in the form of a shorter work week and longer vacations.

Leisure time, however, will not affect everyone equally. The reductions in work will apply mostly to employees whose responsibilities can be measured by the number of hours that they spend on the job (rather than what they accomplish). This would include secretaries, clerks, office managers, foremen, and factory workers. Another group such as salespersons, doctors, politicians, researchers, scientists, inventors, writers, artists, and business executives will probably continue to work longer hours. These people set their own goals and do not mind spending the extra time striving to attain them.

Curiously, increased leisure time is not welcomed by all groups of society. Immigrants who have recently arrived in Canada, for example, tend to use vacation time working at a part-time job to supplement their income.

Other people find that their concept of self-worth is so closely related to their job that they feel uncomfortable when they are away from work for long periods of time.

North Americans, historically, have regarded nonworking people as lazy and nonproductive. As a result, people with increased leisure time often feel guilty about not working.

Viewing Leisure Time Differently

Since computerization will increase the amount of time we spend away from work, it is important that negative attitudes towards leisure begin to change. Societies must be taught to view leisure time and working time with equal respect.

Leisure time can be used to indulge in specialized hobbies such as carpentry, sculpturing, competitive chess, oil painting, landscaping, gardening, or continued education.

Eventually, people may spend part of their year working for a company, and the other part teaching a craft to a group, lecturing, travelling, playing for a team, designing a house, spending more time with their children, or writing a book. What a great way for a human being to spend their life compared to a lifetime tied to a dreary job. Instead of just a vacation, we will have the time to do something entirely different and exciting.

Summary

It is not enough to study what uses computers are suited for. Any complex technology, if it becomes popular, can cause dramatic changes in society. As individuals, we may not be able to alter the impact such technology has on our lives. An understanding of its impact, however, will help us to accept and cope with the changes.

Consider the impact of the automobile. It has contributed to the development of highways, suburbs, drive-ins, fast food chains, traffic lights, petroleum processing, tire, battery and automobile manufacturing, air pollution, traffic congestion, and jobs for one-sixth of the North American population.

Computer technology is going to have that kind of widespread impact. It will affect our work habits, leisure time, rights to privacy, method of making payments, education, job productivity, and increase our intellectual capacity to solve ever-greater complex problems.

The most visible impact of computer technology will be to make the job market distinctly different from what it is now. Many traditional roles will become obsolete and cause a great number of workers to be displaced. At the same time, computers will give rise to entirely new electronic software and support industries. Workers must be willing to relocate and retrain to maintain their financial position. If the changeover to new computer systems continues to be a slow evolution rather than a rapid revolution, our society may be able to absorb the displaced workers into new and satisfying roles.

Most of the jobs that people will work at twenty years from now have not been invented yet. It is highly probable that the jobs will be computer-related, and quite possible that computer technology will employ more workers than the entire automobile industry.

Review Questions

These are *general level questions* which may require factual recall, reading comprehension, and some application of the knowledge from this chapter.

1. Why are computers different from other fixed-purpose inventions?

2. "Computer systems increase a worker's productivity." Explain that statement and expand your explanation with an example.

3. Explain the similar effect of both engines and computers on human capabilities.

4. What debate has been created by the possibility that computers may someday think for themselves?

5. "All new technologies cause job obsolescence." Explain that statement. Provide three examples of roles that computers will make obsolete.

6. What must people be willing to do when their jobs become obsolete?

7. Computers are said to be causing people to lose their jobs, yet the unemployment statistics still remain relatively low in North America. Explain that apparent contradiction.

8. Name three reasons which would explain why companies which use computers often cause problems for customers.

9. Why are company clerks not the best people to talk to about a computer-related error? Whom should you talk to? Why?

10. Name and define the computer process which may eventually cause a "cashless society."

11. How might people make purchases in the future if they do not carry credit cards, cheques, or cash? Give a typical example to explain how this would work.

12. Why might centralized data banks be feared by many individuals? Explain.

13. Why is there a tendency for computerized records to be negative in their description of people? What effect might this have on potential employers?

14. List the following types of data files. Beside each one, name the type of agency or individual who should be the only ones to have access to the informaton.
    (a) school marks
    (b) medical history
    (c) criminal records
    (d) credit ratings
    (e) tax payments

15. What is a computer ombudsman? What powers should he or she have?

16. Who in the future, probably, will have more leisure timè as a result of increasing productivity? Who, probably, will still work "long hours"?

17. Give three reasons why not all people would want more leisure time.

18. What change must be made in our attitude towards leisure? Why?

Applying Your Knowledge

These *advanced level questions* assume an understanding of the material presented in this chapter, and provide new situations which may require evaluation, analysis, or application of that knowledge.

1. Complex technologies, if they become popular, can cause changes in society. Consider the impact of (a) automobiles and (b) computers on jobs in the following way. For each one, list five jobs that the invention has made obsolete, then list five new jobs that it has created.

2. This chapter mentions that computers expand our mental capabilities. Identify three mental capabilities that a computer can imitate and expand. What types of mental activities does the computer allow humans to do that we previously could not?

3. Norbert Weiner predicted that "as machines learn, they develop unforeseen strategies at rates that baffle their programmer, and go beyond the limitation of their human designers." Why do many people find this idea frightening?

4. Describe the computer hardware that would be necessary for a retail store and a bank to establish an electronic funds transfer system.

5. How would messages about customer transactions get to the bank from the retail store? How would this EFT system work if the bank closed while the store still remained open?

6. What advantages do you think EFT provides? Name two disadvantages.

7. George Orwell's novel *1984* described a government which kept a large centralized data bank. Suggest why many people, including writers, fear the establishment of government-operated, computerized information centres.

8. Suppose that you discovered that a data file about you contained false information, or someone's opinion rather than facts. What would you do? Explain.

9. In the future, increased productivity caused by computers may allow people to work for part of the year, then do something else for the remainder. Suggest three different things (other than watching TV or doing nothing) that you would do if you had three months each year to pursue other activities.

Individual Projects

1. Presentation of a Novel

Many writers have strong fears of the uncontrolled use of computers and robots. Often, science fiction writers include them as either a villain or as part of the story's setting.

Read one of the following stories. Prepare a short summary to present to the class. Identify the role of the computer or robot in the story (villain or setting) and explain the fear(s) that the author is attempting to communicate to the reader.

(a) *2001: A Space Odyssey*, Arthur C. Clarke
(b) *Rossum's Universal Robots*, P. Selver and N. Playfair
(c) *The Hummanoids*, Jack Williamson
(d) *Player Piano*, Kurt Vonnegut
(e) *1984*, George Orwell
(f) Any other science fiction novel, with permission of your teacher, that concentrates on robots or artificial intelligence.

2. Great Thinkers on Computers— Research Report
Advanced level

Research information about the ideas one of the following people have written. Prepare a summary for the class. In your report, concentrate on the person's ideas, rather than their biography.

Great Thinkers

(a) Norbert Wiener
(b) John Von Neumann
(c) Alan M. Turing
(d) Norman Cousins
(e) Arthur L. Samuel

Suggested Sources

(a) *Computers and Man*, Richard C. Dorf
(b) *The Computer and the Brain*, John Von Neumann
(c) *The Human Use of Human Beings*, Norbert Wiener
(d) *Scientific American*, Reprints on specific authors
(e) *The Computer Prophets*, Jerry Rosenberg
(f) *God and Golem, Inc.,* Norbert Wiener

14

A Structured Approach to Planning Solutions

Objectives

An understanding of the reasons for the development of a structured approach to planning computer programs

A working knowledge of the three basic control structures—Sequence, Repetition, and Selection

A working knowledge of some applications of structured programming

The major cost of most computer installations stems from the development of application software. New planning and programming techniques are required to reduce the time and cost of such development.

Courtesy of Honeywell Inc.

Chapter Fourteen

A Structured Approach to Planning Solutions

People who write programs without considering the costs of debugging and modification are similar to golfers completing a game without counting the strokes. Neither group is very effective in its performance.

In the past, good programmers were thought to be those who, without planning, wrote clever, tricky code that took up the least amount of main memory and ran in the least possible time. Now that computers contain large main memories and fast microprocessors, this type of thinking is discouraged. In fact, programmers using that approach often cause more problems than they solve.

Insufficient planning, for example, may lead to a program which requires so many changes to correct errors or omissions that it resembles a patchwork quilt. In addition, patchwork coding is often held together by several **goto** statements. When the need arises for a change in such a program, other programmers usually find it difficult to read and understand. Because of the interconnecting **goto** statements, a single modification may affect several parts of the program at the same time. All these factors contribute to long and costly delays in the development of high quality and usuable software. Some company managers have indicated that the costs of updating and modifying a program can be three to five times as much as it took to produce the original program.

What Is the Alternative?

To eliminate the problems created by old-style programs, most computer installations are switching to a technique referred to as **structured programming**. It requires programmers to plan, code, and test computer programs in a systematic and organized way.

One of the most visible characteristics of a structured program is that it consists of independent **blocks**, or **modules**, of code. When a block of code is altered, it does not affect the other sections of the program. This allows programs to be corrected and modified in a relatively short period of time.

When good programming techniques are added to the block appearance, the result are programs which are readable, easy to understand, and easy to modify.

Structured languages such as recent versions of FORTRAN, BASIC, and PASCAL contain new instructions for decision making and looping. These instructions help to create the blocks or modules of code.

This chapter explains one planning technique which is well-suited to structured programs, namely, structured flowcharting.

Flowchart Symbols

A structured flowchart only uses seven symbols in its construction. Each symbol represents a different type of action that the computer must perform.

Those readers who are familiar with traditional flowcharting should note the new uses for both the decision symbol and the exit symbol. The successful design of a structured flowchart depends strongly on the new applications of these two symbols. The following chart illustrates all of the structured flowchart symbols as well as a sample of their application.

Figure 14.1
Symbols Used in Structured Flowcharting

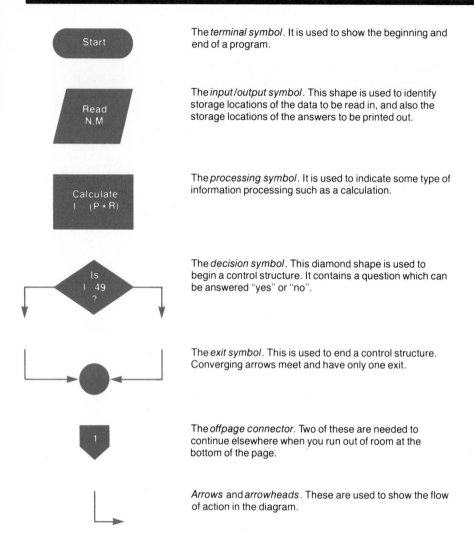

The *terminal symbol*. It is used to show the beginning and end of a program.

The *input/output symbol*. This shape is used to identify storage locations of the data to be read in, and also the storage locations of the answers to be printed out.

The *processing symbol*. It is used to indicate some type of information processing such as a calculation.

The *decision symbol*. This diamond shape is used to begin a control structure. It contains a question which can be answered "yes" or "no".

The *exit symbol*. This is used to end a control structure. Converging arrows meet and have only one exit.

The *offpage connector*. Two of these are needed to continue elsewhere when you run out of room at the bottom of the page.

Arrows and *arrowheads*. These are used to show the flow of action in the diagram.

Program Structures

The idea of structured programming was introduced in 1964 by two mathematicians, **Corrado Bohm** and **Guiseppe Jacopini**. They discovered that three basic structures could be used to express any programming logic, no matter how complex. These basic control structures are : (1) Sequence; (2) Selection: (3) Repetition. **Structured programming** can be defined as a method of programming which uses these three basic control structures to form readable blocks of code.

Sequence

Sequence is the simplest of the three control structures. One event occurs immediately after the other. Rectangular boxes contain the processing steps which the computer is to perform.

Figure 14.2
Sequence Structure

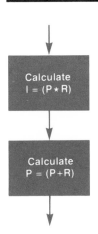

Selection

The second control structure provides the computer with two alternatives. If a certain **test condition** is true, one alternative is carried out. If the condition is false, the other alternative is performed.

In structured programming, an *if-then-else* block of code is used to provide the alternatives. These coding commands can be superimposed onto the flowchart to illustrate the actions to be taken with each alternative. The *if then* alternative represents the actions the computer must take if the "test" condition is true, while the *else do* alternative represents the actions that computer must take if the "test" condition is false. It is possible for one of the alternatives to contain nothing at all. This is referred to as a **null alternative**. In that situation, the *else do* command in actual coding is left out. In the flowchart, the false alternative continues in a pattern similar to the other side, but contains no instructions.

For example, if a program is reading in employee records, one at a time, the condition may be to determine "is the employee male?." A yes answer to that "test" condition would cause the *if then* portion of the program to operate. If the answer happens to be no, the *else do* portion of the program would be executed.

Figure 14.3
Selection Structure

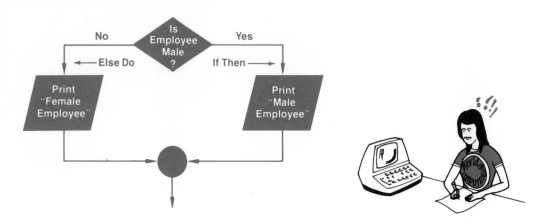

Repetition

The third logical structure, the repetition structure, is used to permit looping. **Looping** refers
to a sequence of instructions which are
repeated as long as a certain condition
remains true. During the looping process, the
computer must be given a logical way to exit
from the loop. Without this information, the
computer would continue to process the same
set of instructions over and over and produce
some undesirable results. A loop which does
not have a logical way to exit is called an
infinite or **endless loop** and occurs as a
result of poor program design.

There are two ways to prevent infinite
loops from occurring during the design of repetition structures. The first method is to use a
counter. This concept requires three components: an equation to count the number of
loops; a storage location with an initial value to
store the answers produced by the equation; a
test condition to allow a logical exit from the
loop.

Each time the computer repeats a set of
instructions, the counter adds the value one to

the storage location, and then the test condition is performed. If the required number of loops has occurred, the computer is instructed to exit from the loop.

Suppose, for example, that the phrase "Charlie is a nice person" is to be printed ten times. To achieve this, a counter can be used. The letter C (one of the many possible storage locations in main memory) is assigned an initial value of one. This is referred to as **initializing the counter**. A test condition checks to see if the counter is less than or equal to ten. If the answer is yes, the computer prints the phrase, adds the value one to the counter, and then returns to the test condition. This looping process continues until the condition is no longer true. Then the computer is instructed to stop.

Figure 14.4

Repetition Structure—Counter Method

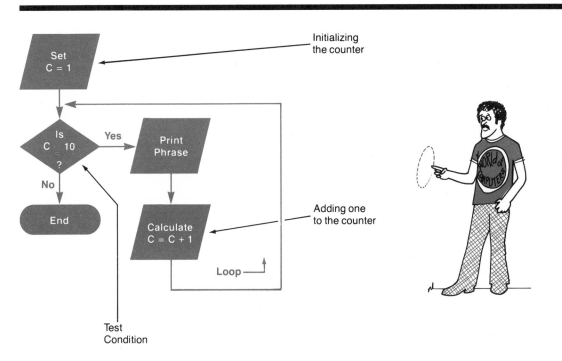

A second method to prevent an infinite loop is to use an end-of-file check. It can be used when a list of items are being read into the computer a few items at a time. A computer needs to be informed when the end of the list occurs; otherwise, it will attempt to continue reading even though there is no more data. To inform the computer of the end, an arbitrary dummy name, in this case the word *last*, is placed at the end of the list. The computer is then instructed to continue looping as long as the word *last* is not encountered. This particular process is referred to as an **end-of-file check**.

Figure 14.5
Repetition Structure—End-of-File Method

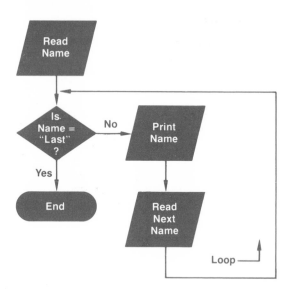

Putting the Structures To Use

The three basic structures described above can be used to plan the solution to any computer problem. Suppose that you were required to plan the solution which would print ten different answers to the equation $T = (10 * B) + 18$, where B is a variable which begins with the value of one and increments one at a time. The plan would appear as shown below.

Planning for Problem Using Three Basic Structures

Problem Definition

Print ten different answers to the equation $T = (10 * B) + 18$ where B increments one at a time.

Data Values

$B = 1$

Figure 14.6

Flowchart for Problem Using Three Basic Structures

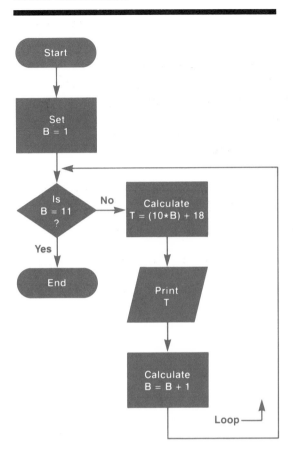

You may have noticed that the solution used a **counter**, namely, (B = B + 1), to keep track of the numbers of answers being printed. The first B in the equation is the unknown. The second B was previously defined at the beginning of the program to have a value of one.

In a structured flowchart, the left-hand side of the diagram is the **main line** of the program, while the steps within any *repetition* structure are offset to the right. The loop itself is almost completely enclosed by a right-side flowline, which returns to the main line of the program.

Including the Selection Structure

Suppose you were required to write a program which would read a list of names and marks, one record at a time, and from the list select only those students who obtained marks of 80% or better. These names are to be printed under the title *Honour List*.

Planning for Honour List Including the Selection Structure

Problem Definition

Under the title Honour List, print only those names and marks of students who obtained over 79%.

Dummy Record : "LAST", 00

Typical Data Record

N = Student's name
M = Student's mark

Figure 14.7

Flowchart for Honour List Including the Selection Structure

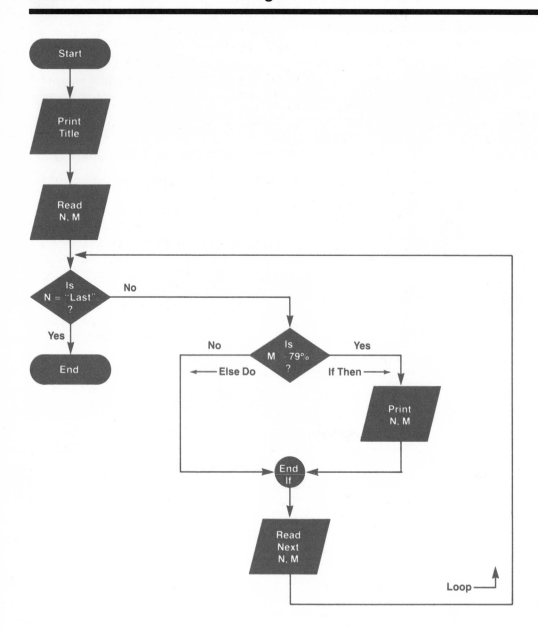

The purpose of the *repetition* structure is to allow a series of steps to be repeated several times until a certain condition is met. In the last flowchart, a list of names and marks are being read, one record at a time, until an arbitrary dummy name is encountered. When that happens, the computer is instructed to stop.

The *selection* structure is designed to make a comparison between a given constant and the latest variable. Alternative programming choices are provided, depending on whether the constant is equal to, greater than, or less than the variable. In the *Honour List* problem, each student's mark is compared to the constant value 79%. If the student's mark is greater than 79%, the computer is instructed to print the record. If the student's mark is 79% or less, the computer is told to simply read the next student's name and mark.

Multiple Selection Structures

Most programs contain more than one selection structure. If several programming structures are encountered, each additional structure is placed within the first one. This makes is easy to see where one structure begins and ends within the body of the program. This is an important concept, because each structure has a definite beginning and end in actual programming.

Female Honour List Problem

To illustrate how multiple structures would appear in a flowchart, suppose that the *Honour List* problem is redefined to print only a list of students who are both female and have a mark greater than 79%. The data record, in this case, would need to contain the student's name, code 0, or 1, representing male and female, respectively, and the student's mark.

In the solution to this problem, there are two *selection* structures to determine the selection of the requested students, and one *repetition* structure to continue the looping process until all data records have been read and processed.

Figure 14.8
Flowchart for List of Female Honour Students Problem

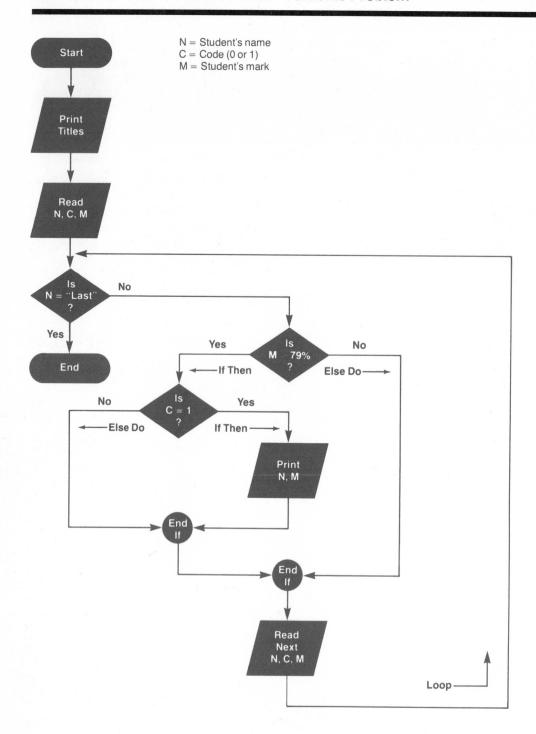

N = Student's name
C = Code (0 or 1)
M = Student's mark

Summary

A traditional knowledge of how to write programming code, however clever, is not enough to meet the needs of today's working world.

Writing computer programs without first planning the steps usually leads to long delays while the frustrated programmer spends hours correcting errors and omissions. The result is often a program with so many modifications that it resembles a patchwork quilt. Typically, the program is both difficult to read and difficult to modify.

In 1964, two mathematicians introduced a planning technique referred to as structured programming. This method of program design uses three basic control structures to express any programming logic, no matter how complex. The three control structures are the Sequence; a method of looping called the Repetition structure; and a method of providing programming choices called the Selection structure.

Whichever planning technique a programmer eventually chooses, successful application can only come with practice. There are also other planning techniques (see Chapter Three) available to people who wish to learn structured programming, including top down development, Warnier-Orr diagrams, structure diagrams, and pseudo-code.

Review Questions

These are *general level questions* which may require factual recall, reading comprehension, and some application of the knowledge from this chapter.

1. What type of skills were formerly considered to be sufficient for a computer programmer?

2. Give two reasons why the old approach to programming causes more problems than it solves.

3. What method has been proposed to eliminate problems created by old-style programs? Explain.

4. What advantage does structured programming provide? How is this done?

5. Who introduced the concept of structured programming? Why is it considered to be a simple method?

6. Name three basic control structures.

7. Using a flowchart template, plan the *sequence* solution to the following problem. A sum of $500 was invested at a 12% annual rate of interest. Calculate and print the dollar amount of interest for one year.

8. Plan the flowchart *sequence* to the following problem. Bob Smart's term marks are: English 68, Math 71, French 78, Computers 84. Read in the data, then calculate and print his term average.

9. Plan the flowchart *sequence* for this problem. Betty Feldon purchased on credit a video tape recorder worth $985 to attach to her television set. If the department store charged 24% annually, calculate
   (a) the dollar amount of monthly interest;
   (b) the balance owing (if left unpaid) by the end of the first month. .

10. Flowchart **only** the *selection* structure for this situation: a decision which asks "Is the number equal to 100?" If the answer is yes, calculate N = N + 1. If the answer is negative, no processing takes place.

11. Flowchart **only** the *selection* structure for this situation: a decision which asks "Is the mark greater than 70%?" If the answer is yes, print "The student is recommended." If the answer is no, print "Must write final exam."

12. Flowchart **only** the *selection* structure for this situation: a decision which asks "Is the employee female?" If the answer is yes, print "Female" and calculate $F = F + 1$. If the answer is no, print "Male," and calculate $M = M + 1$.

13. Flowchart the steps related to this *repetition* structure: a decision which asks "Is the name equal to Last?" If the answer is yes, instruct the computer to stop. If the answer is no, print Name, Mark, read next name and mark, and then loop back to the decision.

14. Flowchart the steps related to this *repetition* structure: a decision which asks "Is C $= 10$?" If the answer is yes, instruct the computer to stop. If no, calculate $T = 50 * W$; print T; calculate $C = C + 1$; loop back to the decision.

15. Flowchart the steps related to this *repetition* structure: a decision which asks " Is C $= 000$?" If the answer is yes, instruct the computer to stop. If no, print the Product Name, and Cost; calculate $T = T + C$; read next name and cost; loop back to the decision.

Applying Your Knowledge

These *advanced level questions* assume an understanding of the material presented in this chapter, and provide new situations which may require evaluation, anaylsis, or application of that knowledge.

1. **Term Report**

   The office of a local high school wants a program which would read in each student's name, along with four subject marks. Once the average has been calculated, the student's name and term average is printed. The program must be able to handle over 900 students.

2. **Changing Variable Problem**

   Solve the following equation which contains the variable X beginning at the value 5, and increasing five at a time until a total of 50 answers has been printed.

   Equation: $A = 2250 /(2.5) * (X)$

   Print both the value of X and the answer to the equation each time.

3. **Bank Investment**

   Norbert Casey invested a sum of $5000 in a savings account which paid 14% annual rate of interest, compounded semi-annually. Calculate the interest and accumulated balance for each half year for a total of five years.

4. **Positive or Negatives**

   Plan a program which will read in a series of numbers, one at a time; determine whether it is a positive number or a negative number; then either print it in the first column under the title Positive Numbers, or in the second column under the title Negative Numbers.

5. Metric Conversions

A government consumer agency wants to convert all its consumer information into metric measurements. At present, some weights have been expressed as pounds, while others are shown in kilograms. Plan a program which will read in two items at a time. The first item is a one-letter code with the letters M or C. The letter M means that the weight is already in metric and nothing is to be changed, The letter C means that a conversion must take place. The second item is the weight itself. (Note: 1 pound = 0.45 kg)

6. Sorting Numbers

A company needs a program which will read in any three numbers, sort and print the numbers from highest to lowest. Use an end-of-file check to make sure that the computer does not read empty space as the next set of numbers are being read.

7. The Credit Card Company

A well-known credit card company has just hired you to plan a program which would determine whether a customer's credit limit (the amount of credit still available to a customer making purchases) is positive or negative. If the credit limit is still positive, print the phrase "Thank you." If the credit limit is negative, print the phrase "Credit limit is exceeded." The program must be capable of reading in a customer's name and credit limit, perform that operation, read the next name and credit limit, then continue that series of events until all credit card customers for that day have been processed.

8. Inventory Reorder List

One manufacturer has a computer card for every product in inventory. Each card contains *Product Name*, *Original Quantity*, *Quantity on Hand*, and *Status*. Status is a one-digit number. The number one means that the product is to be reordered; whereas, the number two means that the product is no longer popular and is not to be reordered. Print a list which would contain each product and the amount to be reordered if the quantities are to be returned to their original levels. If the product is no longer popular, under amount to be reordered, print *No Order*.

15

Structured Basic

"BASIC" was designed as an introductory computer language for beginners. People of all ages find it easy to learn and manipulate.

Objectives

An understanding of the need to eliminate spaghetti programming

An awareness of the four characteristics of a structured program

A working knowledge of the loop structure and the need for a test condition within each loop

A working knowledge of the selection structure

Chapter Fifteen
Structured Basic

Improper use of the goto *command can create troublesome "spaghetti programs."*

Structured BASIC, developed by the University of Waterloo, is a particular version of that computer language. It can be used only if your microcomputer contains software capable of understanding structured BASIC commands. (Such software is available from that university in the form of a single ROM chip.)

Structured BASIC is presented as an independent topic because of its special programming features. It allows programmers to indent instructions to make them more readable. Also, its particular looping and decision instructions form **blocks**, or modules, of code which reduce the time that it takes to correct or modify a program.

This chapter contains only those features which are different from ordinary BASIC. Before studying these features, it is recommended that you practise the introductory programming concepts presented in Chapter Four, as well as the three basic control structures presented in Chapter Fourteen.

Eliminating Spaghetti Programming

The great disadvantage of ordinary BASIC is that a particular command called *goto* allows a programmer to link different parts of a program without regard to the program's overall design. Because it is easy to use, programmers often insert a large number of these commands into a program. The result is a network of criss-crossed *goto* commands which, if they were connected by pencil lines, would give the program the appearance of a plate of spaghetti. Unfortunately, when one error is corrected, or a single modification is required, the interconnected "spaghetti network" causes several other parts of the program to default. Many frustrating hours are spent at the keyboard by unknowledgeable spaghetti programmers.

Structured Thinking

Structured programs contain four noticeable characteristics. The first is that the program is composed of independent *blocks* or *modules of code*. Each block performs a specific function such as making a decision, or repeating a set of instructions. It is possible to test and modify each block as an independent unit without altering the rest of the program. This feature tends to increase a programmer's productivity.

The second feature is its **top down design**. Structured programs tend to be designed in modules which can be processed from the top to the bottom of the program rather than in a multi-directional "spaghetti" fashion. This is possible because the *goto* instruction is eliminated. The program's logic is therefore much easier to follow.

The last two characteristics, *spacing* and *indenting*, are included in the program to make the code easier to read and to debug. The blocks of code can be indented from the main line of the program, and highlighted by leaving spaces before and after each block in the program listing. The main line of the program always remains without indentation at the left-hand margin, while additional structures such as loops and decisions are indented towards the right-hand margin.

Together, these four characteristics produce programs which are readable, easy to understand, and easy to modify.

What Makes Up a Block of Code?

A block or module of code is a series of instructions that go together as a unit. **Programmer comments** such as the program title, the programmer's name, and program description would represent the first block of code.

The **main line of the program** sometimes represents one, two, or three separate blocks of code. They would contain such items as output titles and subtitles, initializing values, calculations, final print statements, and data values.

Two other programming features, **loops and decisions**, are displayed as indented modules. Loops require the computer to repeat a set of instructions. Decisions require the computer to compare two items and then choose alternative programming instructions as a result of the comparison.

Loops — Increasing Your Programming Power

Once you have mastered the simple instructions such as *read, print, tab, end*, and *data*, you are ready to proceed with more powerful programming statements. If your programs have loops or decisions in them, they are more powerful than programs without them. Loops and decisions are capable of getting the computer to do a great deal of processing with very few instructions.

A **loop**, also known as a **repetition struc-ture**, refers to a set of instructions with a defi-nite beginning and ending, which are repeated until a certain test condition is satisfied.

All loops must contain a **test condition**. This is an instruction which allows the com-puter to exit from the loop once a certain con-dition is met. Loops with a poorly designed or absent test condition may cause the looping process to continue far beyond the needs of the program. That situation is referred to as an **infinite** or **endless loop** and is avoided by good programmers. Consider the following example of a test condition.

```
50   IF C = 25 THEN QUIT
```

This line instructs the computer to com-pare a number stored in memory location C. If the number is equal to 25, the computer is then instructed to quit looping. If the number stored in C is not equal to 25, the computer will continue to repeat the set of instructions con-tained within the boundaries of the loop. Con-sider this second example.

```
50   IF N$ = "LAST ONE" THEN QUIT
```

This second test condition illustrates how the computer can compare a variable to a word. If the variable stored in memory location N$ is equal to the phrase *last one*, the com-puter is instructed to quit looping; otherwise, the computer is to continue repeating the set of instructions within the loop.

Loop ... Endloop

A loop or repetition structure can be designed with *loop ... endloop* commands. These are the beginning and ending commands which enclose a set of instructions which are to be repeated a number of times. The example shown below illustrates how these commands are used as "bookends" to enclose the instruc-tions. See if you can figure out what the com-puter is required to do.

```
45   C = 0
50   :
55   LOOP
60      IF C > 100 THEN QUIT
65      PRINT C
70      C = C + 2
75   ENDLOOP
```

If you understood those instructions, you would have concluded that the computer is instructed to print all the even numbers from 0 to 100.

The additional line which came before the loop structure, C = 0, is necessary to tell the computer what value to begin the loop with. This statement is referred to as **initializing the counter**. The counter in this example is the letter C, which increases by the value 2 each time a loop is completed. Counters do not have to start at one. In this case, the value one happened to be appropriate.

Consider the following sample problem which uses a *loop ... endloop* structure as well as a test condition in its solution.

The Lottery Problem

Suppose that you have just won $50 000 in a lottery, and invested the cash at an interest rate of 15%, compounded annually. What would be the value of your investment at the end of ten years?

Coding for the Lottery Problem

```
05    REM   ******************************
10    REM     THE LOTTERY PROBLEM
15    REM   *****************************
20    :
25    :
30    C = 0
35    R = 0.15
40    P = 50000
45    :
50    :
55    LOOP
60      IF C = 10 THEN QUIT
65      I = (P * R)
70      P = (P + I)
75      C = (C + 1)
80    ENDLOOP
85    :
90    :
95    PRINT "THE VALUE OF THE INVESTMENT WOULD BE " ; P
100   END
```

Notice the characteristics of structured programming in the solution to the *Lottery Problem*. Colons are used to create the spaces before and after each block of code. While the top and bottom "bookends" to the loop remains at the left-hand margin, the instructions within the loop are indented towards the right-hand margin.

Practice Assignment

Prepare a program which would print a table to show the equivalent temperatures in Fahrenheit and Celsius. Display the temperatures in five-degree intervals from 0°F to 100°F. Note that C = 1.8 * (F − 32). The table should appear with headings as shown.

FAHRENHEIT	CELSIUS
0	—
5	—
1 0	—
(e t c .)	—

Loops and Data Statements

When a program is required to read and process a series of data records, the same *loop . . . endloop* structure can be used. The test condition is modified to cause the computer to exit from the loop if a dummy record is encountered. A **dummy record**, or **trailer**, refers to an arbitrary name or number placed at the end of a list of items. Its purpose is to inform the computer that there is no more data to be processed. A dummy record must contain the same type and number of items as a typical record. Consider the following problem which requires the computer to process both words and numbers by means of a *loop . . . endloop* structure.

The Term Report Problem

Suppose that you are required to design a program which would read and print four subject titles and their corresponding marks, one set at a time. Once the list is completed, the phrase *Term Average Is* and the answer is to be printed.

Structured BASIC Coding for the Term Report Problem

```
05     REM   ******************************
10     REM      TERM  REPORT  PROBLEM
15     REM   ******************************
20     T = 0
25     :
30     REM ***PRINT SUBJECTS AND ADD MARKS***
35     LOOP
40       READ N$, M
45       IF N$ = "LAST" THEN QUIT
50       PRINT N$, M
55       T = T + M
60     ENDLOOP
65     :
70     REM ***CALCULATING AVERAGE***
75     A = (T/4)
80     PRINT
85     PRINT "TERM AVERAGE IS   "; A
90     :
95     :
100    REM *****DATA RECORDS*****
105    DATA "GEOGRAPHY", 64
110    DATA "POLITICAL SCIENCE",
115    DATA "INTRODUCTION TO BUSINESS", 83
120    DATA "ENGLISH", 69
125    DATA "LAST", 00
130    END
```

Practice Assignment

For this program, you will need the names and ages of five people. Design a program which will read the list of names and ages, one set at a time, then calculate the year of their birth by subtracting their age from the current year.

Remember to include a test condition to prevent an infinite loop. The output is to appear as follows:

```
* * * * * * * * * * * * * * * * * * * * * * * * * * * *

NAME        AGE      YEAR  OF  BIRTH

  * * *      —             —

  * * *      —             —

(etc.)       —             —


* * * * * * * * * * * * * * * * * * * * * * * * * * * *
```

Modifying the Loop Structure

It is possible to combine the test condition and a loop command by using a *while .. endloop* structure. See if you can predict what the output will be from the following program.

```
40    C  =  0                Line 55 serves as both a test
                             condition and the beginning
45    :                      of the loop structure.
50    :
55    WHILE  C  <  11
60        PRINT  C
65        C  =  C  +  1
70    ENDLOOP
```

In the above example, the test condition to prevent an infinite loop and the beginning loop command are combined into one *while* structure.

There are several other variations on the loop structure in structured BASIC. Although the ones illustrated in this chapter should be sufficient to solve most computer problems, programmers who wish more flexibility should consult their computer manual.

Programming Decisions

A decision structure, also known as a selection structure, refers to instructions with a definite beginning and ending, which require the computer to compare two or more items, and then provide alternative programming choices for the computer to perform. Which choice the computer would select would depend on the results of the comparison. It is this type of structure that gives computers their apparent ability to "think."

Decision structures in structured BASIC are written with *if...endif* commands. These are the beginning and ending commands which enclose a set of instructions which will be performed if the *if* condition is true. Consider the following example of an *if...endif* structure.

```
50    IF  B < 0
55        PRINT  "ACCOUNT  OVERDRAWN"
60    ENDIF
```

In this example, the computer has been given two choices. If the value of B (a customer's bank balance) is less than $0.00, the computer is instructed to print the phrase "account overdrawn." If the value of B is equal to or greater than that amount, the computer will ignore the entire structure, and continue with the rest of the program.

If...Else...Endif

A similar selection structure can be used to provide two programming alternatives within the same block of code. To achieve this, an *else* command is inserted between the two choices. For example.

```
50    IF < 0
55        PRINT  "ACCOUNT  OVERDRAWN"
60    ELSE
65        PRINT  "ENTER  TRANSACTION"
70    ENDIF
```

In this example, the computer is instructed to compare the customer's balance with the value $0.00. If the customer's balance is less than that value, the first phrase is printed. If the customer's balance is equal or greater than that amount, the second phrase is printed.

Combining Loops and Decisions

Decisions are often part of a loop within a program. When coded, the decision or selection structure would be highlighted with spaces and indented further towards the right-hand margin than the loop which contains it. Consider the following problem and solution which is illustrated with all the problem-solving steps—problem definition, list of the values, planned solution, and coded solution.

Positive and Negative Answers Problem

Plan and code a program which would read in a list of twelve numbers, three at a time, then add the numbers together. If the sum of the numbers is positive, print the answer in the first column under the title *Positive Answers*. If the sum of the numbers is negative, print the answer in a second column labelled *Negative Answers*. When the computer has completed this task, have it print a bottom row of stars to highlight the two columns.

Planning for Positive and Negative Answers Problem

Problem Definition:

Print two column headings—*positive answers* and *negative answers*. Determine whether the sum of each set of three numbers is positive or negative, and print the sum under the appropriate heading. Print a bottom row of stars.

$S = (A + B + C)$; Dummy Record: 0,0,0

Typical Data Values

A = first number
B = second number
C = third number

Figure 15.1
Flowchart for Positive and Negative Answers Problem

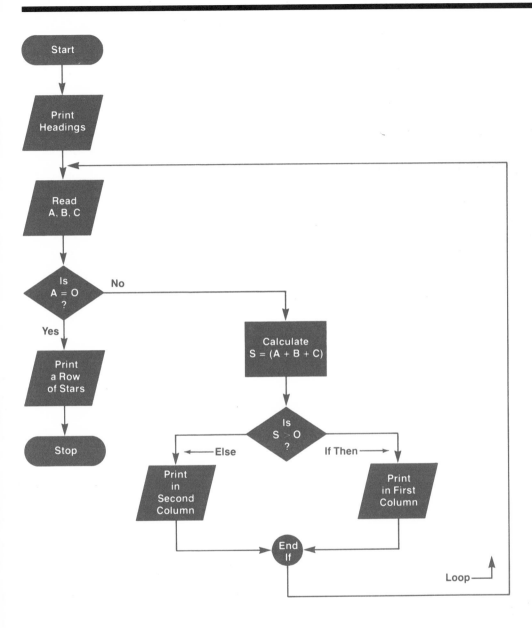

Basic Coding for the Positive and Negative Problem

```
05    REM  *************************************
10    REM   POSITIVE AND NEGATIVE PROBLEM
15    REM  *************************************
20    REM   *** PRINT COLUMN TITLES ***
25    PRINT TAB (5) "POSITIVE ANSWERS" ; TAB (25) "NEGATIVE ANSWERS"
30    :
35    REM *** READ VALUES; CALCULATE SUM ***
40    REM *** PRINT SUMS IN PROPER COLUMNS ***
45    LOOP
50      READ A, B, C
55      IF A = 0 THEN QUIT
60      S = (A + B + C)
65    :
70    :
75        IF S > 0
80          PRINT TAB (10) S
85        ELSE
90          PRINT TAB (30) S
95        ENDIF
100   :
105   ENDLOOP
110   :
115   :
120   REM *** DATA VALUES ***
125   DATA -4,   6,  -9
130   DATA  9,  -8,  -6
135   DATA  5,   8,   4
140   DATA  6,   4,   7
145   DATA  0,   0,   0
150   END
```

Summary

Structured BASIC is a unique version of that computer language. It contains loop and decision structures that are different from any other version of BASIC.

It was created to accommodate a new approach to writing computer programs called top down design. This feature requires the logic of the program to progress in an orderly manner from the top to the bottom of the program. To achieve this feature, the *goto* command, common to most versions of BASIC, is eliminated.

In its place, self-contained blocks, or modules, of code with specific beginning and ending commands are used. These commands only allow one entry and one exit point from each structure.

Programmers also indent loop and decision structures towards the right-hand margin, and highlight them by inserting spaces before and after each block of code.

Top down programming reduces the free-style, spaghetti-like programs that regular programmers encounter. As a result, programmers who use structured BASIC are able to produce better programs in a shorter period of time than traditional programmers.

Review Questions

These are *general level questions* which may require factual recall, reading comprehension, and some application of the knowledge from this chapter.

1. Suppose that a computer enthusiast was planning to purchase a microcomputer, and program in *structured* BASIC. What things should that person consider before making the purchase?

2. What is "spaghetti programming"? Why is it a poor way to design programs?

3. Briefly name and describe four noticeable characteristics of a structured program.

4. Name four different sections of a program which could be represented as individual blocks, or modules, of code. Which modules are indented?

5. Define a *loop structure*.

6. What is a *test condition*? Suppose a computer was processing a loop which did not contain a test condition. What would happen?

7. Explain what the following statement requires the computer to do.

```
60   IF W > 15 THEN QUIT
```

8. Write a line of code which would require the computer to quit a loop if the word *dumbo* is encountered. Use line number 30.

9. Design a repetition structure which would begin with the number one, add all the odd numbers from one to fifty, then print the final answer.

10. Design a repetition structure which would calculate the interest on an investment of $800 for ten years, if the rate of interest is 15% compounded annually. Have the computer print both the annual interest and principal each year for ten years.

11. What does the phrase *initializing the counter* refer to? What is the purpose of a counter when considering a loop structure?

12. Define and explain the purpose of a *dummy record*.

13. Suppose the following list of items represents the data for a program. Design a suitable dummy record for the data file.

```
80   DATA  "WALLY",  83
85   DATA  "SUE",  76
90   DATA  "ZIGFREED",  68
```

14. What characteristics, in your opinion, should an acceptable dummy record contain?

15. What is wrong with this loop? Why?

```
35   LOOP
40       READ N$, M
45       PRINT N$, M
50       S = S + M
55   ENDLOOP
```

16. Modify the following loop structure to combine the beginning loop command and the test condition into one *while* statement. Assume that the counter C begins with the value of zero.

```
55   LOOP
60       IF  C > 20  THEN  QUIT
65       PRINT  C
70       C = C + 1
75   ENDLOOP
```

17. Define a *decision structure*.

18. Explain the choices the following decision structure provides for the computer.

```
30   IF  M > 79
35       PRINT  "HONOUR  STUDENT"
40   ENDIF
```

19. Design a decision structure to provide two programming alternatives within the same block of code. The two choices would be as follows: if a counter contains a value greater than ten, the computer is to print the phrase *processing completed*; otherwide, the computer is to add the value one to the counter.

20. If a decision structure is to be included within a loop, what can be done to ensure that both parts can be easily read and understood by someone else?

21. Design a loop structure which reads a list of 100 items, four values at a time. Each set of four values is to be added together. If the sum of the four numbers is greater than the value 50, print the sum; otherwise, print the word *insufficient*. Remember to include a test condition to prevent an endless loop.

Applying Your Knowledge

These questions assume an understanding of the material presented in the chapter, and provide new situations which may require evaluation, analysis, or application of that knowledge. Section One contains *general level questions* on specific statements or programming techniques. Section Two contains *advanced level questions*, which require the planning and coding of complete problems.

Section One

1. Identify the sections of this program which indicate poor programming techniques. Suggest ways to make the program more readable, easier to understand, and easier to modify.

```
05    REM  JOHN  GREVEN
06    READ  P ,  R
07    C  =  0
08    LOOP
09    IF  C  =  10    THEN  QUIT
10    I  =  ( P  *  R )
11    P  =  ( P  +  I )
12    C  =  ( C  +  1 )
13    ENDLOOP
14    PRINT  " THE  BALANCE  IS  " ;  P
15    DATA  800 ,  .14
16    END
```

2. Rewrite the following program to make it more readable, easier to understand, and easier to modify.

```
05    X = 10
10    PRINT "VALUE OF X", "VALUE OF Y"
15    LOOP
20    IF X > 100 THEN QUIT
25    Y = (425) / (X * 1.4)
30    PRINT X, Y
35    X = X + 10
40    ENDLOOP
45    END
```

3. Rewrite the following program to make it more readable, easier to understand, and easier to modify.

```
05    REM U.H. GALLSTONE
10    READ N$, H, R
15    LOOP
20    IF N$ = "LAST ONE" THEN QUIT
25    G = (H * R)
30    IF G > 125
35    PRINT TAB(20) G
40    ELSE
45    PRINT TAB(5) G
50    ENDIF
55    READ N$, H, R
60    ENDLOOP
65    DATA "B. TOOLOOSE", 40, 4.65
70    DATA "O. GRAHAM", 42, 4.31
75    DATA "C. BREEZE", 36, 3.89
80    END
```

4. Write the appropriate *while* loop structure for the data provided. Have the program read in the values two items at a time, multiply the two values, print the answer, then continue by processing the next two values.
   169, 41
   863, 128
   447, 931
   299, 872

5. Write the appropriate loop structure for the data provided. Have the program read in one record at a time, multiply the quantity times the unit price, then print both the name and the cost of each item.

ITEM	QUANTITY ORDERED	UNIT PRICE
CEILING TILES	1000	0.42
CONTACT CEMENT	4 TUBES	1.95
FOUR-INCH NAILS	8 BOXES	6.25
PLYWOOD #4	12 SHEETS	14.10

Section Two—Problems for Programming
Advanced level

Plan and code the solutions to the following problems. For the planning stage, define the problem, list the values, plan the solution with a diagram, and code into *structured* BASIC. Remember to include the coding techniques which help to make the programs readable, easy to understand, and easy to modify.

1. Loan Payment Schedule

The manager of a local bank has hired you to program their computer with a loan payment schedule. This schedule shows the total amount which must be repaid by customers on loans kept for either twelve months, eighteen months, or twenty-four months. The interest rate is 18% annually or 1.5% compounded monthly. The amounts borrowed are shown in the sample schedule.

AMOUNT OF LOAN	MONTHS 12	18	24
$ 500	—	—	—
$1500	—	—	—
$2000	—	—	—
$5000	—	—	—

2. The 24-Hour Clock

A national railway company has purchased several table-top microcomputers for its smaller railway stations. The company needs someone to develop a program for these microcomputers which would display both the twelve-hour clock and the twenty-four hour clock which the railway uses.

Design a program which would display only the time from noon to midnight for both time references. The words *noon, midnight*, and *pm* must appear in the twelve-hour display. The output would appear as shown:

REGULAR TIME	RAILWAY TIME
NOON	12 : 00
1 PM	13 : 00
2 PM	14 : 00
(etc.)	—

3. The Telephone Company

The telephone company needs a program which would read in customer information, and then print an invoice in the format shown below. The company charges a flat rate of $16.00 for telephone usage, and an additional $0.35/min on all long distance calls. Each invoice, when completed, would have the appropriate customer information inserted.

```
* * * * * * * * * * * * * * * * * * * * * * * * * * *
MA BELL TELEPHONE COMPANY
CUSTOMER:
PHONE # :
FLAT RATE  LONG DIST.  TOTAL
$ —        $ —         $ —
* * * * * * * * * * * * * * * * * * * * * * * * * * *
```

Data File

CUSTOMER NAME	PHONE NUMBER	LONG DIST. IN MIN.
R. WILKINSON	921-2265	120
B. HERD	665-5521	360
P. GERRARD	405-3039	170
J. MCKNIGHT	790-4352	285

4. Machine Milling Simulation

A specialty milling company uses a computerized metal lathe to cut metal shapes for customers upon request. The operator keys in the parameters for the job, which are a combination of cutting depth (in millimetres) and cutting time (in seconds). This particular job calls for 60 s at a cutting depth of 3 mm and 100 s at a cutting depth of 4 mm.

Plan and code a program which would keep track of the time and have these commands printed when required.

TIME	COMMAND
0	"LOWER CUTTING EDGE TO 3 M
60	"LOWER CUTTING EDGE 1 MM"
160	"RAISE CUTTING EDGE"

5. Customer Accounts

The credit department of a local retail store wants you to design a customer account program which would read in and process information about its credit card customers. The output is to contain *customer name, interest* (if any), *account balance* (interest added on), and any phrases that the company wishes printed. The following rules are to be incorporated within the program.

Credit Rules

Balances less than or equal to 30 d, print *no charge*.
Balances 31-60 d, add 2% interest.
Balances 61-90 d, add 2% interest, and print *your account is now overdue*.
Balances 91-120 d, add 2% interest and print *your credit is discontinued, pending payment*.

Data File:

CUSTOMER	BALANCE	DAYS WITHOUT PAYMENT
K. HEER	$450.	29
G. SMITH	$136.	35
V. D. VALLE	$ 45.	61
D. HAYNES	$875.	105

16

Structured Fortran

Objectives

An understanding of the general features of a structured program

A working knowledge of the loop structure

A working knowledge of the selection structure

A working knowledge of *formatted* read and print statements

Because of its portability and long history of service,
"FORTRAN" is frequently used in large computer centres.

Courtesy of Digital Equipment Corporation.

Chapter Sixteen
Structured Fortran

The problem with traditional programs is that they are difficult to read and modify.

One of the earliest high-level languages developed for computers was FORTRAN, an acronym meaning FORmula TRANslation. It was developed by IBM, and released in 1957 as a programming language to be used by scientists, engineers, mathematicians, and the military. The language is noted for its ability to manipulate mathematical expressions easily.

Although FORTRAN was not intended to be a universal language, by the early 1960s, virtually all manufacturers had developed some version of FORTRAN. A committee was established to develop standards for the language which would specify which commands were acceptable.

This standardization has made FORTRAN a **portable computer language**. This means that programs written for use on one computer could be run on another computer with very little modification. Also, as new refinements were accepted by the committee (ANSI — American National Standards Institute) they were simply added to the existing versions. This allowed programmers to write in both old and new styles of FORTRAN using the same machine.

One disadvantage of FORTRAN is that it is not easily adapted to business applications. Programs written to handle alphabetic data (words) and printed reports tend to be technical and awkward in construction. With a little ingenuity, however, business applications can be mastered.

Another disadvantage of FORTRAN is that it was not originally designed to be an interactive language. This means that a program must be completely coded and entered into the computer before any errors are discovered. This limitation makes the correcting of errors a time-consuming process. It is this second disadvantage that structured programming attempts to minimize.

This chapter contains only those features which are different from ordinary FORTRAN, specifically the repetition and selection structures. Before studying these features, it is recommended that you practise introductory programming concepts from sources outside this textbook, as well as the three control structures presented in Chapter Fourteen.

Programmers thinking of adopting structured programming concepts should be aware that a specific version of manufacturer's software is needed to translate your programs. These versions, WATFOR and WATFIV compilers, for example, are available from the University of Waterloo.

What Is Structured Fortran?

This structured version of FORTRAN was created to accommodate a new approach to writing computer programs called **top down design**. This feature requires the logic of a program to progress in an orderly manner from the top to the bottom of the program. To achieve this feature, self-contained **blocks**, or **modules, of code** with specific beginning and ending commands are used. These commands only allow one entry and one exit from each structure.

Programmers also indent **loop** and **decision structures** towards the right-hand margin, and highlight them by inserting **spaces** before and after each block of code.

Programs produced in a structured style tend to be readable, easy to understand, and easy to modify. As a result, structured programmers are able to produce better programs in a shorter period of time than traditional programmers.

What Makes Up a Block of Code?

A block, or module, of code is a series of statements that go together as a unit. **Programmer comments** such as the program title, the programmer's name, and program description would represent the first block of code.

The **main line of the program** may contain several blocks of code grouped according to their function such as *input, processing*, and *output*. These modules would contain

such items as initializing values, titles and subtitles, calculations, final print statements, and data values.

Two other programming features, **loops and decisions**, are displayed as indented modules. Loops require the computer to repeat a set of instructions. Decisions require the computer to compare two items, and then choose alternative programming instructions as a result of the comparison.

The blocks are separated from each other in the program with spaces. The *comment* statement, used to create these spaces, can also be used to describe the purpose of each module. Both concepts make a program easier to read and to understand.

The following example illustrates how even a simple program can be made more readable with spacing and modular design.

Bank Interest Problem

Fritz Hinklemier deposited $800 into a term account. The trust company offered to pay a rate of interest of 18%, compounded annually. Plan a program which would print the balance of his account at the end of one year.

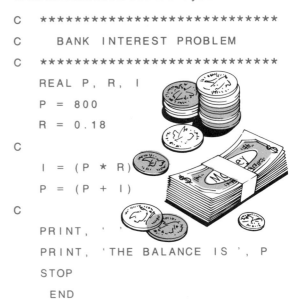

```
C     **************************
C        BANK  INTEREST  PROBLEM
C     **************************
      REAL  P ,  R ,  I
      P  =  800
      R  =  0.18
C
      I  =  ( P  *  R )
      P  =  ( P  +  I )
C
      PRINT ,  ' '
      PRINT ,  'THE  BALANCE  IS ' ,  P
      STOP
      END
```

The *Bank Interest Problem* has been divided into three logical modules—*input, processing*, and *output*. Notice the letter C which appears down the left-hand margin. This letter appears when the programmer has used the *comment* statement to space items in the program listing, or to insert **program documentation** such as the title to explain the purpose of the program. These *comment* statements have no effect on the program's output or on the execution of the program. They are simply inserted to improve the readability and appearance of the program listing.

Declaring Variables

FORTRAN programs must declare whether the values in the program will be whole numbers or decimal numbers. This is necessary because the computer uses a different method to store and process each type of number.

Declarations are always the first executable statement in a program. Comments may come before them because they are not part of the program's executable logic.

Although variables beginning with the letters I, J, K, L, M, N are assumed to be whole numbers automatically, it is wise to declare all variables to be *real* or *integer*. This gives the programmer the freedom of choosing the letters which best represent the items being considered. For example, the letters P, R, and I are good choices to represent Principal, Rate of Interest, and the dollar amount of Interest, respectively, in finance-related problems. Consider the following rules about variables.

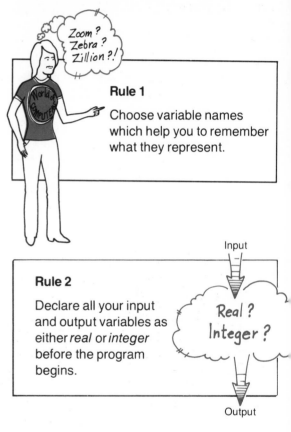

Rule 1

Choose variable names which help you to remember what they represent.

Rule 2

Declare all your input and output variables as either *real* or *integer* before the program begins.

Figure 16.1
Declarations

Integer	This statement tells the computer that certain variables are to be treated as whole numbers.	**Integer C,M** eg., 24, 506
Real	This statement tells the computer that certain variables are to contain decimals.	**Real I, P. R** eg., 90.00, 500.00 0.18

Practice Assignment

Ann Gelica works as a computer programmer for a manufacturing company. She works 42 hours a week at a rate of $8.35 per hour. Plan a program which would print out the phrase *gross pay is* and the answer. Use appropriate letters to represent the variables in the solution.

Expanding Your Programming Power

Once you have mastered the more common FORTRAN statements such as *comment, read, data, print, stop, end, integer, real*, and arithmetic expressions, you may wish to learn more powerful programming instructions. If your programs have loops or decisions in them, they are more powerful than programs without them. Loops and decisions are capable of getting the computer to do a great deal of processing with very few instructions.

A **loop**, also known as a **repetition structure**, refers to a set of instructions with a definite beginning and ending which are repeated until a certain test condition is met.

A **test condition**, which is a comparison between two or more items, provides a logical way for the computer to exit from the loop. Loops which have a poorly designed or absent test condition may cause the looping process to continue far beyond the needs of the program. That situation is referred to as an **infinite** or **endless loop**, and is avoided by good programmers.

"I figure it will pay for itself in the money we'd save on chalk."

While Do...Endwhile

A loop structure can be designed with *while do...endwhile* commands. These are the beginning and ending commands which enclose a set of instructions that are to be repeated a number of times.

The example shown below illustrates how these commands are used as "bookends" to enclose the instructions. See if you can figure out what the computer is instructed to do.

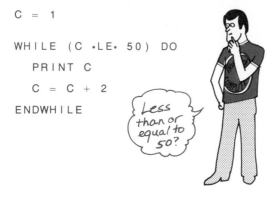

```
C = 1

WHILE (C .LE. 50) DO

    PRINT C

    C = C + 2

ENDWHILE
```

If you understood those instructions, you would have concluded that the computer is instructed to print all the odd numbers from one to fifty.

The additional line which came before the loop structure, C = 1, is necessary to tell the computer what value to begin the loop with. This statement is referred to as **initializing the counter**. The counter in this example is the letter C which increases by the value two each time a loop is completed. Counters do not have to start at one. In this case, the value one happened to be appropriate.

The test condition in the loop was contained in the following statement ...

```
WHILE (C .LE. 50) DO
```

This statement is translated to mean "While the value stored in C is less than or equal to 50, do the following...." If that statement was true, the computer would perform whatever instructions were contained within the loop structure. If the statement was false, the computer would quit looping and continue with the rest of the program.

Logical Operators

When comparing items in a FORTRAN statement, logical operators are used. These are the two letters which express the relationship between the items being considered. Figure 16.2 illustrates the possible relationships which can be used in comparisons.

Figure 16.2

Logical Operators

Operator	Meaning
.EQ.	Equal to ...
.LT.	Less than ...
.GT.	Greater than ...
.LE.	Less than or equal to ...
.GE.	Greater than or equal to ...
.NE.	Not equal to ...

Consider the following sample problem which uses a *while do...endwhile* structure as part of the solution.

The Gas Consumption Chart

A major oil company knows that a typical sub-compact car consumes 4.76 L of gas every hour travelling at 50 km/h. For each additional 10 km/h in speed, the car will consume an extra 0.5 L.

The marketing department wants a chart which will illustrate the relationship between *speed* and *gas consumption*. The chart is to display speeds in intervals of ten, ranging from 50 to 100 km/h.

Fortran Coding for Gas Consumption Chart Problem

```
C     ****************************************
C       GAS CONSUMPTION CHART
C     ****************************************
      REAL GAS
      INTEGER SPEED
      READ, SPEED, GAS
C
C
      PRINT, ' ****************************************'
      PRINT, 'SPEED', 'GAS CONSUMPTION'
      PRINT, ' '
C
C
      WHILE (SPEED .LE. 100) DO
         PRINT, SPEED, GAS
         SPEED = SPEED + 10
         GAS = GAS + .5
      ENDWHILE
C
C
      PRINT, ' '
      PRINT, ' ****************************************'
      STOP
      END
      $ ENTRY
      50, 4.76
      $ END
```

Gas Consumption Chart—Output

```
* * * * * * * * * * * * * * * * * * * * * * * * * * * * *
        SPEED           GAS  CONSUMPTION
         50                   4 . 76
         60                   5 . 26
         70                   5 . 76
         80                   6 . 26
         90                   6 . 76
        100                   7 . 26
* * * * * * * * * * * * * * * * * * * * * * * * * * * * *
```

Practice Assignment

Prepare a program which would print a weight table to assist employees in the post office. The table is to contain equivalent weights in both ounces and grams in intervals from 0.5 ounce to 10 ounces. Note that 0.5 ounce is equal to 14.2 g. The final output should appear with headings as shown...

```
OUNCES          GRAMS

0 . 5           14 . 2

1 . 0             —

1 . 5             —

(etc.)            —
```

Programming Decisions

A **decision structure**, also known as a **selection structure**, refers to instructions with a definite beginning and ending, which require the computer to compare two or more items. The structure also provides alternative programming choices for the computer to perform based on the results of the comparison. It is this type of structure that gives computers their apparent ability to "think."

Decision structures in structured FORTRAN are written with *if (   ) then do...endif* commands. These are the beginning and ending statements which enclose a set of instructions which will be performed if the *if* condition is true. Consider the following example of this type of structure.

```
IF  (AVER .GT. 79)  THEN  DO
     PRINT,  'HONOUR  STUDENT'
ENDIF
```

In this example, the computer has been given two choices. If the value of the variable *aver* (representing a student's average mark) is greater than 79%, the computer is instructed to print the phrase "Honour student." If the value of the variable *aver* is not greater than 79%, the computer will ignore the entire structure, and continue with the rest of the program.

If (   ) Then Do...Else...Endif

A similar selection structure can be used to provide two programming alternatives within the same block of code. To achieve this, an *else* statement is inserted between the two choices. Consider the following example of a selection structure which is part of a program for a customer's invoice.

```
IF (BAL .GT. 1000) THEN DO
    PRINT, 'YOU HAVE EXCEEDED YOUR
               CREDIT LIMIT'
ELSE DO
    PRINT, 'THANK YOU FOR SHOPPING
               AT SEARS'
ENDIF
```

In this example, the computer is instructed to compare the customer's account balance, represented by the variable *bal*, with the value $1000. If the customer's account balance is greater than that value, the phrase "You have exceeded your credit limit" is printed. If the customer's account balance is equal to or less than that amount, the second phrase is printed.

Combining Loops and Decisions

Decisions are often part of a loop within a program. When coded, the decision or selection structure would be highlighted with spaces and indented further towards the right-hand margin than the loop which contains it. Consider the following problem which is illustrated with all the problem-solving steps —problem definition, list of values, planned solution, and coded solution.

The Questionnaire Problem

A government agency is interested in the response to one particular question from a national census. This question had asked the respondants to enter their gross annual salary.

Plan a program which would produce the following output from a sample population of 10 000 citizens.

```
********************************************

    NUMBER  OF  SALARIES  >  $35000

    NUMBER  OF  SALARIES   $0  to  $35000

    AVERAGE  ANNUAL  SALARY

********************************************
```

Planning for the Questionnaire Problem

Problem Definition:

Print three phrases with answers . . .
Number of Salaries $35 000
Number of Salaries $0 to $35 000
Average Annual Salary
for a total of 10 000 people.

Total = Total + Salary
Aver. = Total / 10 000

Data Values

Salary = variable

Initial Values

Total = 0
High = 0
Low = 0
C = 0

Figure 16.3
Flowchart for the Questionnaire Problem

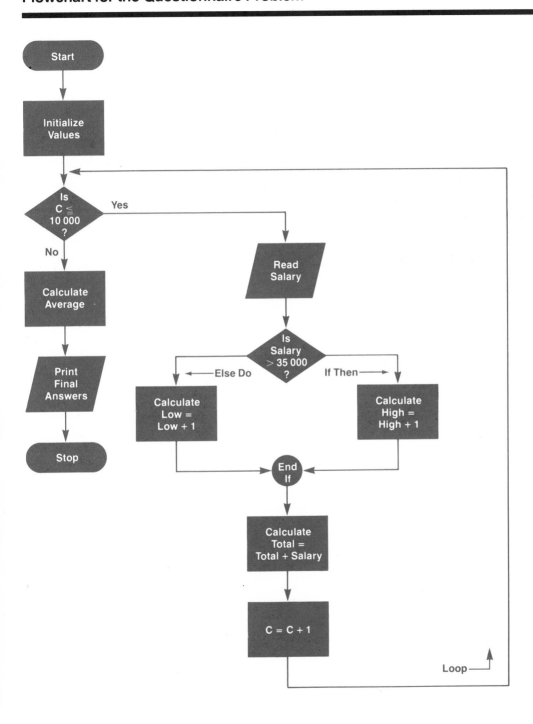

FORTRAN Coding for the Questionnaire Problem

```
C     **************************************
C           THE QUESTIONNAIRE
C     **************************************
      INTEGER * 4 SALARY, TOTAL
      INTEGER HIGH, LOW, C
C
C     ***INITIALIZING VALUES***
      TOTAL = 0
      HIGH = 0
      LOW = 0
      C = 0
C
C       ***READ LOOP WITH***
C     ***SELECTION STRUCTURE***
      WHILE (C .LE. 10000) DO
        READ, SALARY
C
        IF (SALARY .GE. 35000) THEN DO
          HIGH = HIGH + 1
        ELSE DO
          LOW = LOW + 1
        ENDIF
C
        TOTAL = TOTAL + SALARY
        C = C + 1
      ENDWHILE
C
C     ***CALCULATE AVERAGE SALARY***
      AVER = TOTAL / 10000
C
```

Integer * 4 is needed to store numbers larger than 32767.

Continued...

```
C   ***FINAL OUTPUT***
    PRINT,  ' ****************************************'
    PRINT,   'NUMBER OF SALARIES > $35000 =' , HIGH
    PRINT,   'NUMBER OF SALARIES $0 to $35000 =' , LOW
    PRINT,   'AVERAGE ANNUAL SALARY =' , AVER
    PRINT,  ' ****************************************'
    STOP
    END
```

Practice Assignment

A geography class just completed a term test. You have been asked to design a Test Diagnostic program which would read in the term marks, one at a time, and produce the following output.

```
******************************
NUMBER OF PASSING GRADES—
NUMBER OF FAILING GRADES—
AVERAGE MARK FOR THE CLASS—
******************************
```

These are the marks that the students achieved on the term test : 52, 85, 41, 66, 78, 73, 69, 61, 56, 58, 64, 91, 88, 63, 50, 74, 49, 67.

Greater Print Control

Most printed answers look much better if they contain titles and subtitles to explain what they represent. To achieve greater print control, the FORMAT statement must accompany the *print* command. The FORMAT instruction specifies exactly how the answer is to appear on the page.

A row of asterisks (stars), for example, can be used to highlight answers. Below are shown two methods of obtaining the same output. The first method is a simple print line. The second method uses the *format* statement.

Method One

```
PRINT, ' ****************************************** '
```

Method Two

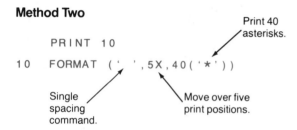

Print 40 asterisks.

```
      PRINT 10
10    FORMAT ( ' ' , 5X , 40 ( ' * ' ) )
```

Single spacing command.

Move over five print positions.

In method two, the statement, PRINT 10, instructs the computer to perform some printing function as specified on line ten. The line number is arbitrary and is invented by the programmer. The next statement, identified on the left as line ten, instructs the computer to use single spacing, move the print head over five print positions, and then print a total of forty asterisks.

The first item in every print *format* statement must be a carriage control character. The carriage is the mechanism which guides the print head over the paper. Figure 16.4 contains five items which can be used as a carriage control character.

Figure 16.4
Carriage Control Characters

Character	Meaning to the Printer
'1'	Skip to the top of a new page
' '	Single spacing
'0'	Double spacing
'_'	Triple spacing
'+'	Stay on the same line as the previous print command.

Once one of the above carriage control characters are placed in the *format*, the programmer can then choose from several other *format* instructions to help with the printing. For example:

```
        PRINT 20
20      FORMAT ('1',45X,'TABLE OF SPECIFICATIONS',3(/))
```

These two lines require the computer to skip to the top of a new page, move over 45 print positions, print the phrase "Table of Specifications", and then skip three lines before beginning anything else. The slash symbol (/) can be used by itself for one line, or inside brackets for multiple lines of vertical spacing. Note, however, that all items inside a *format* statement are separated by commas.

Practice Assignment

Plan a program which would centre the following report title in the middle of a new page. The title and the rows of stars to highlight it must be the only printed matter on the page.

```
* * * * * * * * * * * * * * * * * * * * * * * * * * * *

        CHICKADEE  COMPANY  LTD.

        HATCHED  PROJECTIONS

        TO  THE  YEAR  1990.

* * * * * * * * * * * * * * * * * * * * * * * * * * * *
```

Data Formats

In addition to positioning titles and subtitles, the *format* statement can also be used to manipulate input and output data. *Format* statements give the programmer greater control over how data files are read, and how answers will appear on a printout.

This statement requires that the type of data being processed be clearly specified as either an integer, a real number, or as alphabetic data. Figure 16.5 shows the letter codes used to indicate data types.

Figure 16.5
Format Data Codes

Letter Code	Meaning	Sample of Use
I	Integer variable	I4
F	Floating-point decimal variable	F5.2
A	Alphabetic data	12A1 (WATFOR) A12 (WATFIV)

Integer Format

Whole numbers are the easiest to format. The letter I, meaning integer, is followed by the number of spaces reserved for the number. Consider these examples of formats for integer numbers.

Number	Format Code
28	I2
403	I3
13978	I5

Decimal Format

Computers go through several stages when processing numbers which contain a decimal point. As a result, they need to know two things about a decimal number. First, how many digits, including the decimal point, are in the entire number. Secondly, it also needs to know how many digits appear to the right of the decimal point. Consider these examples.

Number	Format Code	
0.25	F4.2	Number of digits which appear to the right of the decimal.
189.005	F7.3	
10500.006	F9.3	

Number of print positions needed to store the entire number.

Alphabetic Format

Words or phrases are called **character strings** in FORTRAN. You can think of words as a series of characters, including spaces, all strung together. When referring to alphabetic data, the number of characters (letters, numbers, spaces, or special characters) must be specified along with the letter "A." Consider these examples which illustrate the format code for alphabetic data represented by the variable *name*. The first group of examples in Figure 16.6 illustrate the WATFOR method of representation. The second group in Figure 16.7 has the same examples, but with the WATFIV compiler requirements.

Figure 16.6
WATFOR Method

Data	Declaration	Format Code (WATFOR)
J. Wilson	Dimension *Name (9)*	9A1
Tool Kit #14	Dimension *Name (12)*	12A1
16 Main St.	Dimension *Name (11)*	11A1

Figure 16.7
WATFIV Method

Data	Declaration	Format Code (WATFIV)
J. Wilson	Character *Name * 9*	A9
Tool Kit #14	Character *Name * 12*	A12
16 Main St.	Character *Name * 11*	A11

Reading Mixed Data Records

When using the *format* statement to read or print data, it is important to place the data into fixed-length fields. A **data field** is a specified number of spaces which are required to hold the largest variable in that section. For example, consider the following three data records which describe items stored in a warehouse.

INVENTORY ITEM	QUANTITY IN STOCK	COST PER UNIT
TOOL KIT # 14	65	24.80
MEASURING TAPE	400	9.50
CIRCULAR SAW	20	89.98

14 character field	3 character field	5 character field

It would take fourteen spaces to hold the largest inventory item, three spaces to hold the largest quantity, and five spaces (including the decimal point) to store the largest cost per unit figure. Numbers, or course, are always **right-justified** in a field. This means that if a number is too small to fill a data field, it is placed in the right-hand side of the field. The computer always assumes that the remainder of the field is filled with zeros. Alphabetic data is left-justified. The field for the Inventory records shown earlier would be specified in a *format* statement as shown.

```
    READ 10, ITEM, QUANT, COST
10  FORMAT (14A1, I3, F5.2)
```

The following program illustrates the method for reading and printing the Inventory Items with a *while do* loop.

```
C   ****************************************
C       INVENTORY PROBLEM
C   ****************************************
    DIMENSION ITEM (14)
    INTEGER QUANT, C
    REAL COST
C
    C = O
C
    WHILE (C .NE. 3) DO
            READ 10, ITEM, QUANT, COST
10          FORMAT (14A1, I3, F5.2)
            PRINT 12, ITEM, QUANT, COST
12          FORMAT (45X, 14A1, 10X, I3, 10X, F5.2)
            C = C + 1
    ENDWHILE
    STOP
END
```

Practice Assignment

The mass of a planet determines the pull of gravity, and therefore the weight of a person standing on the surface. An astronaut, for example, would feel lighter standing on a small planet than on a larger one.

Design a program which would determine how much you would weigh on various planets. Assume that your weight relates directly to a planet's size. The following planets are expressed as a percentage of the earth's size: Moon 16%, Mars 38%, Venus 85%, Jupiter 264%.

The program should read in that data, and then produce the following output. (Use your weight as the starting value.)

PLANET	YOUR WEIGHT
EARTH	—
MOON	—
MARS	—
etc.	—

Summary

FORTRAN, one of the earliest high-level languages developed for computers, must be completely coded and entered into the computer before any errors are detected. This limitation makes debugging a time-consuming process. To minimize this disadvantage, a new style of writing code called "structured programming" was introduced.

Structured programming displays four prominent features. It includes the concept of top down design. This means that the logic of the program progresses in an orderly manner from the top to the bottom of the program.

The program is also organized into modules, or blocks, of code. Each block contains statements of a similar nature. One possible organization of a program would be by function such as *input*, *processing*, and *output*.

Programmers indent loop and decision structures towards the right-hand margin, and highlight them by inserting spaces before and after each block of code. Loop and decision structures also have specific beginning and ending statements with only one entry and one exit point per structure.

Programs written in a structured style tend to be readable, easy to understand, and easy to modify. As a result, programmers who use structured commands produce better programs in a shorter period of time than traditional programmers.

There are only three type of structures in a structured program, namely, the Sequence (one step after the other), the Repetition Structure, and the Selection Structure. These three structures are sufficient to solve any computer problem, however complex it may be.

Although FORTRAN was not designed for business applications, data records and printed reports can be processed with practice and a thorough knowledge of FORMAT statements.

"I didn't understand all that stuff he said between 'Good Morning, Class' and 'That concludes my lecture for today'."

Review Questions

These are *general level questions* which may require factual recall, reading comprehension, and some application of the knowledge from this chapter.

1. Explain two advantages and two disadvantages of FORTRAN as a computer language.

2. Briefly name and describe four noticeable characteristics of a structured program.

3. (a) Define a module of code;
   (b) Name three sections of a program which may appear in modules;
   (c) Which modules are idented?

4. Define *integer*. Define a *real* number.

5. Classify the following numbers as either *real* or *integer*: 0.24; 50.65, 2098; 3; $1.98.

6. In one student's solution to a bank interest problem, the variable names for Principal and the Rate of Interest were listed as A and B. Explain why those letters are poor choices for variable names in this case. What variable names would be more appropriate?

7. Define *repetition structure*.

8. What is a *test condition*? Suppose a computer was processing a loop which contained an incorrect test condition. What might happen?

9. Analyze the loop structure given below, then answer the questions which follow it.

```
C = O
WHILE (C.LE.10) DO
    PRINT, C
    C = C + 0.5
ENDWHILE
```

   (a) How many answers will this loop print?
   (b) What will be the value of the last answer?

10. What does the phrase *initializing the counter* refer to? What is the purpose of a counter within a loop structure?

11. Design a repetition structure which would print all the even numbers from zero to ten.

12. Design a repetition structure which would begin with the value zero, add the even numbers from zero to fifty, then print only the final answer.

13. Design a repetition structure which would calculate the interest on an investment of $900, if the rate of interest is 18% compounded annually. Have the computer print both the annual interest and the balance each year for ten years.

14. What is wrong with this loop? Why?

```
C = 1
WHILE (C .LE. 10) DO
   READ, M
   S = S + M
ENDWHILE
```

15. Define a *decision structure*.

16. Explain the choices the following decision structure provides for the computer.

```
IF (MARK .GT. 49) THEN DO
   TOTAL = TOTAL + MARK
ENDIF
```

17. Design a decision structure to provide two programming alternatives within the same block of code. The two choices are as follows: if the counter contains a value greater than ten, the computer is to print the phrase *first stage completed*; otherwise, the computer is to add the value one to the counter.

18. If a decision structure is to be included within a loop, what can be done to ensure that both parts can be easily understood by someone else?

19. Design a loop structure which would read a list of 200 items, four values at a time. Each set of four values is to be added together. If the sum of the four numbers is greater than the value 50, print the sum; otherwise, print the word *insufficient*. Remember to include a test condition to prevent an endless loop.

20. Write two lines of code using the *print* and *format* statements to produce this output.

```
*  THISTLE  FURNITURE  CO.  LTD.  *
```

21. Write the appropriate lines which would produce these headings. They are to begin four lines from the top of a new page, in the centre.

```
         LOAN  REPAYMENT  SCHEDULE
12 MONTHS  18 MONTHS   24 MONTHS
```

22. Code the *read* and *format* statements which would enter the following set of data into the computer.

```
14.62          100          0.25
```

23. Code the *read* and *format* statements to enter these data records into the computer, one line at a time.

Student	Number of Credits	Term Average
Jim Nasium	14	83.5
Al Kapone	09	51.2
Joan Rivers	15	75.4

24. Write the corresponding *declaration* statements which would appear at the top of a program for the data given in the last question.

Applying Your Knowledge

These questions assume an understanding of the material presented in the chapter, and provide new situations which may require evaluation, analysis, or application of that knowledge. Questions 7 to 10 should be considered *advanced level questions*.

Note: the problems in this section deal entirely with repetition and selection structures. If you wish to begin with simpler problems, refer to those at the end of Chapter Four. For additional problems requiring repetition or selection structures, refer to those at the end of Chapters Nine and Fifteen.

Problems for Programming

Plan and code the solution to the following problems. (Remember to include the coding techniques which help to make the program readable, easy to understand, and easy to modify.)

1. Braking Distance

The braking distance for the average car is 0.06 times the square of the car's speed, that is...$D = 0.06*S^2$. Design a program which will print the braking distance for speeds ranging from 30 to 100 km/h in intervals of ten. The output should appear as shown below.

SPEED	BRAKING DISTANCE
3 0	—
4 0	—
5 0	—
(etc.)	—

2. My, But She's Growing!

A human baby tends to grow at a rate of 3% per week for the first half year. Plan a program which would print the weight of a baby each week for 25 weeks if the baby's weight at birth was 3.37 kg.

After this chart is completed, convert the final answer into pounds. (1 kg = 2.197 lb)

WEEK	WEIGHT
1	3 . 37
2	—
3	—
(etc.)	—

WEIGHT IN POUNDS =

3. The Mortgage Dilemma

One problem with the purchase of expensive homes is that the current interest rates often make the payments beyond the reach of the average home owner. Jolleen Sitler, for example, has $85 000 left to pay on her home. The interest rate has changed to 18.75% compounded annually. Jolleen, however, is still making payments which total $12 800/a. If the bank adds on the interest before deducting the payment, print a chart as shown (for a period of twenty years) which would illustrate the dilemma that Jolleen is in.

YEAR	INTEREST	BALANCE
1 .	$ —	$ —
2 .	—	—
(etc.)	—	—

4. Population Growth

Hamilton's population is 320 000 and is growing at the rate of 2%/a. Waterloo's population is 50 000 and is growing at the rate of 15%/a. List the years, and the population of each city. Continue to print the population figures until the year in which Waterloo's population is larger than Hamilton's, as shown below.

** GROWTH COMPARISON CHART **

YEAR	WATERLOO	HAMILTON
1 9 —	—	—
1 9 —	—	—
1 9 —	—	—
(etc.)	—	—

Note: The declaration *integer* * 4 is needed to handle the large values in this problem.

5. Shipping Rates

Packages are shipped from Toronto to Halifax by rail at the following rates: for packages up to 20 kg—$0.65/kg; for packages exceeding 20 kg—$0.80/kg. Plan a program which would read the following package weights, one at a time, and produce this chart :

PACKAGE WEIGHT	COST
—	$ —
—	$ —
(etc.)	$ —

Data

14, 80, 21, 50.5, 100, 40.65

6. Odds or Evens

Plan a program which will read in the series of numbers, one at a time. The solution should determine whether each number is even or odd, then either print it in the first column under the title *evens* or in the second column under the title *odds*.

Data

65, 20, 41, 39, 34, 58, 99, 82

7. Educo Book Company

The Educo Book Company supplies schools and libraries with textbooks. It offers reduced rates on orders of 50 or more copies of the same book. A certain book is priced as follows:
up to 50 copies   ... $18.95 per copy
over 50 copies   ... $18.25 per copy.

Design a program which would print the *customer name* and *total cost* for the customers listed below.

Data

Customer Name	Quantity Order
Leduc Secondary	60
Winnipeg Public Library	4
Victoria Collegiate	120
Dartmouth High	48

8. Binary to Decimal

Computers manipulate numbers in binary (base 2) rather than in decimal (base 10). Plan a program which would convert the binary numbers listed below into their decimal equivalents. Hint: The six-digit binary numbers can be read as a six-part number (A B C D E F) with different variable names for each binary digit in the number. To find its decimal equivalent, the following expression may be used.
Number = $(A * 2^5) + (B * 2^4) + (C * 2^3) + (D * 2^2) + (E * 2^1) + (F * 2^0)$. The output should appear as shown.

BINARY NUMBER	DECIMAL NUMBER
—	—
—	—
(etc.)	—

Data

001011
110101
111000
111111

9. Sorting Numbers

Plan a program which would read the following six numbers in the order given, then sort and print the numbers from highest to lowest. Invent an appropriate title for the printout.

Data

408, 310, 390, 250, 525, 701.

10. Delnite Mining Co.

Hy. O. Silver is the payroll officer for a gold mining company. He needs a program which would print the *Employee Name* and *Gross Pay* for the company employees each week.

If an employee works 40 hours or less each week, he is paid his hourly rate. If the employee works more than 40 hours, he is paid 1$\frac{1}{2}$ times his regular hourly rate for each hour over 40 hours. This amount is then added to his "40-hour salary." For this problem, use the data below:

Data

Employee	Regular Rate	Hours Worked
Scott Bowman	$8.50	40
Jacque Ducarme	$7.75	44.6
Rennie Lafave	$8.90	36.5
Tony Dececchi	$9.25	48

17 Controversial Issues Involving Computers

Objectives

An awareness of controversial issues usually avoided by conventional computer scientists

An understanding of some of the indirect societal impacts of computer systems

An awareness that people should consider the consequences before embracing new technologies

Computer technology is viewed with mixed emotions by most members of our society, including the scientist and layman.

Courtesy of ITT Industries Canada Ltd.

Chapter Seventeen

Controversial Issues Involving Computers

One of the reasons why our society confronts so many unexpected problems is that we tend to develop and adopt new technologies before considering possible consequences.

This chapter presents several short articles which deal with issues that have aroused much debate over the years. The articles are concerned with the legal, moral, and philosophical impacts computers may have on our society. These are the long-run issues which computer scientists usually neglect to consider when designing computer systems. Although the issues themselves may be serious, their presentation is often positive and sometimes light-hearted.

Most of the questions which follow the articles are divided into two groups. The first group is concerned only with the reader's understanding. The second group, entitled *Getting at the Issues*, invites the reader to analyze and evaluate the underlying assumptions.

Can Computers Think?

A British mathematician, Alan Turing, proposed a test for computer intelligence, even before computers became popular. Turning stated that the question of a computer's intelligence could be answered by means of an "imitation game." He suggested that a researcher use a keyboard terminal to communicate with two people hidden in another room. If a computer could be substituted for one of the hidden people, and the machine continued the conversation undetected for some time, it would be considered to be thinking.

One clever application of this test is a program called "Doctor." This program allowed a computer to conduct psychiatric interviews with several patients. Afterwards, when the patients were told that they were not "conversing" with a real psychiatrist, but rather a computer, 60% of the people refused to believe it.

Systems analysts are now discovering ways to provide a computer with various levels of thinking which allow a computer to perform complex tasks. Computers are now available which use their own chess strategy to beat human opponents. Robot devices can now navigate around objects, climb stairs, or think of ways to build ramps to obtain some object just out of its reach.

It may be only a short time before characteristics normally attributed to humans—intelligence, intuition, and creativity—will be displayed by computers.

Norbert Wiener, a pioneer in robotic theory, believes that this trend in computer development is dangerous. Computers which appear to go beyond the limitations of the people who designed them may become uncontrollable.

An opposing opinion is held by a scientist named Arthur L. Samuel. The fact that some computers can beat humans at chess, and appear to be thinking, is irrelevant. The person who created the chess program gave computers that ability. The computer's level of artificial intelligence was decided ahead of time by its designer.

Checking Your Reading

1. What test did Alan Turing propose? What was he trying to prove?

2. What human characteristics may soon be displayed by computers?

3. Why does Norbert Wiener think increased computer intelligence may be dangerous?

4. Why is Arthur Samuel not concerned with "thinking computers"?

Getting at the Issues

5. Is there anything wrong with Turing's test for computer intelligence? Explain.

6. Why, in your opinion, would some patients refuse to believe that the psychiatrist was a machine, rather than a real person?

7. Suppose that you owned a computer which displayed intelligence, intuition, and creativity. Do you think that it would be a dangerous machine to be around? Explain.

8. In your opinion, can computers think? Give reasons for your answer.

Computer Theft

It has been estimated that the total losses due to computer-related crimes since 1965 has amounted to $300 million. No one really knows for sure. One study has indicated that the average "take" from a computer-related theft is 43 times as much as from a traditional armed bank robbery. Yet these stories rarely appear in the newspaper. Few criminals are ever brought to trial. The corporate victims fear the bad publicity which the court appearances may cause.

One embezzler used a bank's computer to withdraw twenty or thirty cents at a time, at random, from several hundred chequing accounts. The money was then diverted into a dummy bank account which the embezzler had opened up at the same branch. The criminal was careful never to divert money from any particular account more than three times a year.

The victims, the bank customers, often either assumed the 30-cent difference was due to their own poor arithmetic, or simply did not find it worthwhile to argue the point with the bank manager. As a result, little by little, the embezzler became rich.

This "salami technique" (a little slice at a time) can become almost invisible to both customers and bank personnel. A computer program can be modified to truncate all bank interest calculations. For example, if interest owed to you amounts to $95.845, the computer transfers the $95.84 to your account, and the remaining $0.005 into a dummy account. The thief then patiently waits to collect the steadily growing sum of money.

Computer theft has not been restricted to just money. In the early 1970s, officials of the Pennsylvania Central Railroad were surprised to discover that 217 boxcars had disappeared. When U.S. federal agents had finally located them, the boxcars had been repainted and sold to another railway. Someone had been able to reroute the boxcars by providing the company's computer with false information.

In another case, a university student was charged with stealing $1 million worth of electronic equipment from a major telephone company. He had gained access to the company's computerized ordering service with a portable keyboard terminal. Unaware of the situation, the company's own trucks delivered expensive equipment to empty warehouses, where the thief stored them temporarily until a sale could be made.

Checking Your Reading

1. Some people think that computer-related theft is insignificant. Is that true? Explain.

2. Why are the facts of computer crimes generally not made public?

3. How is an "electronic thief" able to embezzle money from so many bank accounts and not get caught?

4. How did the boxcar theft occur?

Getting at the Issues

5. Suggest how an accountant with programming knowledge could detect the "salami technique" of embezzlement.

6. Suppose the facts about computer frauds were reported regularly in the newspaper and on television. Explain one negative impact and one positive impact that this might have.

7. Explain who suffers when a bank is subject to "electronic theft."

8. What could individual customers do to reduce the number of computer-related crimes? Explain.

"Our next speaker will talk on the subject of 'the pitfalls of electronic funds transfer systems'."

Robots

"Hold it Ribley!" the executive called out. "I have another parcel for the fourth floor."

"Yes, sir," came the response. Its mechanical rotor stopped and Ribley waited patiently while the executive found room for the package among those already stuffed into its parcel bin.

"O.K., off you go," the executive said, and he returned to his office.

Its quiet whirring slowly faded as the robot disappeared down the corridor towards its next delivery point.

As the short story above indicates, office robots are now being used for delivering mail in large office buildings. Other robots are designed to make and deliver coffee to people at their work stations. In factories, durable industrial robots are gaining popularity by doing such hazardous jobs as welding, spray painting, hot-oven work, and handling dangerous chemicals, explosives, or nuclear material. The next generation of robots may be the type designed specifically for home use. These domestic robots could be a companion to the children, teach, and do housework. Most likely, they will be programmed with a high level of intelligence, and have the ability to communicate easily in a natural language.

The capacity of a computer to interact with children was demonstrated in 1965 in a New York City hospital. A computerized typewriter had remarkable success in radically improving the condition of several autistic children. These are children who, for some reason, refuse to communicate with people, or even respond to the world around them. What amazed a number of psychiatrists is that the children's improvement occurred without psychotherapy. The machine, by being able to talk, respond to touch, comment, explain, and draw pictures, helped the children come out of their inner world, and enjoy being with people once more.

A series 2000 "Unimate" industrial robot is used to automate the hot and difficult job of die casting.

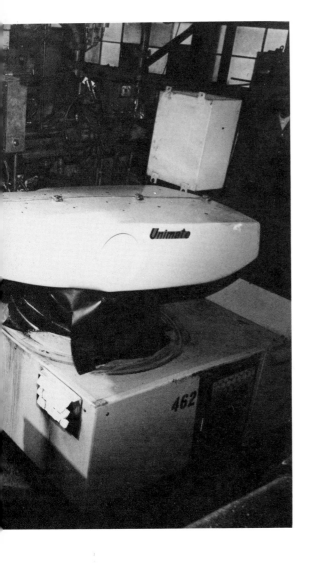

Checking Your Reading

1. Name two jobs which office robots can perform. Think of another similar job which they could also perform in office buildings.

2. What are some examples of jobs which industrial robots are designed to do?

3. What is a domestic robot? What things might it do for the people who owned it?

4. List two abilities which domestic robots probably will need.

Getting at the Issues

5. Why do you think that children like to communicate with robots?

6. Suggest some tasks, other than those already mentioned, which robots could assist in performing around the house.

7. Besides the two characteristics mentioned in the article, what other abilities would be helpful if they were programmed into a domestic robot?

8. Some people are genuinely concerned about robots being placed in offices and factories. Suggest some reasons why these people might be worried.

Computers and the Courtroom

The dependence on computer systems can lead to some unusual shifts in attitude about who is responsible in certain situations. This impact of computers is illustrated in the following fictional civil cases.

Case One

Dr. T. Unger, a doctor in a large urban hospital, is being sued for malpractice. This is a situation in which negligence is suspected in the treatment of the patient.

During the court proceedings, it was revealed that Dr. Unger had relied on the responses of a computer terminal for treatment of the patient. The terminal provided hospital staff with access to a "medical diagnosis" program. This program was designed to make a diagnosis and recommend treatment on the basis of the patient's medical data. The system was thought to be reliable, since it had been used successfully for several years. Therefore, the defendant's lawyer argued, the doctor is not the one who is at fault for the poor medical treatment; the computer is.

Case Two

Some parents filed a lawsuit against a computer software company which had provided educational cassettes for their child's home computer. The parents claimed that the child had spent some five hours a week during her preschool years studying the information on the cassette tapes. At the time, the child appeared bright and alert.

When the child was enrolled in grade one, however, she received very poor marks, and seemed to lack the ability to understand material suitable for the average student. Both the school principal and the classroom teacher suggested that the child's inability to learn may have been caused by improper teaching techniques used by the computer software company.

Case One Questions

1. What is a medical diagnosis program?

2. Why does a lawyer think that the doctor is not guilty of malpractice?

3. In your opinion, who is at fault—the doctor or the computer? Explain.

4. Suppose a politician claimed that a decision which resulted in a $100 million loss to the country was actually due to a faulty program in a large computer. What similarity is there between this situation and the lawyer's argument for the doctor? Why would this trend in thinking be dangerous for the public?

Case Two Questions

1. Why are the parents suing the computer software company?

2. What makes the parents think that their child is not below average intelligence?

3. Besides the computer software company, who else might be at fault? Give reasons.

4. Do you think that a child who enjoys interacting with a microcomputer will necessarily succeed in school? Explain. What would you recommend to the parents to help the child?

Enhanced Human Intelligence

The fictional television hero, the Six Million Dollar Man, was orginally described as a cyborg. Although writers have since adopted the less harsh term "bionic," the term cyborg was probably more accurate. A cyborg is a person who is partly mechanical and partly organic. Both sections of the body can be controlled by the brain.

There are actually hundreds of bionic people in our society. These are patients who have been fitted with electronic eyes, touch-sensitive skin, battery-powered pacemakers, artificial hearts, kidneys and limbs. These adaptations to the human body require that both the brain and the body's chemical defences accept the foreign object as natural.

The next step in this man-machine evolution may be a tiny computer chip connected to the brain. Such miniature circuits could enhance human intelligence by providing additional memory, or ultra-high speed processing areas. Imagine the possibilities of "instant knowledge" by implanting a memory circuit containing millions of facts and figures. A human being could, for the first time, have immediate access to the entire storehouse of human knowledge.

One argument against implanted circuits is that this type of processing and memory capability could just as easily be carried around in the form of a powerful pocket computer.

Other opponents argue that this trend toward more durable and efficient mechanical parts in our body may change the way in which we view ourselves. Instead of considering humans to be valuable living organisms, people may be treated as merely stylish entities with disposable, replaceable human parts.

Checking Your Reading

1. Define a cyborg. What other computer-related term mentioned earlier in this text is the word "cyborg" related to?

2. Do bionic people really exist? Explain.

3. What may be the next step in this man-machine evolution?

4. What other invention may be used instead of implants? Suggest some capabilities that invention should have to be useful.

Getting at the Issues

5. Would there be any advantage in having an implanted computer, as opposed to a pocket computer? Explain.

6. In your opinion, should medical engineers continue to experiment with enhanced human intelligence. Why?

7. Why would the viewpoint: "People may be treated as stylish entities with disposable, replaceable human parts" be considered a poor one?

8. Suppose that you had the opportunity to triple your factual knowledge, and to be able to multiply ten digit numbers in your head. Would you consider having an implanted circuit to achieve this? Why?

The Controlled Society

The most persistent fear which writers have concerning computers also is the one most likely to come true. This would be a society in which computer systems are used to direct and control the population. Usually this results in a loss of privacy and freedom of expression.

This fear is reflected repeatedly as a theme or setting in science fiction novels. Sometimes it is the governments which misuse computers to produce a distorted society such as those in *Logan's Run* and *1984*. In other novels, it is the computers themselves which dictate how people are to behave, live, or die. Notable examples include *The Forbin Project*, *Space Odyssey 2001*, and *Vulcan's Hammer*.

At present, governments have countless information data banks containing statistics on individual citizens, and a growing number of interconnecting computer networks. These data banks include information on taxes, school achievements, criminal records, medical history, birth, death, marriage and divorce certificates, and records of all financial transactions and bank accounts.

If people were required to carry a plastic identification card at all times, government agencies could determine where you shopped, ate lunch, went on vacation, which airline you used, and in which hotel you slept. In fact, the electronic funds transfer sytem recommended by computer companies (the use of a plastic bank debit card to pay for everything) is an excellent way to painlessly create such a society. Each time you purchase an item, you leave an electronic trail.

Ironically, it will probably not be a wicked dictatorial government that imposes such a system, but rather a naive, passive population which eagerly embraces a technology without considering the consequences.

Checking Your Reading

1. Describe the fear which many writers have about computers.

2. What do governments already have which would contribute towards a more controlled society?

3. How would a compulsory plastic identification card help suspicious government agencies?

4. Explain the concept of "electronic funds transfer system."

Getting at the Issues

5. Why would writers, in particular, fear a computer-controlled society? Who else would suffer? Explain.

6. Explain the meaning of the last paragraph in the article, in your own words.

7. Do you believe what was stated in the last paragraph? Give reasons.

8. Suggest some additional ways, not mentioned in the article, by which governments could use computers to gain greater control over its citizens.

18 The Future

Objectives

An awareness of developmental trends in computer hardware and computer software

An awareness of communication media such as optical fibres and communication satellites as common data carriers

An awareness of possible future developments in computers from 1990 to 2005

An appreciation of the problems which may be created by the widespread adoption of industrial robots and EFT systems

Chapter Eighteen
The Future

There are many possible futures. An intelligent society will aim not just for the most promising technological future, but also for the one which will be the most socially acceptable for its citizens.

Computers and related communication technologies are continuously being improved to meet people's rising expectations. About every five and a half years, a new generation of computers is introduced which usually displays an improvement in speed and reliability by a factor of ten and an increase in memory capacity by a factor of twenty. By the year 2000, the computer systems now in use will appear as crude and unsophisticated as the Wright brothers' first airplane.

This chapter is concerned with predictable short- and long-term trends in areas related to computers. Topics will include computer hardware, computer software, communication networks and their impact on society, trends in specific applications, and some of the problems which people likely will be faced with as a result of widespread computer use.

Hardware Trends

Holographic Storage

In the future, mass storage of information may be accomplished by a technique called **holographic storage**. This refers to a device which etches varying laser light patterns onto a negative plate surface called a **hologram**. To retrieve information, a less intensive laser beam is directed to the appropriate hologram. This image is then projected onto sensors, which translate the wave patterns into digital data for the computer to use. A single beam of light immediately can transfer a complete page of data at one time.

Internal Memory

Magnetic bubble memory is expected to be more reliable and lower in cost. Bubble memory is favoured over traditional semiconductor memory (RAMS and ROMS), because the former can potentially store over a million bits of information on a single chip. One or two of these memory chips would give a pocket computer the capacity of a complete information library.

Present-day semiconductor devices will probably give way to three-dimensional **memory cubes**. In other words, a cube of material will be filled with electronic circuits, rather than confining two-dimensional electronics to the flat surface of a chip.

Logic Circuits

Experimenters have discovered that electrical circuits work about 100 times faster when they are supercooled. Manufacturers are currently designing machines which will keep the logic circuits at very low temperatures to take advantage of this difference in speed. These special circuits are called **superconductive cryogenic devices**.

Although at present all computers operate binary circuits, this may change. Binary electronic logic may be replaced with **quarternary logic** or more complex levels of electronics. Dr. Tich Dao of Signetics Inc. is one of the pioneers of this application of computer logic.

Most computers today contain only one processor (that is, one miniature computer chip). In the future, most computers will contain several processors. Some of these computer logic circuits will be arranged in a series for rapid multiple calculations, or distributed decision making. Other processors will be dedicated to particular jobs such as helping to keep track of requests from several terminals, job scheduling, or operating several I/O devices at the same time. Desk-top computers could easily contain the power and complexity of current mainframe systems with this design.

Software Trends

Computer technology will make much greater use of **firmware**, also called **stored logic** or **microprograms**. These are instructions that are permanently stored inside the computer system by the manufacturer. As the cost of internal memory decreases, manufacturers will begin to store more and more software into the computer's circuits, rather than keeping the programs on tape or disk. Programs such as operating systems, language processors, and common library routines will become standard firmware features in every new computer. This will make computers less complicated to operate, and decrease the need for external storage devices.

Most internal software such as operating systems, language processors, and graphic instructions are permanently stored in circuits. Such software is referred to as firmware or microprograms.

Courtesy of National Semiconductor.

Computer Languages

At present, computers generally operate with high-level languages, which require a fairly extensive training program for potential users. FORTRAN, COBOL, PASCAL, and APL are of this nature. Modern COBOL, the most widely used programming language for business applications, is very similar to the first version introduced some twenty years ago. BASIC, the language used in microcomputers, is an attempt to make programming easier for people to understand.

It has been estimated that a typical industrial programmer produces only eight to ten debugged lines of code per day when working on a programming project. Although structured design and structured programming are aimed at improving programming productivity, there is still much improvement to be made.

As computers become more widespread and gain popular acceptance in homes, there will be a tendancy for computers to respond to natural language instructions such as English. Computer systems which operate by voice imput will become more common.

Communication Networks

It is not just the technology which will change. People will rely, to a greater degree, on information networks to move information, almost instantaneously, from one part of the world to another. All forms of communication media will be actively involved in the transmission of computer data. These media include telephone lines, coaxial cable, microwave towers, and orbitting satellites.

Optical fibre, hair-thin glass strands along which laser light can travel, will slowly replace coaxial cable. A single strand of optical fibre can transmit twenty times the data that an ordinary copper wire can carry, and is immune from normal electromagnetic disturbances such as lightning.

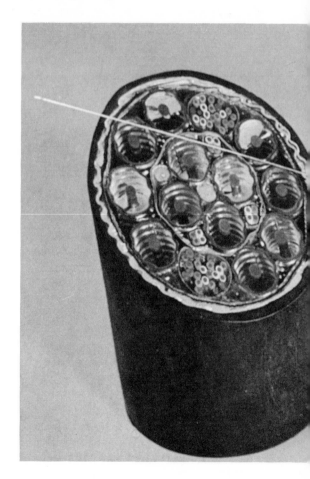

A single glass strand of thin optical fibre is compared to the older type of data carrier—coaxial cable—which it is replacing.

Courtesy of The Computer Communications Group.

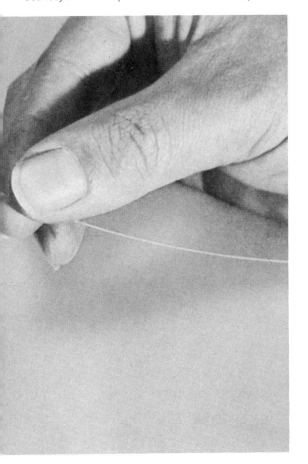

Canada is one of the world's leading producers of communication satellites.

Three **communication satellites** are all that is needed to completely "wrap" the world in an information network. Their stationary orbits would keep them above the same points on the earth at all times. The satellites can then be used to "bounce" messages from one ground station to another. Someday it may be a common occurrence, for example, for a student living in Edmonton to have access to a computer data base located in London, England, in order to complete a research paper.

The Canadian philosopher, Marshall McLuhan, referred to this electronic shrinking of the world as a trend towards a "global village." People from other continents will become as familiar as our next door neighbours.

Adapting to an Information-Rich Society

New consumer products and services will arise as a result of a combination of old technologies. Television companies will offer such options as hard-copy printers, joysticks for games, a typewriter keyboard for data entry, or a telephone response system built into the television's electronics. Telephone companies will compete for this profitable market by offering a communication device which is a combination of a telephone, a video screen, and a keyboard.

Several companies will provide specialized computer cable services to customers for a fee. Students could use interactive terminals to research information for school projects. Lawyers, doctors, scientists, and business analysts will have access to large data banks operated by companies that store specialized information relating to their particular profession.

In an information-processing society, an increasing amount of paper-related information can be transmitted electronically. Cable services could deliver electronic mail and electronic newspapers.

There will be less need to travel as access to information becomes more readily available. Office work could be accomplished through a computer terminal located somewhere in the home. Shopping could be done by viewing the latest selections on a video screen, then entering requests to the store's computer by means of a home terminal keyboard.

Hidden Helpers

Microprocessor chips will be built into most future electronic devices. These **dedicated processors**, so called because they operate on a fixed set of instructions, will improve the reliability and accuracy of most devices, for example, radio receivers, televisions, video recorders, cassette decks, record changers, toys, clocks, microwave ovens, refrigerators, and stoves.

It will also be common for new suburban homes to have built-in microprocessors which control and monitor the environment. They would automatically control the heating in the winter and the air conditioning in the summer.

Generally, dedicated processor circuits are hidden from view, and the user is unaware of their operation. The influence of computers in the home will be more apparent with the addition of either a microcomputer or a home terminal. A personal microcomputer can be used to run computer programs for entertainment or household management. A home computer terminal, with the help of a television set, will allow people to interact with outside data banks.

The Vista project, operated by the Bell Telephone Company, is a pilot project which offers information to people who have both a telephone and a television set. Using the telephone as a communication link, the subscriber can key in numerical codes on a remote control device to manipulate the type of information desired on the television screen. The information is stored in data banks sometimes hundreds of miles from the subscriber.

This modem or acoustic coupler may become a common sight in future homes. The device allows a computer terminal to be linked with a distant computer system by means of the telephone. The telephone headset is placed inside the pockets in the modem, which then converts a computer's digital signals into the type of analog signals used in telephone lines.

Courtesy of APF Ltd.

Looking Into the Future

Forecasting the future is at best a risky venture. Computer futurists must consider not only the types of machines which will be available, but also the extent to which a society will be willing to accept a particular computer application.

Although many computer developments are technically possible, not all developments are socially desirable. Just because a manufacturer discovers a new use for a computer, it does not automatically follow that society must accept that particular application.

Many things may prevent technical achievements from being adopted by a society. For example, if politicians were convinced that industrial robots would lead to massive unemployment, laws may be legislated which would prohibit their widespread use.

If citizens perceive electronic funds transfer systems as a threat to their future privacy because of the possibility of electronic surveillance, that computer application may not be fully used.

Consider Figure 18.1, entitled *Future Computer Developments*. It projects possible technical achievements and applications from the year 1990 to the year 2005. All achievements are given a 50% chance of becoming commonplace by some particular year. The approximate years are indicated along the bottom line. The higher an item appears in the chart relative to the left-hand column, the greater the probability it has of becoming a commonplace event.

Figure 18.1
Future Computer Developments

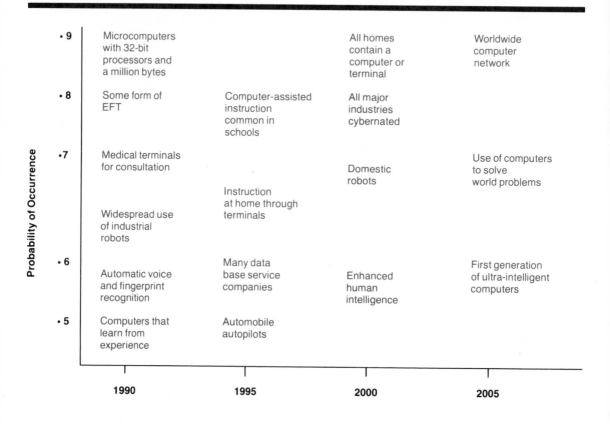

Industrial Robots: New Blue Collar Workers

Japanese manufacturers have already begun to use industrial robots to assemble cars, toys, calculators, computers, and operate entire processing, chemical, and steel plants. North American manufacturers are retooling factories with the same type of machines. Company officials have discovered that reprogrammable robots make excellent workers. They do not sleep, take coffee breaks, require vacations, or retirement benefits.

The problem with using industrial robots on assembly lines is that they displace human workers. Some forecasters have predicted 25% to 50% of the work force will be unemployed by 1990 due to this type of technological displacement. What will people do?

One solution may be to reduce the number of hours a person works each week. The standard work week may be four instead of five days. Also, people may be urged to retire at 55 instead of 65. These two changes would spread the available work among more people.

To provide retirement benefits for those who retire early, and be able to pay unemployment benefits to those people who are not working, the robots could be taxed.

Whatever solutions may be found, widespread use of industrial robots will create a society profoundly different from the one which we are in now. The use of human beings for assembly line production may become obsolete. All jobs may be of the white collar variety—office work, sales, and various services. For the unskilled, blue collar factory workers who become displaced by technology, there will be difficult years of retraining, relocation, and frustration.

ETF—The Hidden Threat

Banks and computer companies are presently advocating the use of computers (and telephone lines) to move money electronically from one place to another. This computer application, referred to as electronic funds transfer, could make paper money and coins almost obsolete as a medium of exchange.

The system has several advantages. Certain types of crimes would be reduced: cheque forgery, fraud, and armed robbery. Computer embezzlement, however, may increase. An advantage for businesses is that they are paid at once, instead of waiting for customers to pay their bills. This provides stores with the necessary purchasing power to buy more merchandise for resale.

The hidden threat of electronic funds transfer is that all purchases by customers leave an electronic trail. Government agencies such as the tax department and various investigative agencies could conduct secretive electronic searches of the computer networks to determine your actual buying power (as opposed to reported income), types of purchases made, and even your present location.

In a television interview, a tax auditor was asked how "tax loopholes" could be prevented. He replied that an EFT system of payment could probably remove 99% of all tax evasions. After some thought, the tax auditor added that, unfortunately, this increase in efficiency would cost society a great deal of individual freedom and privacy.

Summary

Computer technology rapidly becomes obsolete as new innovations replace the old. Most of the changes have occurred with the hardware devices and computer circuitry. There is a general trend towards faster, more accurate computers, with a greater memory capacity.

Computer languages have changed relatively little over the past twenty years. They still remain complex and difficult to learn. For widespread adoption, computer devices will have to respond to natural language instructions, for example, that require little or no programming experience by the user. To achieve this, future software will either be in the form of stored logic or easy to insert ROM cartridges.

It is not just the technology which will change. People will rely, to a greater degree, on information networks to move information from one part of the world to another. Optical fibres, laser light, and communication satellites will become the common carriers of global information.

People will adapt their lifestyles to an information-rich society. Video screens and printers will be substituted for home mail delivery and the traditional morning and evening newspaper. Information will be conveyed to fellow office workers just as easily over several kilometres as it would be in person. Home terminals will reduce the necessity for the daily time-consuming, and often frustrating, ritual of travelling to work.

Although many future computer developments are technically possible, not all developments may be socially desirable. When people believe that the adoption of a technology is inevitable, it becomes a self-fulfilling prophecy. At that point, even when privacy, freedom, and dignity are challenged, individuals will feel powerless to intervene.

It is important, therefore, that computer scientists, industrialists, politicians, and those studying computer systems consider two things about promising new computer developments. They should not only ask the first question: "Is it possible?" but also, and perhaps more important, ask the second question: "Is it socially desirable?"

Review Questions

These are *general level questions* which may require factual recall, reading comprehension, and some applications of the knowledge from this chapter.

1. What does *holographic storage* refer to?

2. Why is bubble memory favoured over traditional memory chips by computer manufacturers?

3. How will future memory circuits differ from present-day devices?

4. Describe three changes which may effect logic circuits in the future.

5. Define *stored logic*. Why is this concept becoming more important in computer design? What effect will this have on computers?

6. (a) How efficient is the average industrial programmer?
   (b) How does that compare to your own programming speed?
   (c) What efforts are being made to increase programming productivity?

7. In order for computers to gain popular acceptance, what trend will there be in computer devices?

8. In what way are optical fibres and communication satellites associated with computers?

9. Eventually, it will become popular to transmit paper-related information electronically. Describe two noticeable effects that this may have on society.

10. (a) What is a *dedicated processor*?
    (b) Suggest at least three products which contain a dedicated processor. (c) Will people usually be aware of these processors while thay are in use? Explain.

11. List three items from the "Future Computer Developments" chart which will have a very high possibility of occurring by the year 2000. List one item that, in your opinion, will not occur. Explain why.

12. What is the problem with industrial robots? Suggest three things which might be done to solve the problem.

13. Describe some effects that widespread use of industrial robots may have on traditional blue collar workers.

14. What does *electronic funds transfer* refer to? Why might it be considered to be a hidden threat?

Applying Your Knowledge

These *advanced level questions* assume an understanding of the material presented in this chapter, and provide new situations which may require evaluation, analysis, or application of that knowledge.

1. Suppose that you were given the task of designing a microcomputer for the typical Canadian home. What features would you include in the computer that would make it easy to operate, and acceptable to even those families who have no knowledge of programming, or any type of experience with a computer?

2. In what way does Marshall McLuhan's description of the world as a *global village* seem an appropriate term for the world of the future?

3. Suppose that scientists sent a communication satellite into orbit around the earth. The scientists want the satellite to remain above the same point on the earth at all times so they can "bounce" messages off it. How can this be accomplished if the earth keeps rotating every 24 hours?

4. Many people believe that the widespread use of industrial robots will cause massive unemployment among blue collar workers. In your opinion, what effects would the widespread use of *domestic robots* (robots in the home) have on society? Give reasons.

5. The "Future Computer Developments" chart shows the "use of computers to solve world problems" as a possible application by the year 2005. Describe several world problems which, in your opinion, computers could be used to solve.

6. Obviously, the "Future Computer Developments" chart is incomplete. Many possible items were omitted. Suggest some additional developments which may occur. Classify your suggestions as either high or low probability.

7. If you had complete control of society today, what would you do to prevent the high unemployment predicted as a result of the widespread use of industrial robots? Why are similar steps not being taken by our society?

8. Draw a two-columned chart which illustrates several Advantages and Disadvantages of allowing networks of electronic funds transfer systems to operate in our country.

Individual Projects

1. ## A Science Fiction Story

   Plan and write a science fiction short story using computers or robots as either characters or part of the story's setting. In your plan, consider the various possible future computer developments which you could include to add technical realism to the story.

2. ## Inventing Possible Futures

   Futurists often use a technique of predicting possible futures called a scenario. A scenario is a description, in this case, of how the world might appear in the year 2005. Use either a positive or negative view to describe how you think the world will appear at that time.

Appendix A
Recommended Reference Books on Basic Programming

Basic Programming Primer, by Mitchell Waite and Michael Paradee, Howard W. Sams & Co., Inc. (1978). An excellent, easy-to-read introductory book for beginners. Good use of cartoons and quick wit to lighten the text.

Computer Graphics Primer, by Mitchell Waite, Howard W. Sams & Co., Inc. (1979). An easy-to-understand book about the use of graphics for microcomputers.

Radio Shack BASIC Computer Language, Dr. David Lien, Tandy Corp. (1977). An excellent, light-hearted booklet for the beginning programmer who has a Radio Shack computer.

PET/CBM (Personal Computer Guide), by Adam Osborne and Carroll S. Donahue, 2nd. edition, Osborne/McGraw-Hill Book Company, (1980). A thorough presentation of BASIC for owners of Commodore computers.

BASIC and the Personal Computer, by Thomas Dwyer and Margot Critchfield, Addison-Wesley Publishing Company, (1978). Some excellent project ideas in large paperback format. Examples include gaming, graphic art, data bases, and simulations.

The Mind Appliance: Home Computer Applications, by T.G. Lewis, Hayden Book Company, Inc. (1978). Excellent projects for microcomputers around the home, including recipe storage, word processing, business processing, graphics, and others.

The Most Popular Subroutines in BASIC, by Ken Tracton, Tab Books (1980). A listing of countless subroutines for mathematics, metric conversions, graphs, electronics, science, and other topics.

Appendix B
Recommended Books On Structured Programming

Structured FORTRAN With WATFIVs, by Paul Cress, Paul Dirkson, Wesley Graham, Prentice-Hall, Inc. (1980). A readable text for instructors on Structured FORTRAN.

A Structured Approach to Programming, by Joan K. Hughes and Jay I. Michton, Prentice-Hall, Inc. (1977). A recommended text for instructors who wish a thorough understanding of the theories and application of structured concepts.

Appendix C
Where to Purchase Robotic Turtles

Terrapin, Inc.
678 Massachusetts Avenue, #205
Cambridge, Massachusetts
U.S.A. 02139

$995.00 for robot, cables, interfaces, software, and manuals. (Slightly cheaper for self-assemble "turtle kit.") Cost subject to change.

Glossary

Acoustic Coupler A device into which a telephone headset can be placed to link a computer terminal with a distant computer. Also called a modem.

Acronym A word or short form derived from the first letter (or letters) of each word in a phrase or name. Typically, no period follows the letters when typewritten, for example, CRT (which means Cathode Ray Tube).

Ada A computer language developed by the U.S. Department of Defense. It is a structured language similar to PASCAL. It was named after Ada Lovelace, Lord Byron's daughter, who was a major intellectual inspiration and patron of Charles Babbage's Analytical Engine.

Aiken, Howard (1900–1973) In affiliation with IBM, Aiken built an electromechanical computer called the Mark I.

Algorithm A general name for any set of well-defined rules or procedures in the solution of a problem.

Alphanumeric A term for any set of alphabetic letters (A through Z), numbers (0 through 9), and special characters (−,+,/,$, etc.) which can be machine-processed.

ALU An acronym for arithmetic logic unit. The logic circuitry designed to perform operations such as addition, subtraction, multiplication, and division. Also, it can perform logical comparisons.

Analog computer A device which measures physical quantities including air pressure, temperature, or velocity, and compares the measurement to some preset level. The device usually triggers some system into action if the comparison is not equal. Example: a thermostat measuring room temperature.

Application Programs Programs often tailored to the user's need. These programs perform tasks unrelated to the operation of the computer itself. Example: payroll program.

Arithmetic Operator A symbol used to indicate a math operation such as + for addition.

Artificial Intelligence A machine's ability to make decisions on its own, often developing strategies beyond its original programming.

ASCII (pronounced "asskey") An acronym for American Standard Code for Information Interchange. Originally a 7-bit code, it is often used in keyboards and IBM equipment to represent data. Also available in an 8-bit code called ASCII-8.

Audio Response Unit Circuitry capable of imitating human speech as a form of computer output.

Automated Teller Terminals Computer terminals located on the outside wall of banks to allow customers to process banking transactions after closing time. Also called 24 hour cash dispensers.

Auxiliary Storage Extra storage devices, such as magnetic tape drives, which can be added to a computer system.

Magnetic Tape Unit.

Babbage, Charles (1792–1871) A British mathematician and inventor. He designed a "difference engine" for calculating logarithms to twenty decimal places, and an "analytical engine" that was the forerunner of the modern digital computer. His designs were ahead of the technology of his day.

BASIC An acronym for Beginner's All-Purpose Symbolic Instruction Code. A computer language designed in 1964 to provide an introductory language for people without a background in computer studies. Presently, the most popular computer language used in personal computers.

Batch Processing A method of grouping jobs of a similar nature to assist in their processing.

Binary A number system composed of just two numbers, 0 and 1. All computers process information coded into some form of binary representation.

Bionics The study of living systems for the purpose of relating their characteristics to the development of mechanical and electrical hardware.

Bit A binary digit. One storage position in a computer circuit which can be either electrically "on" or "off." Several bits are required to represent a number or letter in a computer system.

Bubble Memory A type of computer memory circuit which uses an electromagnetic field to store and move magnetic spots (called domains) around a tiny chip of magnetic material. The domains resemble tiny bubbles when viewed through a microscope; hence, its name. Generally designed as a sequential access device. Also called magnetic bubble memory.

Bug A term used to denote a mistake in a computer program or system, or malfunction in a computer hardware component.

Byte The number of bits which are needed to code one character (a letter, number, or symbol) in a particular computer.

CAI An acronym for computer-assisted instruction. An application of various programming techniques including conversational programming to provide self-learning lessons on some topic for students.

CRT An acronym for cathode ray tube. An electronic output device used to visually display answers on a screen. Also called visual display terminal, or display screen.

Centralized Data Banks The concept of combining several different data files on citizens into one massive cross-index data base, accessible by a variety of government agencies.

Checksum A method of adding the number of bits required to internally represent a computer program. Its purpose is to assist the verification of programs transferred between storage devices and main memory.

COBOL An acronym for Common Business-Oriented Language, a high-level computer language originally developed for business data processing applications.

Coding The process of writing a problem solution into some particular computer language.

COM An acronym for computer output microform units—devices which reduce computer output to miniature images on negative film for future reference.

Common Data Carrier A communication medium, for example, telephone lines, routinely used to transmit computer data.

Communication Satellite An earth-orbiting device capable of relaying communication signals over long distances.

Communication Satellite.

Computer Applications The uses that people find for computers in society.

Computer Generation A series of computers using a specific design which is characteristic of that group. A term generally used to identify each major technological innovation in the computer industry.

Computer Graphics Images drawn by a computer program, including graphs, artistic designs, cartoons, maps, etc.

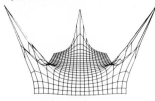

Computer Graphics.

Computer Language A set of instructions, construction and syntax rules which are needed to communicate with a particular computer system. Examples: BASIC, COBOL, FORTRAN.

Computer Model A series of mathematical equations which represent variables in a real-life situation. By altering the variables in the model, a researcher can determine the effect on the entire situation.

Computer Ombudsman An appointed official who can intervene in any civil matter on behalf of individuals who have been unfairly treated as the result of computerized information.

Computer Operator A person who makes certain that a computer system operates correctly and without delays.

Computer Programmer A person who plans and codes computer programs, employing problem-solving skills and a thorough knowledge of the rules of some particular computer language.

Conversational Programming A particular technique of writing programs which requires the end-user of the program to make active responses to the instructions which appear on the screen.

Computer Simulation The use of a computer to imitate real-life situations, often for the purpose of experimentation or training. Simulations can be dynamic video screen displays or elaborate computer-controlled environments such as a pilot-training simulator.

Computer Terminal A general name for any input/output device directly linked to a computer system.

Console Station A general name for an interactive computer terminal containing a keyboard and visual display screen.

Control Unit The hardware logic circuitry which controls the sequence of operations in a program.

CP/M A popular operating system developed by Digital Reseach Inc. for microcomputers.

Counter An arithmetic statement used to keep track of a series of events. Example: $C = C + 1$.

CPU An acronym for central processing unit. See Processor Unit.

Cybernation A combination of the words automation and cybernetics. It refers to a computer-controlled factory which employs automated devices such as industrial robots to produce assembly-line products.

Cyborg A person who is partly mechanical or electrical and partly organic, both parts controlled by the brain.

Data The values or variables used in computer programs.

Data Base A large collection of data stored on magnetic disks.

Data Base Management A software program which allows a computer to select parts of several different disk files and combine them to form a report.

Data Entry Clerks People who enter information directly into a computer system (onto disks) using a typewriter keyboard and a visual screen to edit the entries before they are stored.

Data Processing A phrase traditionally applied to the application of computers to the processing of information related to the operation of a business. Examples: accounting, production figures.

Data Processing Manager A person who is responsible for the successful operation of a computer department. This person hires the data processing staff, supervises their training, recommends the purchase of new equipment, and prepares the annual department budget.

Debug To detect, locate, and remove all mistakes in a computer program.

Debugging a Program.

Decision Table A chart-style planning technique used to plan the solutions to problems which contain multiple decisions and outcomes, but appear to lack a clear mathematical solution.

Dedicated Processor A miniature logic chip with a limited set of instructions which aids in the operation of some device such as a digital clock or toy.

Demand Report A request to the computer to select information from several files and combine them in a particular order before displaying them for the user.

Diskette A circular disk composed of flexible, mylar plastic and a thin coating of metallic oxide. It stores information by means of coded magnetic spots. Also called a floppy disk.

Diskette or Floppy Disk.

Documentation Various items related to a computer program which are stored together in an organized manner for future reference.

Domestic Robots The use of robot devices in the home.

DOS An acronym for Disk Operating System. A collection of programs stored on disk which operates computer system.

Dumb Terminal A computer terminal that totally relies on a computer system for its operation. It has no logic or control circuitry of its own.

Dummy Record An arbitrary name or number placed at the end of a list of items which are to be read into a computer. Its purpose is to inform the computer that there is no more data to be processed. Also called a trailer record or dummy variable.

EBCDIC An acronym for Extended Binary Coded Decimal Interchange Code. An 8-bit code used to represent data in modern computers. EBCDIC can represent up to 256 distinct characters, and is the principal code used in many of today's computers. Pronounced "ebb see dic."

EFT An acronym for electronic funds transfer system. It refers to a network of computer systems which allows consumer purchases to cause an immediate reduction in that person's bank account.

Electromechanical A device which is partly electrical and partly mechanical.

Electronic Mail The immediate transfer of traditional letters or memos from one location to another, using teleprocessing and computer systems.

EOF Check An acronym for end-of-file check. This is a statement within a program which requires the computer to check for a specific record in a list of data. (The programmer deliberately places the item that the computer is checking for at the end of the list of data.) The purpose of this statement is to prevent an infinite loop from occurring during the reading process.

EPROM An acronym for erasable, programmable read only memory. It is a semiconductor memory chip which can be erased with ultraviolet light.

Error Diagnostics Messages from the language processor indicating that a programming error has occurred.

File A collection of related records treated as a unit. Example: List of all credit customers.

Firmware Instructions permanently stored inside a computer system by the manufacturer in the form of integrated circuits. Also called stored logic or microprograms.

Fixed Point Arithmetic Arithmetic involving whole numbers (integers). There are no fractions.

Flight Simulator An imitation cockpit of an airplane or other flying craft which is used to train pilots. A computer is used to create visual and motion effects as the pilot manipulates the flight instruments.

Floating Point Arithmetic Arithmetic involving decimal fractions. This is a necessary feature for scientific and business applications.

Flowchart A diagram which uses arrows and special symbols to represent the steps in a problem solution.

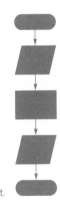

Flowchart.

Fortran A combination of the words FORmula TRANSlation, it is one of the earliest computer languages originally designed for use by engineers, scientists, and the military.

General-Purpose Computers Computer systems which can be adapted through a change in software to a variety of applications.

GIGO An acronym for Garbage In-Garbage Out! It refers to the necessity to accurate input to a computer system in order to arrive at the correct answer.

Graphics Terminal A special CRT with stored logic programs capable of producing graphs, charts, and diagrams with relative ease.

Hacker A person who spends all of his or her time programming a computer. A computer enthusiast who is capable of fixing any computer problem but is unable to communicate to you how it was done.

Hard Copy Terminal An output device capable of printing answers from a computer onto sheets of paper.

Hardware All the electrical and mechanical parts that make up a computer system. Example: CRT; printer.

Hollerith, Herman (1860–1929) A statistician with the U.S. census bureau who designed a method of storing coded information on cardboard cards in the form of punched holes. The code and computer card were eventually adopted by IBM and still bear his name.

Holographic Storage A technique of converting digital messages into laser light patterns on negative film for future reference. Also called laser storage.

Hopper, Grace A mathematician and programmer who developed programs for the Mark I and early Univac computers. A pioneer in the field of computer languages, Hopper wrote the first practical "compiler" program and helped to develop the COBOL programming language.

Hung A word to describe a computer system which appears to be doing nothing, although it is in the middle of a program. This state can be caused by a programming error such as an infinite loop, or an incomplete *input* command. Also, the system may be waiting until the user turns on a peripheral device.

Hybrid Computer System A combination of both the analog and digital computers. Analog devices usually act as peripherals, while the digital computer provides the processing and instructions for the system. Example: Automatic feedback systems on a cybernated assembly line.

IBM An acronym for International Business Machines Ltd., a company which has dominated the computer market for 25 years because of superior marketing strategies and innovative designs.

Idiot-Proofing The process of designing procedures to handle unexpected responses from the user of a conversational program to prevent the program from "crashing."

Impact Printer An output device which contains a printing head which must physically strike the paper in order to form a character.

Infinite Loop A situation in which a computer continues to follow a series of instructions without a logical way of stopping. Also called endless loop.

Input Device A general name for any hardware device which can be used to enter information into a computer system. Examples: keyboard; card reader.

Input Medium The material on which information is stored before it is entered into a batch-style computer system. Examples: Computer cards; magnetic tape; magnetic disks.

Industrial Robots Robotic devices with interchangeable, multi-purpose arms, and reprogrammable memories which can perform a given task repeatedly with great efficiency.

Integer A whole number that may be positive, negative, or zero. It does not have a fractional part.

Integrated Circuits Miniature electrical circuits contained in a tiny chip of silicon or some other material.

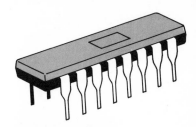

Integrated Circuit Inside Protective Plastic Module.

Intelligent Terminal A computer terminal which contains logic and control circuits similar to a computer.

Interactive Processing A type of processing involving a continuous dialog between the user and the computer. As the user makes an entry, the computer responds almost immediately.

Joystick A type of input device that is manipulated to produce different graphics on a display screen.

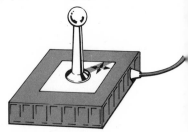

Joystick.

Keypunch Machine A data preparation device in which the user keys information to be encoded onto cardboard computer cards in the form of punched holes.

Keytape Machine A data preparation device which can be used to key in information to be encoded onto reels of magnetic tape.

Key Words Variable names used to identify a particular concept or process.

Language Processor A type of manufacturer's software designed to translate the instructions the user provides into electrical impulses which can operate a computer's circuits. Examples: FORTRAN compiler; BASIC interpreter.

Library Functions Prewritten subroutine programs provided by the manufacturer to make programming easier. Examples: *sine, cos* functions; *randomize; renumber.*

Light Pen An electrical device which resembles a pen used to write or sketch on the screen of a cathode ray tube.

Logic Error An error in program organization such as instructions out of sequence or an illogical request.

Logical Operators Symbols used to indicate a relationship between two or more items. Also called relational operators.

Loop A series of instructions that the computer is required to repeat until a certain test condition is met. Also called a repetition structure.

Magnetic Disk A circular magnetic storage medium comprising a hard metal base with a coating of metallic oxide and plastic on both sides. Magnetic disks are available in hard disks and flexible, smaller diskettes. Also spelled disc (British).

Magnetic Tape A magnetic storage medium comprising two layers of material. The base is a thin, plastic called mylar. One side of the plastic is coated with powdered metallic oxide. The metallic oxide can store data in the form of coded magnetic spots.

Reel of Magnetic Tape.

Mainframe Computer System The largest type of computer system which derives its name from its oversized processing unit. Each of the computer's basic functions (input, output, processing, storage, and control) has its own separate floor-model machine which usually operates at very high speeds. Often, the computer hardware will occupy an entire room.

Main Memory The part of a computer which stores programs and data while the computer uses them. Also called primary memory or internal memory.

Management by Exception A time-management concept which specifies that a manager should concern himself/herself with only the exceptions to the rule or items requiring immediate attention.

Mark I The first electromechanical computer developed under the direction of Howard Aiken at Harvard University.

Mark Sense Card A computer card which requires pencil marks to encode information for a card reader to interpret.

Mass Storage Device A particular storage device which contains thousands of magnetic tape cartridges stored in a honeycomb-like container. A minicomputer is required to operate the search mechanism. Also a general name for any auxilary storage device.

Mauchly, John Co-inventor with J. Presper Eckert who together designed a computer called ENIAC which was America's first completely electrical computer. It weighed 30 t and contained 18 000 vacuum tubes.

Menu A screen of options which list the various programs or files that the user can request by means of a key word. Similar in concept to a restaurant menu. Whatever you order will be brought to you.

Microcomputer A portable, desk-top model computer generally consisting of a CRT, keyboard, and some table-top peripherals such as a printer or cassette deck. Often called a personal computer because only one person can use the machine at a time.

Table-top Microcomputer.

Microcomputer Chip A miniature integrated circuit which contains an entire computer on a single chip. It comprises an arithmetic logic unit, control circuits, and some main memory. Also called a computer chip. Compare to microprocessor.

Microprocessor A sophisticated logic chip which contains the control and logic functions for a computer system.

Microsecond One-millionth of a second, or 1×10^{-6}.

MICR An acronym for magnetic ink character recognition unit. This is a machine used by banks and clearing houses to encode and sort cheques, using a series of specially shaped, magnetized characters placed along the bottom edge of cheques.

Magnetic Ink Characters.

Millisecond One-thousandth of a second, or 1×10^{-3}.

Minicomputer A floor-model computer which generally uses hard disk drives, and character or line printers. Typically applied to medium volume jobs. It can be adapted to batch processing or multiple-user interactive processing.

MPU An acronym for microprocessing unit. This refers to a computer's control and logic circuits contained on a single chip. Also called a microprocessor.

Nanosecond One-billionth of a second, or 1×10^{-9}.

Neumann, John Von (1903 – 1957) A brilliant mathematician who invented the stored program concept. Also one of the first people to use flowcharting as a problem-solving tool.

Nonimpact Printer An output device which uses various methods of printing answers on paper without physically striking the paper with a print hammer.

Number Cruncher   A phrase applied to computers designed to process huge quantities of mathematical calculations at high speed. Example: Cray 1.

Numerical Control Operator   This person translates the details of a blueprint into computer commands and stores them on magnetic tape or paper tape. When the tape is completed, it is fed into a computer-controlled machine which follows the instructions to cut, grind, or shape raw material into finished products.

OCR   An acronym for optical character recognition device. This machine uses photoelectric cells to interpret the shape of characters for a computer to use.

Operating System   A program prepared by the manufacturer which supervises the way in which a computer handles information. One popular operating system for microcomputers is called CP/M.

Optical Fibre   Hair-thin glass strands along which laser light can travel. A medium for transmitting information in the form of light.

Output Device   A general name to describe any hardware device which can be used to display answers or information generated by a computer.

Paging   A process which allows an entire "page" or screenful of information to be taken from storage and displayed on a visual screen. A technique of handling a program when main memory is too small to hold the entire program.

Pascal   A complex, structured programming language developed in 1971. Named after an inventor and mathematician from the 1600s— Blaise Pascal.

Picosecond   One-trillionth of a second, or 1×10^{-12}.

Peripheral   Any device attached to a computer. The computer itself is defined as the processing area, control circuits, and main memory.

Pocket Computer   A portable, hand-held, programmable computer.

Pocket Computer.

POS Terminal   A point-of-sale terminal. These are the specialized electronic cash registers used in department stores and grocery stores which also serve as interactive computer terminals.

Plotter   An output device capable of producing diagrams, graphs, maps, and blueprints. A pen is mounted on a mechanism which can be positioned anywhere on the paper under the control of a computer program.

Powers, James   A statistician with the U.S. census bureau who developed a method of coding information onto cardboard cards for ease of machine handling. Ideas were adopted by the Sperry Rand Corporation.

Predictive Reports   A report generated by mathematical equations to forecast trends and to assist planners in making decisions about the future.

Printout   Output from the computer printed on paper.

Problem Definition   A clear statement of the processing and output requirements of a problem.

Process Control   The ability of a computer to operate machinery external to the computer system itself.

Processor Unit   The part of a computer system which is the actual computer. It contains three sections: main memory, control circuits, and logic circuits. Also called central processing unit, or central processor.

Program   A series of instructions designed to guide the computer, step by step, through some process. Also spelled programme (British).

Programmer   A person who plans and codes solutions into a form that a computer can understand. This person requires problem-solving skills and a thorough knowledge of some programming language.

Programmer Comments
Nonexecutable statements inserted into a program to make the program easier to understand.

Program Listing   A complete copy of the instructions in a computer program provided by the computer upon request.

PROM   An acronym for programmable read only memory. It refers to a blank memory chip which can be programmed permanently by a hobbyist or a computer manufacturer.

Pseudo-Code   Literally translated, it means false code. It refers to a program-planning technique which roughly outlines the steps to the solution of a computer program. Short English phrases are used to describe the steps.

RAM   An acronym for random access memory. It is an erasable semiconductor memory chip which is used to temporarily store computer programs. Nicknamed user memory.

Repetition Structure   A set of instructions with a definite beginning and ending, repeated until a certain condition is satisfied. Also called a loop or loop structure.

Simulated Artificial Intelligence   A clever application of conversational programming techniques to give the user the impression that the computer is thinking for itself.

ROM   An acronym for read only memory. This is a semiconductor memory chip which is used to store programs as a permanent part of the computer system. Typically, ROMS contain manufacturer's software such as a language processor or an operating system.

ROM Cartridges   A storage device similar in appearance to an eight-track cassette containing a circuit board and permanent software programs.

ROM or Solid-State Cartridge.

Scrolling The vertical movement of lines on a video display so that the top line disappears and a new line is displayed at the bottom of the screen, or vice versa.

Selection Structure A set of instructions with a definite beginning and ending, which requires the computer to compare two or more items. The computer is then provided with alternative programming choices based on the results of the comparison. Also called a decision structure.

Sequence Structure A straight line segment of a program which contains no decisions or loops.

Sequential Access A process of searching files requiring that the entire file be searched, one record after the other, until the requested item is found.

Semiconductor Memory The type of integrated circuit typically found in most computers. The circuits are composed of layers of partially conductive metals and insulators.

Software All the instructions which make a computer operate in a required manner. A general name for computer programs.

Software Vendor A business which sells application programs to people who own computers.

Spaghetti Programming A name applied to unstructured programs which use a great number of *goto* statements. Spaghetti programs are very difficult to debug if they contain major errors in programming logic.

Statement A line of code in a computer program.

Stored Program Concept The idea of entering and storing a program into a computer system before the computer begins to work with it.

String Variable A series of characters (letters, numbers, or special symbols) used as a variable in a computer program. Typically, a word or name.

Strip Coding Patterns of coloured stripes on railway rolling stock designed to be read by optical scanners placed along the tracks. The code provides data for a computer to identify the railway car.

Structured Design A method of planning computer programs using three basic control structures to express all programming logic, no matter how complex. The three structures are: the "sequence," the "repetition" structure, and the "selection" structure.

Structure Diagrams Diagrams with a stick-like appearance used to plan the logic or structure of a computer program. This technique is made up of lines, circles, and short written instructions placed on the lines in the diagram. Nicknamed stick flowcharts.

Structured Programming A systemmatic way of planning and coding computer programs. Structured programs are organized into blocks, or modules of code which are highlighted with spaces placed before and after each block to improve readability. Modules which contain loops or decisions are indented towards the right-hand margin for easier identification.

Subroutine A small program which performs some particular function. It is usually separated from the main program and called into action whenever needed.

Syntax Error An error in the grammatical rules of a particular computer language.

Systems Analyst A person who recommends ways of improving office routines, computer forms, or anything related to the application of a computer system.

System Commands Instructions which require the computer to do something, but cannot be included as part of a computer program. Examples: *list; delete*.

System Crash A phrase used to describe an undefined computer malfunction which has caused the computer to stop running, as in: "The system has crashed," or alternatively "The system is down."

Tape Loop Drives A storage device which uses a wafer-size cassette that contains a continuous tape loop.

Teller Terminals Interactive computer terminals designed to be used by bank tellers to process banking transactions.

Teleprocessing Any processing at a distance. Example: A computer terminal can gain access to the processing power of a computer several kilometres away.

Telidon A Canadian videotext system which is designed to provide homes with computer-based information.

Template A plastic stencil used to draw flowcharts.

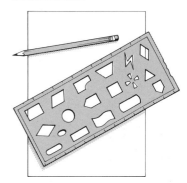

Template.

Test Condition A statement within a repetition structure which provides the computer with a logical way to exit from the structure once a certain condition is met.

Text Editor A software program which allows the user to manipulate and edit information displayed on a visual screen.

Time Sharing A method of sharing a computer facility with several users at the same time. A technique used by banks and airlines.

Top Down Design A chart-style method of planning computer programs by beginning with general statements and progressing to statements with greater and greater detail. Also, a modular method of organizing a computer program into blocks of code arranged into some logical sequence such as input, processing, and output.

Truncate To drop digits of a number which lessens the number's accuracy. Example: If 4.62987 is truncated to two decimal accuracy, it would appear as 4.62.

Univac 1 The first mass-produced model of general-purpose computers. Originally manufactured by Sperry Rand Corporation.

UPC   An acronym for universal product code. It refers to a patch of dark and light vertical lines found on grocery packages. It contains coded information to assist with inventory control.

Universal Product Code.

User Prompts   Messages embedded in conversational programs requiring a response from the user of the program.

Variable Name   A letter or key word invented by the programmer to be assigned to represent the storage location of a particular variable or set of variables.

Variables   Data in a computer program which assume any of a given set of items.

Videodisk   A transparent, plastic platter used to store data in the form of grooves. Information such as complete pictures, data, programs, and sound can be read by an optical laser scanner. Also spelled videodisc (British).

Videotext   A computer and teleprocessing system which transmits and displays information to and from a central computer and home television sets. Example: Telidon.

Virtual Storage   A method of organizing information which allows a computer to run programs normally too large to be stored in main memory. Magnetic disks become an extension of main memory.

Voice Recognition Unit   A device which accepts the human voice as input into a computer system.

Warnier-Orr Diagrams   A technique of planning algorithms in which small groups or sets of instructions are placed inside left-hand brackets. The chart progresses from generalized instructions to more specific detail about the steps in a program.

WATFOR   A verson of structured FORTRAN developed at the University of Waterloo.

WATFIV   A revision of the WATFOR language with additional programming features.

Watson, Thomas J.   The president of IBM until 1952. His motto *Think* often appears in computer cartoons.

Wiener, Norbert (1894 – 1964)   An American scientist who coined the word "cybernetics." The founder of a new branch of science, he believed that many human thought processes could be determined mathematically and adapted for use in computers.

Word Processing   This refers to the secretarial use of desk-top computer systems to type, proofread, edit, electronically file, and print letters and memos.

Word Processing Operator   A secretary who operates a word processing work station, which is a computer dedicated to performing secretarial functions.

Index